MOST IMPORTANT PEOPLE IN KOREAN HISTORY

Influential Figures You Should Know To Understand The Nation

Compiled & Edited by Bridge Education

ISBN: 979-11-88195-30-5
NEW AMPERSAND PUBLISHING

Table of Contents

DANGUN WANGGEOM
The Founding Father of Gojoseon,
The First Ever Korean Kingdom

Dangun (단군;檀君;[tan.gun]) or Dangun Wanggeom (단군왕검;檀君王儉;[tan.gun waŋ.gʌm]) was the legendary founder of Gojoseon, the first ever Korean kingdom, around present-day Liaoning, Manchuria, and the northern part of the Korean Peninsula. He is said to be the "grandson of heaven" and "son of a bear", and to have founded the kingdom in 2333 BC. The earliest recorded version of the Dangun legend appears in the 13th-century Samguk Yusa, which cites China's Book of Wei and Korea's lost historical record Gogi (고기 , 古記).[1]

Mythology

Dangun's ancestry legend begins with his grandfather Hwanin (환인 : 桓因), the "Lord of Heaven". Hwanin had a son, Hwanung (환웅 : 桓雄), who yearned to live on the earth among the valleys and the mountains. Hwanin permitted Hwanung and 3,000 followers to descend onto Baekdu Mountain, where Hwanung founded the Sinsi (신시 : 神市, "City of God"). Along with his ministers of clouds, rain and wind, he instituted laws and moral codes and taught humans various arts, medicine, and agriculture.[2] Legend attributes the development of acupuncture and moxibustion to Dangun.[3]

A tiger and a bear prayed to Hwanung that they might become human. Upon hearing their prayers, Hwanung gave them 20 cloves of garlic and a bundle of mugwort, ordering them to eat only this sacred food and remain out of the sunlight for 100 days. The tiger gave up after about twenty days and left the cave. However, the bear persevered and was transformed into a woman. The bear and the tiger are said to represent two tribes that sought the favor of the heavenly prince.[4]

The bear-woman (Ungnyeo;웅녀 : 熊女) was grateful and made offerings to Hwanung. However, she lacked a husband, and soon became sad and prayed beneath a "divine birch" tree (Hangul:신단수;Hanja:神檀樹;RR: shindansu) to be blessed with a child. Hwanung, moved by her prayers, took her for his wife and soon she gave birth to a son named Dangun Wanggeom.[5]

Dangun ascended to the throne, built the walled city of Asadal situated near Pyongyang (the location is disputed) and called the kingdom Joseon—referred to today as Gojoseon "Old/Ancient Joseon" so as not to be confused with the Joseon that was established much later. He then moved his capital to Asadal on Mount Paegak or Mount Gunghol.[6]

Dating

Emperor Dangun's rule is usually calculated to begin in 2333 BC, based on the description of the Dongguk Tonggam (1485) contrary to the 40th year of the reign of the legendary Chinese Emperor Yao.[7] Other sources vary somewhat, but also put it during Yao's reign (traditional dates: 2357 BC-2256 BC). The Samguk Yusa states Dangun ascended to the throne in the 50th year of Yao's reign, while Annals of the Joseon Dynasty says the first year and Dongguk Tonggam says the 25th year.[8]

Until 1961, the official South Korean era (for numbering years) was called the Dangi (Hangul:단기;Hanja:檀紀), which began in 2333 BC. Followers of Daejongism considered October 3 in the Korean calendar as Gaecheonjeol (Hangul:개천절;Hanja:開天

4

節 "Festival of the Opening of Heaven").[9] This day is now a public holiday in South Korea in the Gregorian calendar called "National Foundation Day". North Korea dates Dangun's founding of Gojoseon to early 30th century BC.[10]

15 March in the year 4340 of the Dangun Era is called "Royal Day Festival" (hangul:어천절 hanja:御天節 romaja: eocheonjeol), the day that the semi-legendary founder Dangun returned to the heavens.

Appearances

The earliest recorded version of the Dangun legend appears in the 13th century Samguk Yusa, which cites China's Book of Wei and Korea's lost history text Gogi (古記).[11] This is the best known and most studied version, but similar versions are recorded in the Jewang Un-gi by the late Goryeo scholar Yi Seunghyu (이승휴:李承休, 1224-1300), as well as the Eungje Siju and Sejong Sillok of the early Joseon. Dangun is worshipped today as a deity by the followers of Cheondoism and Daejongism.[12]

In Taekwondo

Dangun is the second pattern or hyeong in the International Taekwon-Do Federation form of the Korean martial art taekwondo. Students learn that the hyeong represents "the holy legendary founder of Korea in the year 2333 BC."[13] Unusually for a hyeong, all the punches in Dan Gun are high section (eye level) symbolising Dangun scaling a mountain, see Dangun Hyeung.

Mausoleum of Dangun

North Korea's leader Kim Il-sung insisted that Dangun was not merely a legend but a real historical person. As consequence, North Korean archaeologists were compelled to locate the purported remains and grave of Dangun.[14]

According to a publication by North Korea, the Mausoleum of Dangun is the alleged burial site of the legendary Dangun.[15] The site occupies about 1.8 km² (0.70 mi²) on the slope of Taebaek Mountain in Kangdong, not to be confused with the Taebaek Mountain in South Korea. Dangun's grave is shaped like a pyramid, about 22 m (72 ft) high and 50 m (164 ft) on each side. Many observers and historians outside of North Korea, including South Korea, consider the site controversial.

In popular culture

Dangun is a playable character in the computer game Empire Earth II in the first campaign, leading the Korean civilization. The Korean campaign is about early Korean history, from 2333 BC to 676 AD, divided into eight scenarios. The first two scenarios are about the founding of the state of Gojoseon and its first contacts with other Korean states and China, followed by scenarios about Korea's first wars with the Chinese and other Korean states.

JUMONG
The Holy King of The East
(58 BCE – 19 BCE)

Tomb of King Tongmyong, Pyongyang, North Korea (259-298BC)

King Dongmyeong of Goguryeo or Dongmyeongseongwang (동명성왕:東明聖王), which literally means Holy King of the East, also known by his birth name Jumong (주몽:朱蒙), was the founding monarch of the kingdom of Goguryeo,[1][2][3][4] the northernmost of the Three Kingdoms of Korea. In the Gwanggaeto Stele, he is called Chumowang (King Chumo). In the Samguk Sagi and the Samgungnyusa, he is recorded as Jumong with the surname Go. The Samguk Sagi states that he was also known as Chumo or Sanghae (상해:象解). The name is also transcribed in other records as Chumong (추몽:鄒蒙), Jungmo (중모:中牟:仲牟), or Domo (도모:都牟).[5]

Birth

The founding myths of Goguryeo are related in ancient writings, including the Gwanggaeto Stele. The best-known version is found, with slight variations, in the Samguk Sagi, Samgungnyusa, and the "King Dongmyeong" chapter (동명왕편:東明王篇) of the Dongguk Yisang Gukjip (동국이상국집:東國李相國集).

There have been disputes over who the father of Jumong really was. In one legend Jumong is son of Hae Mo-su (해모수:解慕漱) and Lady Yuhwa (유화부인:柳花夫人), the daughter of river deity, Habaek (하백:河伯).[6][7][8][9] Hae Mosu met Lady Yuhwa by a river where she was bathing, but Habaek disapproved of Hae Mosu, who returned to heaven. The river deity chased Lady Yuhwa away to Ubal river (우발수:優渤水), where she met and became the concubine of King Geumwa of Eastern Buyeo. Lady Yuhwa was impregnated by sunlight and gave birth to an egg.[10] Geumwa tried to destroy the egg, and tried to feed it to animals, who instead protected the egg from harm. Geumwa returned it to Lady Yuhwa. From the egg hatched a baby boy, who was named Jumong, meaning "skilled archer" in the ancient Buyeo language.

Leaving Eastern Buyeo, Jumong was known for his exceptional skill at archery . Eventually, Geumwa's sons Daeso and Yongpo became jealous of him, and Jumong left Buyeo to follow Hae Mo-su's dream to unify Gojoseon territories which had been broken up as a result of the Han Dynasty's corrupt government and rescue Gojoseon's population that had been left in Eastern Buyeo. According to legend, as he fled on his horse, he approached a fast-running river. Turtles and creatures of the water rose up and formed a bridge.[11] He entered the land south of the river. In 37 BCE, Jumong became the first king of Goguryeo, and reunited all of the five tribes of Jolbon into one kingdom. Soseono, who was a Jolbon chief's daughter, became his second wife and gave birth to his son, who eventually established the kingdom of Baekje as Onjo of Baekje.

Rule

In 37 BCE, Jumong and his second wife Soseono established Goguryeo and became its first King and Queen. During that same year, King Songyang (송양:松讓) of Biryu surrendered to him after receiving assistance in defeating the Mohe people's invasion. In 34 BCE, along with the palace, Goguryeo's first capital city Jolbon, was completed. Four years later, in 28 BCE, Jumong sent General Bu Wiyeom (부위염:扶尉猒) to conquer the Okjeo.[12][13] During that same year, Jumong's mother, Lady Yuhwa, died in the palace of the Eastern Buyeo, and was given the burial ceremony of a queen consort even though she was only a concubine.

Jumong sent a messenger and numerous gifts to King Geumwa in gratitude for King Geumwa's generosity. In 19 BCE, Jumong's first wife Lady Ye, fled Eastern Buyeo with their son Yuri to Goguryeo. At that time, Jumong's second wife Soseono was queen. When Lady Ye and Yuri arrived in Goguryeo, Soseono gave up her title after realizing that Jumong would make Yuri the Crown Prince and decided to leave Goguryeo. Soseono left Goguryeo with her two sons and some of her subordinates and headed further south into the Korean Peninsula into what is now South Korea. There she established Baekje. Jumong elected his first son, Yuri as the successor to the throne.

Demise

Jumong died in 19 BCE at the age of 40.[14] Crown Prince Yuri buried his father in a pyramid tomb and gave him the posthumous name "Holy King Jumong".

Legacy

Jumong's kingdom of Goguryeo eventually evolved into a great regional territory with considerable power and influence. Goguryeo stood for 705 years and was ruled in total by 28 consecutive emperors in the Go Dynasty until it was conquered by the Silla-Tang alliance in 668. Balhae and Goryeo succeeded it, and the modern descendants of Jumong still bear his family name "Go."

In Goguryeo, Jumong was deified into an ancestral deity and he was worshipped in the Temple of King Dongmyeong next to his tomb.

Tomb of King Tongmyong, Pyongyang, North Korea (259-298BC)

In popular culture

From 2006 to 2007, MBC aired a highly popular 81 episode drama, Jumong, to mark their anniversary. The series took elements from historical records and mythology, and retold the story in a more down to earth manner than found in the myths, recounting how Jumong, the spoiled step-child of the Buyeo royal family, embarks on a journey of self-discovery, becoming a leading figure of Buyeo, but retreating from Buyeo after his step-brothers' betrayal. Relaunching the armed and militarily capable guerrilla fighters' force his biological father Hae Mo-su once headed, Jumong goes on a life-mission to rescue and band together the refugees of the ancient Joseon peoples, leading the fight against the oppression of Imperial China, finally establishing himself as the king of the new nation Goguryeo.

From 2010 to 2011, KBS1 aired King Geunchogo, also known as The King of Legend. In this series, Jumong is portrayed as a tyrant, who could not accept sharing the power over Goguryeo with Soseono and the Jolbon faction. After Yuri of Goguryeo's arrival, the declared crown prince and successor to Jumong's throne, Soseono and all her subordinates and servants decided to leave "their beloved Goguryeo" to establish a new kingdom - one "much more powerful than Goguryeo ever was."

Actors who have played Jumong

Portrayed by Song Il-gook in the 2006-2007 MBC TV series Jumong.
Portrayed by Lee Deok-hwa in the 2010-2011 KBS1 TV series The King of Legend.

KING GWANGGAETO THE GREAT

The Greatest Conqueror in Korean History

(374–413)[1]

Gwanggaeto the Great ([kwaŋ.gɛ.tʰo.dɛ.waŋ] hangul:광개토태왕 hanja:廣開土太王) was the nineteenth monarch of Goguryeo. His full posthumous name means "Entombed in Gukgangsang, Broad Expander of Domain,[1] Peacemaker,[2] Supreme King", sometimes abbreviated to Hotaewang.[2] His era name is Yeongnak and he is occasionally recorded as Yeongnak Taewang ("Supreme King" or "Emperor" Yeongnak). Gwanggaeto's imperial reign title meant that Goguryeo was on equal standing as an empire with the imperial dynasties in China.[1][3][4]

Under Gwanggaeto, Goguryeo began a golden age,[5][6][7] becoming a powerful empire and one of the great powers in East Asia.[8][9][10][11] Gwanggaeto made enormous advances and conquests into: Western Manchuria against Khitan tribes;Inner Mongolia and the Maritime Province of Russia against numerous nations and tribes;[12][13] and the Han River valley in central Korea to control over two-thirds of the Korean peninsula. [3][4]

In regard to the Korean peninsula, Gwanggaeto defeated Baekje, the then most powerful of the Three Kingdoms of Korea,[3] in 396, capturing the capital city of Wiryeseong in present-day Seoul.[14] In 399, Silla, the southeastern kingdom of Korea, sought aid from Goguryeo due to incursions by Baekje troops and their Wa allies from the Japanese archipelago.[4] Gwanggaeto dispatched 50,000 expeditionary troops,[15] crushing his enemies and securing Silla as a de facto protectorate;[4][16] he thus subdued the other Korean kingdoms and achieved a loose unification of the Korean peninsula under Goguryeo.[4] [17][18] In his western campaigns, he defeated the Xianbei of the Later Yan empire and conquered the Liaodong peninsula,[3] regaining the ancient domain of Gojoseon.[4][19]

Gwanggaeto's accomplishments are recorded on the Gwanggaeto Stele, erected in 414 at the supposed site of his tomb in Ji'an along the present-day China–North Korea border. [20] Constructed by his son and successor Jangsu, the monument to Gwanggaeto the Great is the largest engraved stele in the world.[21][22]

Birth and background

At the time of Gwanggaeto's birth, Goguryeo was not as powerful as it once had been. In 371, three years prior to Gwanggaeto's birth, the rival Korean kingdom of Baekje, under the great leadership of Geunchogo, soundly defeated Goguryeo, slaying the monarch Gogukwon and sacking Pyongyang.[23][24] Baekje became one of the dominant powers in East Asia. Baekje's influence was not limited to the Korean peninsula, but extended across the sea to Liaoxi and Shandong in China, taking advantage of the weakened state of Former Qin, and Kyushu in the Japanese archipelago.[25] Goguryeo was inclined to avoid conflicts with its ominous neighbor,[26] while cultivating constructive relations with the Former Qin,[27] the Xianbei, and the Rouran, in order to defend itself from future invasions and bide time to reshape its legal structure and initiate military reforms. [28]

Gogukwon's successor, Sosurim, adopted a foreign policy of appeasement and reconciliation with Baekje,[26] and concentrated on domestic policies to spread Buddhism and Confucianism throughout Goguryeo's social and political systems.[29] Furthermore, due to the defeats that Goguryeo had suffered at the hands of the proto-Mongol Xianbei and Baekje, Sosurim instituted military reforms aimed at preventing such defeats in the future.[28] Sosurim's internal arrangements laid the groundwork for Gwanggaeto's expansion.[1]

Sosurim's successor, Gogukyang, invaded Later Yan, the successor state of Former Yan, in 385 and Baekje in 386.[30][31]

Reign

Rise to power and campaigns against Baekje

Gwanggaeto succeeded his father, Gogukyang, upon his death in 391. Upon his coronation, Gwanggaeto adopted the era name Yeongnak (Eternal Rejoicing) and the title Taewang (Supreme King), which was equivalent to "emperor",[32] affirming that he was an equal to the rulers of China and Baekje.[1][3][4]

In 392, Gwanggaeto led an attack on Baekje with 40,000 troops, capturing 10 walled cities.[33] In response, Asin, the monarch of Baekje, launched a counterattack on Goguryeo in 393 but was defeated.[33] Despite the ongoing war, during 393, Gwanggaeto established 9 Buddhist temples in Pyongyang.[34][35] Asin invaded Goguryeo once more in 394, but was defeated again.[33] After suffering multiple defeats against Goguryeo, Baekje's political stability began to crumble.[18] In 395, Baekje was defeated once more by Goguryeo and was pushed south to its capital of Wiryeseong on the Han River.[33][36] In the following year, in 396, Gwanggaeto led an assault on Wiryeseong by land and sea, using the Han River, and triumphed over Baekje.[33] Gwanggaeto captured the Baekje capital and the defeated Asin submitted to him,[4][37] surrendering a prince and 10 government ministers.[33][38]

Goguryeo at zenith under Gwanggaeto and Jangsu.

By Myself (Own work) [CC BY-SA 3.0 (http://creativecommons.org/licenses/by-sa/3.0)], via Wikimedia Commons

Northern conquests

In 395, while his campaign against Baekje was ongoing to the south, Gwanggaeto made an excursion to invade the Khitan Baili clan to the west on the Liao River,[39] destroying 3 tribes and 600 to 700 camps.[40] In 398, Gwanggaeto conquered the Sushen people to the northeast,[4] who were Tungusic ancestors of the Jurchens and Manchus.[41]

In 400, while Gwanggaeto was occupied with Baekje, Gaya, and Wa troops in Silla, the Xianbei state of Later Yan, founded by the Murong clan in present-day Liaoning, attacked Goguryeo.[42] Gwanggaeto repulsed the Xianbei troops.[19][43] In 402, Gwanggaeto retaliated and conquered the prominent fortress called sukgunseong (숙군성:宿軍城) near the capital of Later Yan.[42][44] In 405 and again in

12

406, Later Yan troops attacked Goguryeo fortresses in Liaodong (요동성:遼東城 in 405, and 목저성:木底城 in 406), but was defeated both times.[42] Gwanggaeto conquered all of Liaodong.[1][4] By conquering Liaodong, Gwanggaeto recovered the ancient domain of Gojoseon;[4][19] Goguryeo controlled Liaodong until the mid-late 7th century.

In 407, Gwanggaeto dispatched 50,000 troops consisting of infantry and cavalry and won a great victory, completely annihilating the enemy troops and pillaging about 10,000 armors and countless war supplies;the opponent can be interpreted as Later Yan, Baekje, or Wa.[42][45]

In 410, Gwanggaeto attacked Eastern Buyeo to the northeast.[42]

Southern campaigns

In 400, Silla, another Korean kingdom in the southeast of the Korean peninsula, request-ed aid from Goguryeo in repelling an allied invasion by Baekje, Gaya, and Wa. Gwang-gaeto dispatched 50,000 troops and annihilated the enemy coalition.[4] Thereupon, Gwanggaeto influenced Silla as a suzerain,[16] and Gaya declined and never recovered. In 402, Gwanggaeto returned Prince Silseong,[46] who had resided in Goguryeo as a political hostage since 392, back home to Silla and appointed him as the king of Silla.

In 404, Gwanggaeto defeated an attack by the Wa from the Japanese archipelago on the southern border of what was once the Daifang commandery, inflicting enormous casual-ties on the enemy.[42][47][48]

Detail of Gwanggaeto Stele

Death and legacy

Gwanggaeto died of an unknown illness in 413 at the age of 39. He was succeeded by his eldest son, Jangsu, who ruled Goguryeo for 79 years until the age of 98,[1] the longest reign in East Asian history.[49]

Gwanggaeto's conquests are said to mark the zenith of Korean history, building and consoli-dating a great empire in Northeast Asia and uniting the Three Kingdoms of Korea under his influence.[4][18] Gwanggaeto conquered 64 walled cities and 1,400 villages.[1][4] Except for the period of 200 years beginning with Jangsu, who would build upon his father's domain, and the golden age of Balhae, Korea never before or since ruled such a vast territory. There is archaeological evidence that Gogu-ryeo's maximum extent lay even further west in present-day Mongolia, based on discoveries of Goguryeo fortress ruins in Mongolia.[50][51] [52] Gwanggaeto established his own era name,

13

Yeongnak Eternal Rejoicing, proclaiming Goguryeo monarchs equal to their counterparts in the Chinese mainland.[1][3][4]

Gwanggaeto the Great is one of two rulers of Korea whose names are appended with the title "the Great", with the other being Sejong the Great of Joseon, who created Hangul the Korean alphabet, to promote literacy among the common people,[53] and made great advances in science.[54][55]

Gwanggaeto is regarded by Koreans as one of the greatest heroes in Korean history, and is often taken as a potent symbol of Korean nationalism.

The Gwanggaeto Stele, a 6.39 meter tall monument erected by Jangsu in 414, was re-discovered in the late 19th century.[20] The stele was inscribed with information about Gwanggaeto's reign and achievements, but not all the characters and passages have been preserved. Korean and Japanese scholars disagree on the interpretation in regard to passages on the Wa.

The Republic of Korea Navy operates Gwanggaeto the Great-class destroyers, built by Daewoo Heavy Industries and named in honor of the monarch.
A prominent statue of Gwanggaeto alongside a replica of the Gwanggaeto Stele were erected in the main street of Guri city in Gyeonggi province.[56][57]

Promotional poster for TV Drama "Dae Jo Young" (Korea Broadcasting System). Actor Choi Soo-jong played Dae Jo-yeong

Dae Joyeong (대조영 : 大祚榮; [tae.dʑo.jʌŋ] or [tae] [tɕo.jʌŋ]; died 719), also known as King Go (고왕 : 高王; [ko.waŋ]), established the state of Balhae, reigning from 699 to 719.[1]

Life

Early life

Dae Jo-yeong was the first son of general Dae Jung-sang of Goguryeo, where he was born in Goguryeo.

After the fall of Goguryeo to the Silla-Tang armies, Dae Jung-sang remained in a part of Goguryeo which had not been attacked during the 3rd Goguryeo-Tang war. Afterward, Dae Jung-sang was opposed to the Tang. In the confusion of the Khitan uprising led by Li Jinzhong against the Tang (Zhou) in May 696, Dae Jung-sang led at least 8,000 Goguryeo remnant peoples, the Sumo Mohe people,[2] to Dongmo mountain, and the Baishan Mohe leader Geolsa Biu made an alliance and sought independence.

King of Jin and Balhae

The Tang killed Geolsa Biu, and Dae Jung-sang also died. Dae Jo-yeong integrated the armies of Goguryeo people and some Malgal tribes[3] and resisted Tang's attack. His overwhelming victory over the Tang at Tianmenling enabled him to expand his father's empire. He claimed himself the King of Jin in 698.[4] He established his capital at Dongmo Mountain in the south of today's Jilin province, and built Dongmo mountain fortress, which was to become Jin's capital.[5]

He attempted to expand his influence in international politics involving the Tang, the Göktürks, the Khitan, Silla[6] and some independent Mohe tribes. At first he dispatched an envoy to the Göktürks, allying against Tang. Then he reconciled himself with the Tang when Emperor Zhongzong was restored to the throne.[6]

In 712, he renamed his empire Balhae. In 713 he was given the titular title of "Prefecture King of Balhae" by Emperor Xuanzong.[4] After a period of rest within the empire, King Go made it clear that Silla was not to be dealt with peacefully because they had allied with Tang to destroy Goguryeo, the predecessor of Balhae. This aggressive stance towards Silla was continued on by his son and successor King Mu of Balhae.

Dae Jo-yeong died in 719,[7] and his son Dae Muye assumed the throne.[8] Dae Jo-yeong was given the posthumous name "King Go."

Family

Dae Jo-yeong had at least two wives. His only known sons through his first wife were Dae Muye, and Dae Munye. The sons through his other wife or wives were Dae Chwi-jin, Dae Ho-bang, and Dae Nang-a. The only concrete fact regarding Dae Jo-yeong's sons was that Dae Muye was the firstborn and oldest among them. He had younger brother, Dae Ya-Bal.

Legacy

After the fall of Balhae, the last prince led all of the Balhae aristocracy into the fellow successor state of Goguryeo, Goryeo. Dae Jo-yeong's descendants include modern-day Koreans who bear the surname Tae (태), or Dae (대).

In South Korea, a television drama on KBS1 was launched since September 2006 in his honor. Roughly 30% (based on 2007 survey) of the Korean viewers enjoyed this programme.

ROK navy warship, Dae Jo Yeong in San Diego, USA.

Dae Jo-yeong built a vast army and a powerful navy just as the Taewangs of Goguryeo had done. The third Chungmugong Yi Sun-sin class destroyer commissioned by the Republic of Korea Navy is named Dae Jo-yeong.[9] KDX-II class destroyers are named after significant figures in Korean history such as admiral Yi Sun-sin.

The Chunbun Ancestral Rite is held annually in Balhae Village, Gyeongsaunbok-do in order to commemorate the achievements of Dae Jo-yeong. The Gyeongsan City mayor participates in the event, which is open for public participation.

In popular culture

Portrayed by Choi Soo-jong in the 2006-2007 KBS TV series Dae Jo Yeong.

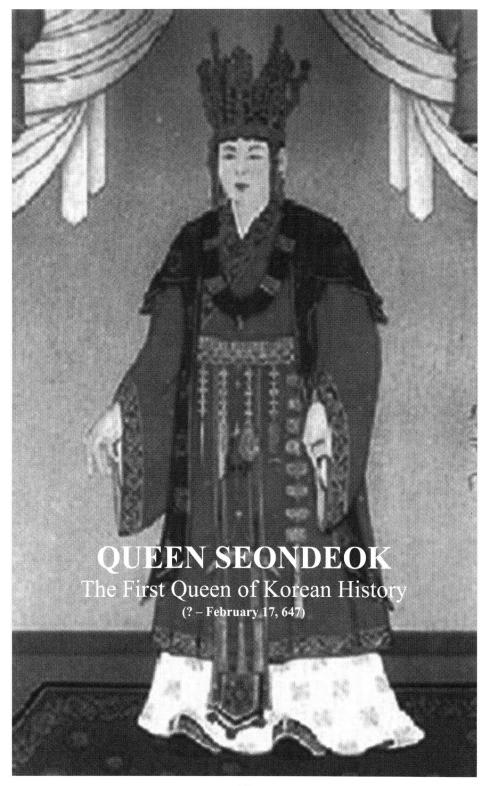

QUEEN SEONDEOK
The First Queen of Korean History
(? – February 17, 647)

Queen Seondeok of Silla (Hangul:선덕여왕 hanja:善德女王)Korean pronunciation: [sʰʌndʌk jʌwaŋ]) reigned as Queen Regnant of Silla, one of the Three Kingdoms of Korea, from 632 to 647.[1] She was Silla's twenty-seventh ruler, and its first reigning queen. She was the second female sovereign in recorded East Asian history and encouraged a renaissance in thought, literature, and the arts in Silla.[2]

Selection as heiress

Before she became queen, Seondeok was known as Princess Deokman. According to the Samguk Sagi, she was the first of Jinpyeong of Silla's daughters, but according to other historical records, she was the second of King Jinpyeong's daughters and much younger than her elder sister, Princess Cheonmyeong. Her nephew, Princess Cheonmyeong's son, eventually became King Muyeol of Silla while Seondeok's other sister, Princess Seonhwa, eventually married Mu of Baekje and became the mother of Uija of Baekje. Seonhwa's existence is controversial due to the discovery of evidence in 2009 that points to King Uija's mother as being Queen Sataek and not Seonhwa as indicated by historical records.

Because he had no sons, Jinpyeong selected Seondeok as his heir. Though unprecedented, this action would probably not have been all that shocking within Silla as women of the period already had a certain degree of influence as advisors, queens dowager and regents - Jinpyeong himself gained the throne as a result of a coup d'état organized by Mishil. Throughout the kingdom, women were the heads of families since matrilineal lines of inheritance existed alongside patrilineal ones. Within Silla, the status of women was relatively high, but there were still restrictions on female behavior and conduct;they were discouraged from activities considered unwomanly. Ultimately, Seondeok's successful reign in turn facilitated the acceptance of two more Queens regnant of Silla.[3]

Rein

In 632, Seondeok became the sole ruler of Silla, and reigned until 647. She was the first of three female rulers of the kingdom (the other two being Jindeok of Silla and Jinseong of Silla), and was immediately succeeded by her cousin Jindeok, who ruled until 654.

Seondeok's reign began in the midst of a violent rebellion and fighting in the neighboring kingdom of Baekje were often what preoccupied her. Yet, in her fourteen years as queen of Silla, she used her wit to her advantage. When Baekje invaded, she sought an alliance with Goguryeo. When Goguryeo also turned on Silla, she strengthened ties with Tang China.[4] She kept the kingdom together and sent royal emissaries and scholars to China. She is also credited with the initial formulation of a Korean chivalric code and sent young Koreans to China for martial arts training.[5]

Like Empress Wu Zetian of the Tang and her own father, she was drawn to Buddhism and presided over the completion of Buddhist temples. Notable amongst Buddhist structures she had built is the nine-story wooden pagoda in Hwangnyongsa. On each story of the 80 meters high structure was the name inscribed of one of the neighbors Silla intended to subjugate.[6] Bunhwangsa and Yeongmyosa were also built under her auspices.

She built the "Star-Gazing Tower," or Cheomseongdae, considered the first dedicated observatory in the Far East. The tower still stands in the old Silla capital of Gyeongju, South Korea. She also worked towards relief of poverty.

In the first lunar month of 647, Bidam led a revolt with the slogan that "female rulers cannot rule the country".[7] Samguk Sagi says that during Bidam's uprising, a star 'fell'. Bidam used it to encourage his followers, saying that it was a sign of the end of the Queen's reign. On the other hand, Kim Yushin advised the Queen to fly a burning kite to signal that 'the star is back in its place'. After that, Kim Yushin's army defeated Bidam's rebel faction. only ten days after Bidam's uprising, he and 30 of his men were executed by Queen Jindeok of Silla on 26 February (Queen Seondeok died on 17 February, Jindeok was then proclaimed Queen of Silla).

Legends

It is believed that Seondeok's selection as her father's successor was justified by her displays of precocious intelligence when she was a princess. One such story (both in Samguk Sagi and Samguk Yusa) recounts that her father received a box of peony seeds from the Emperor Taizong of Tang accompanied by a painting of what the flowers looked like. Looking at the picture, the young Seondeok remarked that while the flower was pretty it was a shame that it did not smell. "If it did, there would be butterflies and bees around the flower in the painting." Her observation about the peonies' lack of scent proved correct — just one of many illustrations of her intellect and hence of her ability to rule.

There are two other accounts of Seondeok's unusual ability to perceive events before their occurrence. In the first it is said that Seondeok once heard a horde of white frogs croaking by the Jade Gate pond in the winter. She interpreted this as an impending attack from the Kingdom of Baekje (the croaking frogs were seen as angry soldiers) in the northwest of Silla (white symbolized the west in astronomy) at the Women's Valley (the Jade Gate was associated with women). When she sent her generals to the Women's Valley, they were able to capture two thousand Baekje soldiers.

The second is an account of her death. Some days before she died, Seondeok gathered her officials and gave the order "When I die, bury me near the Dori-cheon (도리천:忉利天, "Heaven of Grieved Merits")." Decades after her death, the thirtieth king Munmu of Silla constructed Sacheonwang-sa (사천왕사:四天王寺 "Temple of the Four Heavenly Kings") in her tomb. Then the nobles realized that one of the Buddha's sayings, "Dori-cheon is above the Sacheonwang-cheon", was accomplished by the Queen.

KIM YU-SHIN
General Who Led The Unification of Kingdoms
(595 – 18 August 673)

Kim Yushin or Kim Yoo-Shin (김유신;金庾信) was a general in 7th-century Silla. He led the unification of the Korean Peninsula by Silla under the reign of King Muyeol of Silla and King Munmu of Silla. He is said to have been the great-grandchild of King Guhae of Geumgwan Gaya, the last ruler of the Geumgwan Gaya state. This would have given him a very high position in the Silla bone rank system, which governed the political and military status that a person could attain.

Much of what is known about Kim's life comes from the detailed account in the Samguk Sagi, Yeoljeon 1-3, and the much briefer record in the Samguk Yusa, vol. 1.

Early years

Kim Yushin was the son of General Kim Seohyeon (the second son of General Kim Muryeok) and Lady Manmyeong, who was a daughter of Kim Sukheuljong (김숙흘종;金肅訖宗, King Jinheung of Silla's younger brother). He was born in Gyeyang, Jincheon County in 595, became a Hwarang warrior at just 15 and was an accomplished swordsman and a Gukseon (국선;國仙;Hwarang leader) by the time he was 18 years old. By the age of 34 (in 629) he had been given total command of the Silla armed forces. Three years later, Kim Yushin's cousin, Princess Deokman, became Queen Seondeok of Silla and kept Kim Yushin as commander in chief of the royal army. During the reign of Queen Seondeok of Silla (632-647), Kim Yushin owned ten thousand private soldiers, won many battles against Baekje and became one of the most powerful man in Silla.

Military accomplishments

His statue in Namsan Park, Seoul, South Korea

By Integral (Own work) [CC BY-SA 2.0 kr (http://creativecommons.org/licenses/by-sa/2.0/kr/deed.en)], via Wikimedia Commons

Yushin's first military engagement in command is believed to have occurred around 629 AD, and through it he quickly proved his capabilities as a warrior. Silla was in a constant struggle with its neighbor to the west, Baekje, over territory. There had been gains and losses on both sides, and the struggle lasted for many years. It was during this period that Yushin rose through the ranks of the military, rising to the position of general and becoming a skilled field commander.

Baekje and Shilla had formed an alliance to counter Goguryeo's power and its intentions to push southwards, and together they launched a successful attack on it, Silla taking the northern territory and Baekje the one south of the Han river. But Silla broke the alliance and attacked Baekje in order to claim both territories for itself. After this betrayal, Baekje allied with Goguryeo. When Goguryeo and Baekje attacked Silla in 655, Silla joined forces with Tang Dynasty China to battle the invaders. Although it is not clear when Kim Yushin first became a general, he was certainly commanding the Silla forces by this time. Eventually, with the help of the Silla navy and some 130,000 Tang forces, Yushin attacked the Baekje capital, Sabi, in

660, in one of the most famous battles of that century, the Battle of Hwangsanbeol.

The Baekje defenders were commanded by none other than General Gyebaek, although the Baekje forces consisted of about 5,000 men and were no match for Yushin's warriors, which numbered about ten times as many. Baekje, which had already been experiencing internal political problems, crumbled. Kim Yushin's Silla forces and their Tang allies now moved on Goguryeo from two directions, and in 661 they attacked the seemingly impregnable Goguryeo kingdom, but were repelled. The attack had weakened Goguryeo, though. In 667 another offensive was launched which, in 668, finally destroyed Goguryeo.

Silla still had to subdue various pockets of resistance, but their efforts were then focused on ensuring that their Tang allies did not overstay their welcome on the peninsula. After some difficult conflicts, Silla eventually forced out the Tang troops and united the peninsula under their rule.

Legends

Many stories exist about Kim Yushin. It is told that he once was ordered to subdue a rebel army, but his troops refused to fight as they had seen a large star fall from the sky and took this to be a bad omen. To regain the confidence of his troops, the General used a large kite to carry a fire ball into the sky. The soldiers, seeing the star return to heaven, rallied and defeated the rebels. It is also related how General Kim ingeniously used kites as a means of communication between his troops when they had become divided between islands and the mainland.

Another story relates how, while Silla was allied with the Tang Dynasty against Baekje, an argument broke out between Yushin's commander and So Jung-Bang, a Tang general. As the argument escalated into a potentially bloody confrontation, Kim Yushin's sword was said to have leaped from its scabbard into his hand. Because the sword of a warrior was believed to be his soul, this occurrence so frightened the Tang general that he immediately apologized to the Silla officers.

His final years

Throughout his life, Kim Yushin felt that Baekje, Goguryeo, and Silla should not be separate countries but rather united as one. He is regarded as the driving force in the unification of the Korean Peninsula, and is the most famous of all the generals in the unification wars of the Three Kingdoms.

Kim Yushin was rewarded handsomely for his efforts in the campaigns. In 668, King Munmu bestowed upon him the honorary title of Taedaegakgan (태대각간; 太大角干), something like "Supreme Herald of Defense" (literally "greatest-great-trumpet-shield"). He reportedly received a village of over 500 households, and in 669 was given some 142 separate horse farms, spread throughout the kingdom. He died four years later, leaving behind ten children.

Kim Yushin lived to the age of 79 and is considered to be one of the most famous gener-

als and masters of Korean swords in Korean history. He is the focus of numerous stories and legends, and is familiar to most Koreans from a very early age. Following his death on 18 August (the 1st day of the 7th lunar month) 673, General Kim was awarded the honorary title of King Heungmu, and was buried at the foot of Songhwa Mountain,35.8456477°N 129.1911292°E near Gyeongju in southeastern Korea, in a tomb as splendid as that of kings.

Family

Kim Yushin had two sisters, Kim Bohui and Kim Munhui (김문희;金文姬). Kim Munhui, later known as Queen Munmyeong (문명왕후;文明王后), married Yushin's childhood friend Kim Chunchu, King Taejong Muyeol of Silla, who is credited for having led the unification of the Korean peninsula under Silla. Muyeol and Munmyeong were the parents of King Munmu of Silla and Kim Inmun.

Kim Yushin's third wife, Lady Jiso (智炤夫人), was the third daughter of King Muyeol of Silla. Yushin had ten children. His second son, Kim Wonsul, would later play a central role in completing the independence of Silla from the Tang Dynasty.

Legacy

Today, Kim Yushin is remembered by Koreans as one of the greatest generals in Korean history. His ultimate legacy is the first unification of the Korean nation. One of his ten children, his second son Kim Wonsul, became a general during the time of King Munmu of Silla, and he was essential in unifying Silla.

EULJI MUNDEOK
Hero of The Great Battle of Salsu

Eulji Mundeok (을지문덕:乙支文德) was a military leader of early 7th century Goguryeo, one of the Three Kingdoms of Korea, who successfully defended Goguryeo against Sui China. He is often numbered among the greatest heroes in the military history of Korea.

Background

Eulji Mundeok was born in the mid-6th century and died sometime after 618, although the exact date is unknown. Haedong Myeongjangjeon, known as the "Biographies of Famed Korean Generals", written in the 18th century, states that he was from Seokda Mountain (석다산:石多山) near Pyongyang. At the time of his birth, Goguryeo was a powerful state, frequently at war with its neighbors.

In 589, the Sui Empire conquered several surrounding states and launched several large military campaigns against Goguryeo which was unwilling to submit to its dominance.

Eulji Mundeok was a cultured man, skilled in both the martial and literary arts. He eventually rose to become the supreme commander of Goguryeo. The name Eulji may actually be a Goguryeo title.

The Battle of Salsu River

After the founding of Sui in 589, a precarious peace was maintained for several years between the new Chinese dynasty and Goguryeo. However, in 597, Yeongyang launched an attack on the Sui at the Battle of Linyuguan. In response, Sui invaded Goguryeo, but the invasion was defeated due to constant ambushes and unfavorable weather.

In the early 7th century, Emperor Yang learned of a secret correspondence between Goguryeo and the Eastern Turkic Khaganate. Emperor Yang demanded Yeongyang come and submit personally to him or face an "imperial tour of his territories". When Yeongyang failed to do so, Emperor Yang prepared for war. He mustered an army of over 1,133,000 troops and more than 2 million auxiliaries and personally led them against Goguryeo in 612. The Sui army quickly overran Goguryeo's border defenses, then camped on the banks of the Liao River and prepared to bridge it.

Eulji Mundeok, commissioned as the Field Marshal, was called upon to defend the nation. He prepared his troops to meet the numerically superior Sui forces with a strategy of deception, using feigned retreats and sudden attacks. After the Sui forces crossed the Liao River, a small contingent was sent to attack the city of Yodong, but was repulsed by Eulji Mundeok's forces. As the rainy season progressed, the Sui forces launched other small probing attacks, but held off from making any large moves before the end of the rainy season.

When the rains stopped, Emperor Yang moved his forces to the banks of the Yalu River in northwestern Korea and prepared for a major battle. Fighting only small engagements at times and places of his choosing, Eulji Mundeok drew the Sui forces further and further from their supply centers. Emperor Yang sent an advance force of over 305,000 troops to take the city of Pyongyang. After allowing the force to approach the city, Field Marshal

Eulji Mundeok ambushed it. His forces attacked from all sides, driving the Sui troops back in utter confusion. His troops pursued the retreating army, slaughtering them at will. Records claim that only 2,800 men of the massive force returned alive to the main Chinese army. This battle, the Battle of Salsu, came to be known as one of the most glorious military triumphs in Korea's national history.

After the battle, winter began to set in and the Sui forces, short on provisions, were forced to return home in defeat.

Death

Eulji Mundeok managed to protect Sin Fortress from another Sui invasion force, but he died not long after.

The Sui dynasty was beginning to disintegrate and Emperor Yang decided that he urgently needed to expand his empire in order to regain power, but two more attacks on Goguryeo in the following spring were met with similar disasters, and eventually internal rebellion in China forced him to abandon his desire for Goguryeo. By 618, the relatively short-lived Sui dynasty was replaced by the Tang dynasty. Field Marshal Eulji Mundeok's strategy and leadership had protected Goguryeo from Chinese expansion into the Korean peninsula.

Legacy

One of the most distinguished military leaders of the Goguryeo period, Eulji Mundeok's leadership and tactical acumen were the decisive factors in defeating the Sui invasion. Facing numerically superior forces, he developed a strategy that allowed him to secure a decisive victory. Such brilliant tactical success earned him a permanent place among Korea's most famous leaders. Kim Bu-sik, the author of the Samguk Sagi, also attributed the victory over Sui to Eulji Mundeok.

In Korea, Eulji Mundeok is recognized as one of the greatest figures in its national history. During the reign of Hyeonjong in the Goryeo period, a shrine to Eulji Mundeok was built near Pyongyang. In the succeeding Joseon period, he remained just as revered a figure. Yang Seong-ji, a scholar and high-ranking bureaucrat of 15th century Joseon, and An Jeong-bok, a Silhak historian of 18th century Joseon, both thought highly of him. Furthermore, King Sukjong ordered the construction of another shrine in honor of Eulji Mundeok in 1680.

At a time when Korea was suffering under the yoke of Japanese Imperialism, a fuller assessment of Eulji Mundeok was commenced by the Korean historian Shin Chaeho, who published a biography of the famed general in 1908 and held him out as an example of Korea's traditional nationalist spirit. Eulji Mundeok is still celebrated as a national hero. One of the most preeminent Korean scholars of the 20th century, Lee Ki-baik, noted that Eulji Mundeok's efforts in halting the Sui attempt at conquest stand as one of the earliest examples of Korean attempts to fend off foreign domination.

In South Korea, a main thoroughfare in downtown Seoul, Euljiro, is named after Eulji

Mundeok.

The second highest military decoration of South Korea is named after Eulji Mundeok.

The Republic of Korea Navy named a Gwanggaeto the Great-class destroyer in honor of Eulji Mundeok.

Eulji Mundeok's literary work, the Eulji Mundeok Hansi, is one of the oldest surviving poems in Korean literature.

One of the biannual Combined Forces Command exercises between South Korea and the United States was called Ulchi-Focus Lens (UFL) in honor of Eulji Mundeok. It was renamed to Ulchi-Freedom Guardian (UFG) in 2015. UFG is the world's largest computerized command and control exercise, focusing on how US and ROK forces would defend against a North Korean attack.[1]

Modern Depictions

The playable character Mundeok in the popular mobile game Crusaders Quest is based on Eulji Mundeok.

Eulji Mundeok appears in the 2006 television series Yeon Gaesomun.

Euji can be obtained through a seven days log-in event in the mobile game Mini Warriors

YEON GAESOMUN
Goguryeo's Super Hero
Who Saved The Kingdom
(603 - 665)

Yeon Gaesomun (연개소문;淵蓋蘇文) was a powerful and controversial general and military dictator in the waning days of Goguryeo, one of the Three Kingdoms of ancient Korea. In 642, Yeon discovered that King Yeongnyu and some of his official were plotting to kill some of the more powerful military officers, including himself, because they were seen as a threat to the throne. He immediately went to Pyongyang, where his forces killed the king and one hundred government ministers. He placed the king's nephew, Bojang (r. 642-668), on the throne and had himself appointed to the post of Dae Mangniji (대막리지;大莫離支), the highest possible rank of Goguryeo, assuming control over Goguryeo military and political affairs. He successfully repelled invasions of the Tang dynasty in 645, and of a Tang-Silla alliance in 681.

After his death in 666, a power struggle broke out among his three sons. The eldest, Yeon Namsaeng, defected to Tang and then led the Tang invasion which ultimately ended Goguryeo in 668. Yeon Gaesomun has long been a focus of historical controversy. Many historians hold him responsible for the fall of Goguryeo to the Tang. He has become a hero of modern Korean nationalists, for whom he is a symbol of the time when, at the height of their power, the Koreans unambiguously triumphed over the Chinese.

Background

Goguryeo

Goguryeo was the largest of the three kingdoms into which ancient Korea was divided until 668. According to tradition, it was founded in 37 B.C.E., in the Tongge River basin of northern Korea by Chu-mong, leader of one of the Puyo tribes native to the area. Modern historians have dated its origins to the second century B.C.E. A royal hereditary system had been established by the reign of King T'aejo (53–146 C.E.). King Sosurim (reigned 371–384) centralized the authority of the throne and made Goguryeo into a strong political state. Goguryeo expanded its territory during the reigns of King Kwanggaet'o (391–412) and King Changsu (reigned 413–491), and at the height of its influence, the entire northern half of the Korean peninsula, the Liaotung Peninsula, and a considerable portion of Manchuria (Northeast Provinces) were under Goguryeo (Koguryo) rule. During the Sui (581–618) and T'ang (618–907) dynasties in China, Goguryeo (Koguryo) began to suffer encroachment from China. In 668, allied forces of the southern Korean kingdom of Silla and the T'ang dynasty conquered Goguryeo, and the entire peninsula came under the Unified Silla dynasty (668–935).

King Yeongnyu of Goguryeo

King Yeongnyu (영류왕;榮留王; r. 618-642) was the 27th king of Goguryeo, younger half-brother of the 26th king, Yeong-yang (영양왕;嬰陽王), and son of the 25th king, Pyeongwon (평원왕;平原王). He assumed the throne when Yeong-yang died in 618. That same year, the Tang Dynasty replaced the Sui Dynasty in China. Since Goguryeo was recovering from the Goguryeo-Sui War, and the new Tang emperor was still completing the unification of China, and neither country was in a position to initiate new hostilities, Goguryeo and Tang exchanged emissaries. At the request of Tang, a prisoner exchange was carried out in 622, and in 624, Tang officially presented Taoism to the Goguryeo court, which sent scholars to China the following year to study Taoism and

30

Buddhism.

Early life

Yeon Gaesomun was born to an illustrious family who had traditionally been influential in national defense and political affairs. According to one legend, the progenitor of Yeon Gaesomun was a spirit of the lake. From early childhood, Yeon was aggressive, showing no willingness to compromise, and had an overweening pride. According to tradition, at the age of nine years he already carried five swords, and would have men prostrate themselves so that he might use their backs to mount or dismount his horse.

Yeon was born at Goguryeo mountain, which had five beautiful springs of running water, where Yeon practiced martial arts every day. Later, Mongol invaders completely blocked its flow. At fifteen, Yeon tried to inherit his father's political position of "Mangniji." The aristocracy objected, saying that Yeon was cruel and oppressive, upon which Yeon apologized with tears for his defects. The noblemen were touched by Yeon's apology and agreed to appoint Yeon, "Mangniji'."

Rise to power

Very little is known of Yeon's early days, until he became the Governor of the Western province (西部). In 629, Silla's Kim Yu-sin took Goguryeo's Nangbi-seong.

In 631, as Tang gained strength under Li Shimin (Tang Taizong), it sent a small force to destroy a monument commemorating Goguryeo's victory over their predecessors, the Sui. The campaign was unsuccessful for the Chinese, who failed to capture strategic points in numerous attacks. In response, Goguryeo built the Cheolli Jangseong (천리장성;千里長城) a network of military garrisons to defend the western border of the Liaodong area from Tang invaders. The project began in 631, under the supervision of Yeon Gaesomun, and the preparation and coordination was completed sixteen years later in 647. During this time, Goguryeo continued its battles to recover its lost territory from the southern Korean Silla kingdom.

There had been a long-standing power struggle between the military generals and the officials of the Goguryeo court. King Yeongnyu and some of the government officials felt that the army was becoming a serious threat, and plotted to kill some of the more powerful military officers, intending to kill Yeon Gaesomun, whose power and influence were rapidly overtaking the throne's, first. In 642, Yeon discovered the plot, and immediately went to Pyongyang, where he invited one hundred government ministers to a lavish banquet to celebrate his rise to the position of Eastern Governor. Yeon's soldiers ambushed and killed all the ministers present at the banquet. Yeon then proceeded to the palace and murdered the king. According to traditional Chinese and Korean sources, Yeon's men dismembered the dead king's corpse and discarded the pieces.

Yeon Gaesomun took control of the court and placed the king's nephew, Bojang (r. 642-668), on the throne. Yeon then had himself appointed to the post of Dae Mangniji (대막리지;大莫離支), the highest possible rank of Goguryeo, making him responsible for Goguryeo military and political affairs. Yeon assumed de facto control over Goguryeo affairs of state until his death around 666.

Goguryeo-Tang War and Tang-Silla alliance

After defeating Goguryeo's western ally, the Göktürks, the Tang forged an alliance with Goguryeo's rival, Silla. This increased tensions between Tang and Goguryeo.

In the beginning of Bojang's rule, Yeon was briefly conciliatory toward Tang China. He supported Taoism at the expense of Buddhism, and in 643, sent emissaries to the Tang court to request Taoist sages, eight of whom were brought to Goguryeo. Some historians believe this request was simply a tactic to pacify the Tang and allow Goguryeo time to prepare for a Tang invasion, which would inevitably occur if Yeon acted on out his ambitions to annex Silla.

Relations with Tang deteriorated, when Goguryeo launched new invasions of Silla. In 645, Taizong of Tang launched an invasion of Goguryeo, and was successful in conquering a number of major border city fortresses. However, Taizong's main army was held back for several months at Ansi Fortress by the dogged resistance of the Goguryeo general, Yang Man-chun. Yeon Gaesomun defeated the elite marine force sent by Taizong to take Pyongyang, Goguryeo's capital, and, according to the Joseon Sanggosa, immediately marched his legions to relieve Yang's Goguryeo forces at Ansi Fortress. Taizong's forces, caught between Yang's army in the front and Yeon's counter-attack closing in behind them, and suffering from the harsh winter and dangerously low food supplies, were forced to retreat to China. During the retreat, a large number of Taizong's soldiers were slain by Yeon and his pursuing army, but Taizong and the bulk of the invading army escaped. Taizong inflicted heavy casualties to both soldiers and civilians on Goguryeo's side, and Goguryeo was never again able to launch attacks on China, as it once had during the height of its power.

Historians speculate that after Taizong's failure to conquer Goguryeo, Taizong and his son, Gaozong, became involved in a personal rivalry with Yeon. After Emperor Taizong's death in 649, Gaozong launched two more unsuccessful invasions of Goguryeo in 661 and 667. Yeon's legendary defeat of the Tang forces in 662, at the Sasu River (蛇水, probably present-day Botong river), during which the invading general and all thirteen of his sons were killed in battle, is considered by many Koreans to be one of the three greatest military victories in Korean history.

Eventually, faced with increasing domestic problems in China, Tang was forced to retreat. However, the three invasions inflicted sever damage on its economy and the population, and Goguryeo never recovered. Both Silla and Tang continued their invasions for over eight years, ultimately leading to the demise of Goguryeo. As long as Yeon Gaesomun was alive, though, Tang and Silla were not able to conquer Goguryeo.

Death

The most likely date of Yeon's death is that recorded on the tomb stele of Namsaeng, Yeon Gaesomun's eldest son: The twenty-fourth year of the reign of Bojang (665). However, the Samguk Sagi records the year as 666, and the Japanese history Nihonshoki gives the year as the twenty-third year of the reign of King Bojang (664). He apparently died of natural causes.

Fall of Goguryeo

Yeon Gaesomun had at least three sons, (eldest to youngest) Yeon Namsaeng, Yeon Namgeon, and Yeon Namsan. After his death, the country was weakened by a succession struggle between his brother and his three sons and fell relatively swiftly to the Silla-Tang armies.

Yeon Namsaeng (淵男生 연남생 634-679), the eldest son, succeeded his father as the second Dae Mangniji (대막리지, 大莫離支) of Goguryeo. When he was nine years old, his father had begun giving him to official titles, first seonin 先人, and subsequently jungli sohyeong 中裏小兄, jungli daehyeong 中裏大兄, and jungli uidu daehyeong 中裏位頭大兄 (obscure Goguryeo titles whose exact nature is unknown). Yeon Namsaeng, was said to have become Dae Magniji sometime before the death of Yeon Gaesomun, who apparently stepped down from the position and took the honorary position of Tae Dae Magniji.

After the death of his father, Yeon Namsaeng prepared for war with the Tang, and set out on an inspection of the border fortresses in Liaodong, and other fortresses throughout the kingdom. Before his departure, he put his brothers, Yeon Namgeon and Yeon Namsan, in charge of Pyeongyang. Namgeon and Namsan took advantage of their brother's absence to take control of Pyeongyang and the Royal Courts. They falsely accused Namsaeng of being a traitor, and forced the Emperor to order Namsaeng's arrest. At the urging of his son, who had escaped death at the hands of his uncles, Namsaeng fled to Tang China, where he was given a high position in the Tang military. From there, he led a Tang-sponsored military campaign against Goguryeo with the hope of regaining power.

Namsaeng led the Tang army to victory in 668, and ultimately destroyed Goguryeo. Following the surrender of numerous cities in northern Goguryeo, the Tang army bypassed the Liaodong region and captured Pyongyang, the capital of Goguryeo. Yeon Jeongto, the younger brother of Yeon Gaesomun, surrendered his forces to the Silla general Kim Yushin, who was advancing from the south. In November, 668, Bojang, the last king of Goguryeo, surrendered to Tang Gaozhong. Namsaeng died in the domains of the Tang-established Protectorate General to Pacify the East, or Andong Duhufu (安東都護府), the Chinese administration established in Pyeongyang following the fall of Goguryeo in 668, to administer the former Goguryeo domains. He was buried on Mt. Mang (邙山) in Luoyang 洛陽, Tang's eastern capital.

Namsaeng's tomb stele, along with that of his brother Namgeon, has been discovered. Namsaeng's biography (Quan Nan Sheng 泉男生傳) appears in the Xin Tangshu (New History of Tang), book 110. The Chinese rendering of Namsaeng's family name is Cheon 泉 (Chinese Quan) rather than Yeon 淵, most likely because Yeon (Chinese, Yuan) was the given name of Tang Gaozu 高祖 (Li Yuan 李淵), founder and first emperor of Tang, and by Chinese tradition could not be applied to another.

Legacy

The series of wars between Goguryeo and the Tang is one of the most important conflicts in the history of Northeastern Asia. The wars are generally regarded as the main reason for the demise of the once-powerful Goguryeo kingdom, which for several centuries provided a cultural and political counterbalance to China. The suppression of the Goryeo kingdom made China the dominant civilization.

Yeon Gaesomun is viewed by many historians as the chief cause of, as well as a central protagonist in, this important series of wars. It is speculated that his assassination of King Yeongnyu may have been one of the reasons why Tang launched the first failed invasion of Goguryeo in 645. His ambitions to annex Silla were certainly a provocation. Yeon was an able general and succeeded in repelling the Tang invasions in 645 and 662. However, his style of rule as a military dictator caused instability and undermined the traditional system of recruiting officials and administrators from a broad political base, rendering the state less capable of comprehending and responding to new political developments in Tang and Silla. The power struggle which broke out among his three sons after Yeon's death was the final blow; when the eldest son Yeon Namsaeng defected to Tang, he was able to organize the final invasion which crushed Goguryeo.

The repeated wars against Tang were costly, decimating the rural population in the northern regions and weakening Goguryeo's production base.

After the fall of Goguryeo, several attempts were made to re-establish it. In 698, Balhae(Pohai) was founded by Daejoyoung, a descendant of Koguryo. In official documents sent abroad by the king, Balhae (698-926) boasted of itself as the successor of "Goryeo" (Koguryo). The kingdom of Koryo (918-1392), which succeeded Balhae, resurrected the name of "Koryo," which was the state title of Goguryeo.[1]

Historical controversy

Yeon Gaesomun has long been at the center of several historical controversies.

One concerns his personal character and motivation. Later Confucian scholars criticized Yeon for the coup and the regicide that brought him to power, portraying him as a disloyal subject who sought personal power above all else. In particular, extant Tang and Silla sources have consistently portrayed Yeon as a brutal and arrogant dictator. These sources include the story that Yeon carried five swords at a time, and would have men prostrate themselves so that he might use their backs to mount or dismount his horse. Modern nationalist historians dismiss these Tang and Silla sources as biased calumnies, and argue that Yeon's single-mindedness and success in defending Goguryeo testify to his patriotism.

Yeon's detractors blame him for needlessly provoking the Tang to attack Goguryeo and thereby ensuring its downfall. They point out that, while Goguryeo remained a formidable regional power before Yeon assumed power, it was completely destroyed by Silla and Tang within a short time soon after his death. Yeon's defenders claim that the Tang invasion of Goguryeo was inevitable, and that King Yeongnyu's appeasement of Tang bought only a temporary delay.

For many modern Korean nationalists, Yeon is a hero and a symbol of the time when, at the height of their power, the Koreans unambiguously triumphed over the Chinese. During the renascent conflict between South Korea and China over the historical ownership of part of Manchuria, Yeon has undergone a dramatic rehabilitation, and is now admired by many South Koreans, most of whom are descendants of the people of Silla.

Another controversy exists over the sources used to support the defeat of the Tang Dynasty by Goguryeo. Some sources, such as Sin's Joseon Sangosa, claim that Taizong was forced into the outskirts of Beijing, but Sin's account has been challenged on the basis that it lacked support in traditional Korean and Chinese sources. For example, he stated that 100,000-200,000 Tang soldiers died, but both the ancient Korean history Samguk Sagi[2] and ancient Chinese histories Book of Tang,[3] New Book of Tang,[4] and Zizhi Tongjian[5] put the figure at 20,000, stating that there were only 100,000 Tang soldiers in the entire invading army. The modern Chinese historian Bo Yang has speculated that the Yeon may have had the records altered so that he could claim credit for Yang Manchun's victory over Tang.[6]

WONHYO
The Great Master-Monk
(617 – April 28, 686)

Won Hyo (hangul:원효 hanja:元曉) was one of the leading thinkers, writers
mentators of the Korean Buddhist tradition. Essence-Function (體用), a key
East Asian Buddhism and particularly Korean Buddhism, was refined in th
philosophy and world view of Wonhyo.[1]

As one of the most eminent scholar-monks in Korean history, he was an influential
in the development of the East Asian Buddhist intellectual and commentarial tradition.
His extensive literary output runs to over 80 works in 240 fascicles, and some of his commentaries, such as those on the Mahāyāna Mahāparinirvāṇa Sūtra and the Awakening of
Faith in the Mahayana, became classics revered throughout China and Japan as well as
Korea. In fact, his commentary on the Awakening of Faith helped to make it one of the
most influential and intensively studied texts in the East Asian Mahāyāna tradition.[2]
Chinese masters who were heavily influenced by Wonhyo include Fazang, Li Tongxuan,
and Chengguan. The Japanese monks Gyonen, Zenshu and Joto of the Kegon school were
also influenced by him.[3]

With his life spanning the end of the Three Kingdoms of Korea and the beginning of Unified Silla, Wonhyo played a vital role in the reception and assimilation of the broad range
of doctrinal Buddhist streams that flowed into the Korean peninsula at the time. Wonhyo
was most interested in and affected by Buddha-nature, East Asian Yogācāra and Hwaeom
thought. However, in his extensive scholarly works, composed as commentaries and es-
says, he embraced the whole spectrum of the Buddhist teachings which were received in
Korea, including such schools as Pure Land Buddhism, East Asian Mādhyamaka and the
Tiantai.

Biography

Bogwangjeon hall at Bunhwangsa, Gyeongju which is a dedicated shrine to Wonhyo.
Wonhyo was born in Amnyang (押梁), nowadays the city of Gyeongsan, North Gyeongsang Province, South Korea. He had a son, Seol Chong, who is considered to be one of
the great Confucian scholars of Silla.

Wonhyo was famous for singing and dancing in the streets. While the Buddha discouraged such behaviors, his songs and dances were seen as upaya, or skillful means, meant
to help save all sentient beings.

> [Wŏnhyo] tried to embody in his own life the ideal of a bodhisattva who works
> for the well-being of all sentient beings. Transcending the distinction of the
> sacred and the secular, he married a widower princess, visited villages and
> towns, and taught people with songs and dances.
>
> —Hee-Sung Keel[4]

He is thought to have founded Korea's lone riverside temple, Silleuksa, in the late 600s.
While Wonhyo was in Bunhwangsa (in modern Guhwang-dong, Gyeongju), he wrote
a number of books. For such strong association with Wonhyo, a research center and a
shrine named Bogwangjeon hall dedicated to Wonhyo's legacy are located in Bunhwangsa.[5]

.1e wrote commentaries on virtually all of the most influential Mahayana scriptures, altogether including over eighty works in over two hundred fascicles. Among his most influential works were the commentaries he wrote on the Awakening of Faith, Mahāparinirvāṇa Sūtra and Vajrasamādhi sūtra, along with his exposition on the mean-ing of the two hindrances, the ijangui. These were treated with utmost respect by leading Buddhist scholars in China and Japan, and served to help in placing the Awakening of Faith as the most influential text in the Korean tradition.

Wŏnhyo, commonly regarded as the greatest thinker in Korean Buddhism, was a prolific writer who produced no less than eighty-six works, of which twenty-three are extant either completely or partially. By his time, most of the important sūtras and treatises had flowed into Korea from China, and they were causing a great deal of confusion for Silla

A front view of Bogwangjeon hall enshrining Monk Wonhyo at Bunhwangsa temple in Gyeongju

By Alain Seguin from Ottawa, Canada [CC BY-SA 3.0 (http://creativecommons.org/licenses/by-sa/3.0)], via Wikimedia Commons

Buddhists, as they had for the Chinese. It was Wŏnhyo's genius to interpret all of the texts known to him in a way that would reveal their underlying unity of truth without sacrificing the distinctive message of each text. He found his hermeneutical key in the famous Mahāyāna text, the Awakening of Faith (Dasheng Qixin Lun).[6]

Teaching story

Wonhyo spent the earlier part of his career as a monk. In 661 he and a close friend - Uisang (625–702, founder of the Hwaeom) - were traveling to China where they hoped to study Buddhism further. Somewhere in the region of Baekje, the pair were caught in a heavy downpour and forced to take shelter in what they believed to be an earthen sanctuary. During the night Wonhyo was overcome with thirst, and reaching out grasped what he perceived to be a gourd, and drinking from it was refreshed with a draught of cool, refreshing water. Upon waking the next morning, however, the companions discovered much to their amazement that their shelter was in fact an ancient tomb littered with human skulls, and the vessel from which Wonhyo had drunk was a human skull full of brackish water. Upon seeing this, Wonhyo vomited. Startled by the experience of believing that a gruesome liquid was a refreshing treat, Wonhyo was astonished at the power of the human mind to transform reality. After this "One Mind"[7] enlightenment experience, he abandoned his plan to go to China. He left the priesthood and turned to the spreading of the Buddhadharma as a layman. Because of this aspect of his character, Wonhyo ended up becoming a popular folk hero in Korea.[8] An important result of his combined work with Uisang was the establishment of Hwaeom as the dominant stream of doctrinal thought on the Korean Peninsula.

English translation project

Wonhyo's twenty-three extant works are currently in the process of being translated into English as a joint project between Dongguk University and Stony Brook University. The University of Hawaii Press is publishing them in five volumes.[9]

Taekwondo sequence

The International Taekwon-Do Federation pattern "Won-Hyo" is named in Wonhyo's honor. This pattern consists of 28 movements.

The World Taekwondo Federation has a Hyeong or pattern named Ilyeo for 9th Dan black belt which means the thought of the Buddhist priest of Silla Dynasty, Wonhyo.[10]

JANG BO-GO
The Emperor of The Sea
(787 - 846)

Jang Bogo (hangul:장보고 hanja:張保皐), childhood name: Gungbok (궁복:弓福) was a Sillan who rose to prominence in the Later Silla period of Korea as a powerful maritime figure who effectively controlled the Yellow Sea (West Sea),[1] and dominated the trade between Silla, Heian Japan, and Tang China for decades.[2] His impressive fleet of ships was centered in Wando, an island in South Jeolla Province. So influential a figure did Jang become in late Silla politics that he was granted official office as Maritime Commissioner of the Cheonghaejin Garrison (on Wando) and came near to marrying his daughter into the Silla Royal House before his assassination in 846. He was worshipped as a god following his death.

Early years

One of the few sources on his early life is the 12th century Samguk Sagi ("A History of the Three Kingdoms"), which contains a brief biography of Jang compiled three centuries after his death. The biography relates that Jang Bogo was adept in martial arts and that Jang's companion Jeong Yeon (정년:鄭年) could swim five li (about 2.5 km) underwater without taking a breath. The history further records that as young men the two companions, Jang Bogo and Jeong Yeon, traveled to Tang China. Their skills in horsemanship and the handling of spears soon won them military office. They were both named Junior Generals of Wuning District (武寧軍小將) (in what is today Jiangsu province).

Rise to power

By the ninth century thousands of Silla subjects were living in Tang, centered mostly around merchant activities in coastal Shandong and Jiangsu provinces, where they established their own Silla communities often led by Silla officials. Wealthy benefactors (including at one point Jang Bogo himself) even established Silla Buddhist temples in the region, as related by the 9th-century Japanese monk Ennin, whose journal constitutes one of the other rare sources on Jang Bogo.

Apparently, while in China Jang Bogo had become incensed at the treatment of his fellow countrymen, who in the unstable milieu of late Tang often fell victim to coastal pirates or inland bandits. In fact, Silla subjects living in Tang had become a favored target of bandits, who sold their captives into slavery. In 823 the Tang emperor went so far as to issue an edict stopping the slave trade and ordering the return of all abducted Koreans to Silla. [3] Shortly after returning to Silla around 825, and by now in possession of a formidable private fleet headquartered at Cheonghae (Wando), Jang Bogo petitioned the Silla king Heungdeok (r. 826-836) to establish a permanent maritime garrison to protect Silla merchant activities in the Yellow Sea. Heungdeok agreed and in 828 formally established the Cheonghae ("clear sea") Garrison at what is today Wando island off Korea's South Jeolla province. The Samguk Sagi further relates that Heungdeok gave Jang an army of 10,000 men to establish and man the defensive works. The remnants of Cheonghae Garrison can still be seen on Jang islet just off Wando's southern coast.

The establishment of Cheonghae garrison marked the apex of Jang's career. From that moment he can be viewed in the context of the numerous private warlords arising outside the Silla capital who were often backed by formidable private armies. Jang's force, though nominally bequeathed by the Silla king, was effectively under his own control. Jang became arbiter of Yellow Sea commerce and navigation. Another rare account of

Jang and his garrison comes from the journal of the Japanese monk Ennin (Jikaku), who in 840 made a pilgrimage to Tang in search of Buddhist scriptures and relied upon the maritime abilities of Jang to reach China and return. The best evidence of Jang's now high fortunes is his involvement in the volatile factional politics of the Silla court.

Political influence

At the time, Jang Bogo's backing of his own army allotted him immense power in politics. Militarily, he was powerful enough to overthrow the state and become king himself had he wanted to. He was often hated by the Silla royal family members due to his prominent status and the fact that he was born a commoner, not a nobleman.

In 839 Jang proved instrumental in the seizure of power by Silla's King Sinmu following the overthrow of King Minae. Kim Ujing (later King Sinmu) approached Jang for help in taking the throne from the usurper who had killed Ujing's father. Jang is purported to have replied, "The ancients had a saying, 'To see what is right and not to do it is want of courage.' Though I am without ability, I shall follow your orders."[4] Thereupon Jang dispatched a force of 5000 men under the command of his closest companion and adviser Jeong Yeon (who had since also returned from Tang) in support of Sinmu's claim. The success of Sinmu's power grab won Jang Bogo the post of Prime Minister.

Death

The account of Jang Bogo's demise comes from the Samguk Sagi. In 845 Jang overplayed his hand when he maneuvered to marry his daughter to King Munseong (ruled 839-857), son of Sinmu. Aristocratic factions at court, no doubt fed up with the machinations of Jang (a man in all likelihood from obscure provincial origins outside Silla's aristocratic order), then plotted to have him killed. The Samguk Yusa, a late 13th century Korean book that mixes history and tales of marvels and popular legend, relates that the Silla king was pressured by aristocrats to deny Jang his marriage and that as a result Jang began to conspire against the king.[5] Whether it was the Silla king or the aristocracy that was behind Jang's demise is unclear. However, both the Samguk Sagi and Samguk Yusa relate that in 846 Jang was assassinated at his Cheonghae garrison headquarters by Yeomjang (염장: 閻長), an emissary from the Silla court who had arrived concealing a knife in his garments. Gaining Jang's confidence by pretending he had fled from the Silla capital, he then attacked Jang as they shared wine. However, the Japanese history book, Shoku Nihon Kōki (續日本後紀) (Later Chronicle of Japan, Continued), gives Jang's date of death as 841.

In 851 the Cheonghae garrison was disbanded and its troops dispersed. The location of Jang Bogo's burial spot remains unknown.

In Korean Shamanism and Mythology

Jang Bogo was worshipped as a god after his death, especially on the small island of Jangdo. The shamanistic temple on the island worships 'Great General Song';however, according to the islanders, 'Great General Song' is a title of Jang Bogo.

There is a myth about Jang Bogo ('General Jang') and 'General Eom', Jang Bogo's son-in-law, retold in the region.

General Eom, who was General Jang's son-in-law, lived in the Eomnamut Valley. One day, he and General Jang had a contest;who could first raise a flag on that eastern crag? Jang Bogo transformed into a male pheasant and flew to the crag, but General Eom turned into a falcon and killed and ate General Jang in the form of a pheasant. Thus, the crag is still called Kattturiyeo (까투리여, male pheasant crag).

Jang BoGo Memorial Hall

Jang BoGo Memorial Hall, which is a 2F reinforced concrete structure with a plottage of 14,472m², a building area of 1,739m², and an exhibition space of 730m², has on its ground floor Central Hall, Video Room, Special Exhibition Hall, storage, and lounge and on its second floor its permanent exhibition venues of Exhibition Hall 1, Sea Route, and Exhibition Hall 2.

Central Hall on 1F displays 'Trade Ships of Jang BoGo', which was made to one fourth of the actual size by Director Ma Gwang-nam of Cheonghaejin Ship Institute and donated by Sea King Jang BoGo Memorial Society, and a large wooden mural(8m x 2.2m) entitled 'Sea King Jang BoGo', which was created with linden tree by Lu Guangzheng, the Chinese craft art maestro.

The permanent exhibition hall on 2F is divided into the four themes of 'Root', 'Formation of Cheonghaejin', 'Maritime Empire', and 'Voyage', which respectively display relevant exhibits.

Republic of Korea Submarine Chang Bogo (SSK 61) heads out to sea during exercise Rim of the Pacific (RIMPAC)

Cultural references

- Jang Bogo and his exploits were the subject of the 1965 South Korean film, Jang Bogo, directed by Ahn Hyeon-cheol and starring Shin Yeong-gyun and Lee Min-ja. Its English title is Admiral Jang.

- The South Korean navy named the first of its Type 209 submarines 'Admiral Chang Bogo' in Jang's honor.

- A highly fictionalized account of Jang's life was the subject of the 2004 Korean drama Emperor of the Sea,[6] starring Choi Soo-jong as Jang Bogo.

- In March 2009, the Cheonghae Anti-piracy Unit was formed by the Republic of Korea Navy to combat piracy off the coast of Somalia. The unit is named after Cheonghaejin,

the maritime base created by Jang Bogo to combat piracy on the waters of Silla and Tang.
- In Shenyang, a memorial dedicated to Jang Bogo opened in 2007.[7]

"Hae Shin (Emperor of the Sea)" Poster (C) KBS

In popular culture

Portrayed by Choi Soo-jong and Baek Sung-hyun in the 2004-2005 KBS2 TV series
Emperor of the Sea.

GANG GAM-CHAN
The Great General and Hero of Goreyo
(22 December 948 – 9 September 1031)

Gang Gam-Chan Statue atAnguksa shrine in Nakseongdae Park

Gang Gam-chan (강감찬, 姜邯贊) was a medieval Korean government official and military commander during the early days of Goryeo Dynasty (918–1392). Even though he was a career scholar and government official, he is best known for his military victories during the Third Goryeo-Khitan War.

Early life

Gang was born on 22 December 948 into a prominent aristocratic family in the hyeon of Geumju (now Gwanak-gu in Seoul). His father also worked for the King Taejo of Goryeo, and had been awarded for helping establish a new dynasty and unifying the Korean Peninsula. A legend tells that on the day he was born a meteor fell toward his house, and an advisor to the king visited to find that a baby had just been born there, whom he predicted would become great and be long remembered. Gang Gam-chan's birth site is called Nakseongdae (site of the falling star, 낙성대, 洛星岱), near Seoul's Nakseongdae Station on the Line two subway.

As a child, Gang was small for his age, but he showed signs of leadership and loyalty at an early age. At seven he began to learn Confucian philosophy, military tactics and martial arts from his father. After his father's death in 964, he left his household and traveled around the country. In 983 he received the top score in the civil service examination, and qualified as a government official at age thirty-six. In 992 he joined the royal court as a deputy under the Minister of Education.

Goryeo-Khitan Wars

In 993, the Liao Dynasty ordered General Xiao Sunning to invade Goryeo. The opinions among the court officials were divided, either to fight against the Khitans or to negotiate with them. Gang supported the use of negotiations, which was also supported by the king as the official decision. Seo Hui was sent to General Xiao as Korean representative, and the successful truce negotiation led to the withdrawal of Khitan forces and establishment of friendly relationship between Liao and Goryeo.

In 1004, the Khitans defeated the Chinese Song Dynasty and forced its emperor to pay tribute to the Khitan. With Song defeated, the only threat remaining against the Khitans was Goryeo. Also in 1009, General Gang Jo of Goryeo led a coup against the government;he deposed and murdered King Mokjong and began a military rule, and broke the peaceful relationship with the Khitans. The Khitans saw this as their reason to attack Goryeo, and in 1010, Emperor Shengzong of Liao led a massive invasion with a contingent of 400,000 soldiers, commanding the troops himself. Suffering heavy casualties in five major engagements, the Khitans finally defeated the Goryeo army and executed their commander General Gang Jo.

However, Gang urged King Hyeonjong to escape from the palace, not to surrender to the invading Liao troops. The King followed Gang's advice, and managed to escape from the burning capital. A Korean insurgency began to harass Khitan forces, which finally compelled Shengzong to withdraw his army. The Khitans won the war, but gained no benefit from it;rather spending precious resources in vain and reducing the national treasury. Thus another bloody war between the two nations was foreshadowed, and tensions would further lead to the Third Goryeo-Khitan War. Gang was later promoted to Prime Minister.

In 1018, General Xiao Baiya, under orders of the Liao administration, led an expedition to Goryeo with a 100,000 man contingent. This time, many officials urged the king to commence peace negotiations, since the damage from the Second Goryeo-Khitan War had been so great, leaving Goryeo difficult to recover. However, Gang advised the king to declare war against the Liao, since the enemy contingent was much smaller than in previous invasions. He volunteered to be the acting deputy War minister for the duration of the war, at the age of seventy-one. He led about 208,000 men toward the Goryeo-Liao border.

The first battle of the war was the Battle of Heunghwajin, which was a significant victory of Goryeo by blocking the stream and destroying the dam when Khitans were crossing the water. However, General Xiao did not give up the hope of capturing the capital Kaesung, and continued to march south. Later, Xiao realized that the mission was impossible to accomplish, and decided to retreat. General Gang knew that the Khitan army would withdraw from the war, and awaited them at the fortress of Gwiju, where he encountered the retreating Khitans in 1019.

Discouraged and starving, the Khitans were defeated by the Goryeo army. Only General Xiao and few remaining survivors managed to escape from the devastating defeat. This battle is known as the Battle of Gwiju. General Gang returned to the capital and was welcomed as the military hero who saved the kingdom. After the war, Gang retired from both the military and the government to rest, since he was too old, already having become a national hero. He was appointed as Prime Minister in 1030, one year before his death. He died in 1031 on the 20th day of the 8th lunar month (9 September 1031).

Legacy

Statue of Gang Gam-chan in Nakseongdae Park, Seoul, South Korea
General Gang's overwhelming victories in the battles of Kwiju and Heunghwajin are often compared with the victories of General Eulji Mundeok at the Battle of Salsu or Admiral Yi Sun-sin at the battles of Hansan and Myeongnyang, which, like Gang's battles, overcame disadvantages and successfully defended the country. Of course, Gang is regarded as one of the greatest military commanders in Korean history, along with General Eulji and Admiral Yi, even though Gang was never trained as a soldier like Eulji or Yi.

Following his victories in the Third Goryeo-Khitan War, the peace among the three powerful East-Asian empires settled;Goryeo established a peaceful but tense relationship with Liao Dynasty, which gave up the hope of taking over either Song or Goryeo. As a result, Goryeo broke off relationships with Song Dynasty, but continued commercial trading with the Chinese;Song continued to pay tribute to Liao, and Song would also pay tribute to Western Xia, which would pay tribute to the Khitans. The peace lasted for about a century. The Jurchens took advantage of this time to expand their power without any interruption until their establishment of Jin Dynasty. Song Dynasty got the least benefit from the peace, and secretly encouraged the Jurchens to attack Liao, but after the fall of the Khitans, the Jurchens turned on Song and took over its capital, forcing the Chinese to flee southward. The victories of General Gang thus marked the ending point of the chain of wars between countries and was the beginning of a triangle diplomacy (Goryeo, Liao,

Song), setting the scene for the ascendance of the Jurchens.

Gang's shrine, called Anguksa, stands today in Sadang-dong, Gwanak-gu, Seoul. Further to this, the famous Gang Jee Seok is a descendant of the Great Gang Gam Chan.

Also known as devil of war. The South Korean soccer flag which is the Red Devils, the picture is how people saw him.

KIM BUSIK
Great Scholar Who Led The Compilation of The Samguk Sagi
(1075–1151)

Kim Busik (김부식:金富軾) was a statesman, general, Confucian scholar and writer during Korea's Goryeo period. A scion of the Silla royalty and a member of the Kyeongju Kim clan, he was the supreme chancellor in 1136-1142 and was in charge of suppression of the Myo Cheong rebellion. Kim is best known for supervising the compilation of the Samguk Sagi, the oldest extant written Korean history.

Family background and early life

Kyeongju Kim clan were direct descendants of the last Silla king, Kim Pu.[1] The clan seat (pongwan) name[2] derives from Kim's great grandfather, a member of the royal Kim clan, who became the administrator in charge of the former Silla capital (renamed Gyeongju at the beginning of the Goryeo period).[3] The first Goryeo king Taejo married into the Kyeongju Kim,[4] and the clan played a leading role in early Goryeo politics. Three of its members were the officials of the first and second rank during 981-1069.[5]

Kim's father Kim Kun was an official (reached the junior 3rd rank[5]) and a famous poet. When he was a member of an embassy to the Song court, he and the fellow envoy Pak Illyang published a collection of poems that made a deep impression on Song scholars. "The allusions in the poems were so intricate that the most renowned court scholars had to study them in detail before being able to understand them."[6]

The oldest son Kim Bu-pil (? -?) reached the senior 5th rank in 1102,[5] but these were the three younger sons, Kim Bu-il (1071–1132), Kim Busik, and Kim Bu-cheol, also known as Kim Puǔi,[7] (1079-1136) that played an important role in politics and culture of Goryeo. Kim Kun died when Kim Busik was about thirteen, and his widow raised and supervised the education of her younger sons. Later King Yejong rewarded her with a yearly allowance, noting in particular her merit in assisting each of her sons to pass the state examination.[3][8]

Career

Early career, 1096-1122

Kim himself passed the civil service examination in 1096 on the Book of Documents[9] and was appointed as an official in the Anseo prefecture. Subsequently he was selected for a position at the Hallimwon (Academy of Letters),[8] that was also responsible for drafting foreign correspondence. The Kim brothers steadily raised through the ranks of the civil service. In 1115 Kim Busik was appointed to the Office of Remonstrance. Despite their relatively junior ranks, both Kim Busik (senior 6th rank) and Kim Bu-il (junior 5th rank) participated in the meetings of the Privy Council (Chae Chu).

The increasing literary and scholarly reputation of the Kim brothers made them popular lectures on the Confucian classics. In 1116, King Yejong instituted the royal lecture (kyeongyeon) by designating a lecture hall and making a number of appointments to the position of a royal lecturer. Under him and his successor Injong the lectures were held regularly. Such a lecture was a Confucian ritual in which the ruler paid homage to Confucian teachings.[10] Many of the royal lecturers belonged to the Han An-in faction that opposed Yi Cha-gyeom.[11] Both Kim Bu-cheol and Kim Busik delivered royal lectures, expounding the teachings of Confucius and Mencius. Kim Busik lectured on the Book of History and the Book of Changes.[3]

These lectures became a scene of rivalry between Kim Busik and Yun Oni, son of the famous general Yun Gwan. Yun was an influential Confucian scholar and a future supporter of the Pyongyang faction and Myo Cheong. His attacks on Kim may have roots in Yun Gwan's fall and disgrace (1108-1109) that was at least partially precipitated by the court machinations, or in an incident when Kim Busik rewrote a memorial plaque written by the general. During Kim's lessons on various historical topics Yun Oni posed difficult questions, apparently trying to embarrass him and discredit his scholarship.[11] After 1121 Kim Busik was appointed as Royal Diarist, or ji, to the court of Yejong. By 1122 Kim Busik became an executive at the Ministry of Rites (Yebu Sirang),[3] typically an appointment of the 3rd junior rank.

Role in the foreign policy, 1114-1122

The years 1114-1128 saw a major change in the balance of power in North-East Asia. Around the year 1100 the dominant regional power was the Khitan state of Liao. Emperors of Liao and of Song China were officially considered equals.[12] However, Song had to pay an annual tribute (that was not named as such) of 200,000 taels of silver and 300,000 bolts of silk, that was equivalent to several percent of the Song government revenues. Goryeo was a vassal state of Liao, even if the tribute was not paid since 1054. Jurchen tribes were vassals of Liao, that exercised a variable degree of control over their tribal groupings. Jurchen had complicated relationships with Goryeo. These ranged from a tributary status and mercenary service to cross-border warfare and informal alliances, particularly during the reign of King Yejong.[13]

Basic tenets of Goryeo's political theory were expressed in the Ten Injunctions of Taejo. [14] This document advised a cautious following of the Chinese practices, and expressed abhorrence of Khitan, and by extension, other nomadic `barbarians'.[15] The status of Goryeo rulers can be roughly summarized as naeje oewang (emperor at home and king abroad). They were titled kings, were vassals of Khitan Liao dynasty, and were careful to keep these convention in the correspondence with the suzerains. On the other hand, many aspects of the government were fashioned after following the imperial conventions. A majority view of the scholars-officials, including the Kim brothers, was that Goryeo was a realm in itself and thus "a possible center of the world".[16] During this period Kim Busik drafted a significant portion of the diplomatic correspondence with both Liao and Song.

Throughout their careers Kim brothers demonstrated a pragmatic approach both domestically and internationally. At the beginning of the century the Liao Dynasty appeared strong and Kim Bu-il congratulated Emperor Tianzuo of Liao as a ruler who "developed and enlarged [his] territory and made both Chinese and barbarians follow [him] peacefully."[17] In a letter to the Song court Kim Busik derived the Goryeo legitimacy as successors of Jizi (Giji, a semi-legendary sage who is said to have ruled Gojoseon in the 11th century BCE), who was enfeoffed by the Chinese Son of Heaven. After a long and mutually complementary discourse Busik "concluded by stating that it was the barbarians who stood between Goryeo and the Song, literally and figuratively." This letter was written just before Kim Busik finally ensured the recognition by Goryeo of the Jin dynasty ruler as the Son of Heaven in 1126.[18]

Jurchen leader Wanyan Aguda started a successful rebellion against Liao in 1114. While majority of the Goryeo officials were anti-Jurchen, both king's father-in-law Yi Cha-gyeom and Kim Busik aimed to keep Goryeo out of the fray and benefit from the changing geopolitical situation. For example, the first Liao request for help was debated (8th month of the 10th year of Yejong's reign, July 1115) at the extended meeting of the Privy Council that included also the top military commanders. The majority of officials supported sending the troops. The opposition was voiced by a relatively junior associate of Yi Cha-gyeom and by Kim Bu-il and Kim Busik, who argued that 'sending troops for another country could be the cause of trouble and would undoubtedly be dangerous for the future'. They succeeded in stalling the motion.[19] At approximately the same time Kim Busik acknowledged the increasing strength of the Jurchen in the official letters to the Liao court, but swear that Goryeo is loyal to Liao; if not, "may the gods destroy it". [18]

Wanyan Aguda scored a number of victories over Liao; and proclaimed the establishment of the Jin dynasty with himself as its first emperor in 1115. In 1116-1117 Kim Busik was part of the embassy to the Song court. Goryeo consistently refused a military help to Liao and in the wake of the Jurchen advances recaptured the Uiju (Poju) area and once again established the Yalu River as its border.[20] While the majority of the Yenjong's officials believed in the eventual Liao downfall, a crisis in the relationship with the Jurchen was precipitated by the request of Taizu of Jin to be recognized as the 'elder brother' of the Goryeo king in 1117. Majority of the officials opposed this request and even considered beheading the envoy. The factions of Yi Cha-gyeom and Kim Busik factions stalled the rush moves, but the formal submission of Goryeo to Jin was made only during the reign of Injong.

In fact, Kim Bu-cheol (voicing a position of Kim Busik who was at the time in China) submitted a memorandum proposing to accede to the demands of Emperor Taizu of Jin, giving the following rational: "Now even the great Song calls itself the younger brother of the Khitan and they have gotten along peacefully for generations. And although there is nothing under heaven that can measure up to the dignity of the Son of Heaven [of Goryeo], submitting to and obeying the barbarians like this is the proper policy, one that the sages called 'the temporarily putting aside of one's principles as circumstances demand it' and 'the protection of the whole country.'"[18] Later Kim Busik himself provided an example of temporizing in the correspondence with the Jin, arguing why Goryeo cannot be its vassal.[18]

In his book Gaoli tujing Xu Jing (1091-1153), a member of the Song mission to Goryeo in 1122-1123, mentions Kim Busik.[21]

Reign of Injong (1122-1146)

Early ears of the reign of Injong (1122-1126) were dominated by Yi Cha-gyeom, his maternal grandfather. Shortly after Injong took the throne, Kim was an executive, and in 1124 was promoted to the position of the fourth secretary in the Ministry of Rites (Yebu

Sirang). Using his position Kim opposed Yi Cha-gyeom hold on power, aiming at Yi's attempts to enhance his public image. Already in 1122 Kim argued against giving special recognition to Yi Cha-gyeom as king's grandfather. Later he questioned the appropriateness of calling Yi's birthday Insujel (Celebrating Humaneness and Longevity), and a planned performance of the ritual music at the Yi's family graves. Nevertheless, after a failed coup against Yi in early 1126 Kim Busik not only remained in power, but was promoted to the position of the Chief Censor.[22]

The role of Kim Busik in toppling Yo Cha-gyeom is unknown. Kim Bu-il, on the other hand, was one of the intermediaries between Injong and Yi's military supporters, inducing them to defect.[22]

After 1126 Kim brothers advanced through the Security Council into the highest offices.

In 1135-1136 Kim Busik was in charge of suppressing the rebellion of Myo Cheong and rooting out his adherents in Kaesong He became the supreme chancellor in 1136 and dominate the Goryeo government till his official retirement in 1142.

In 1142, Injong ordered the compilation of the Samguk Sagi, a chronicle of events in the Three Kingdoms and Unified Silla. Using Chinese histories (particularly Shiji by Sima Qian), Kim Busik at the head of the fourteen-author team compiled the oldest extant source on Korean history. It was submitted to Injong in late 1145 or early 1146.[3]

Late years

Works

Samguk Sagi("The History of the Three Kingdoms of Korea") is the oldest extant work of Korean history and often the only written source of information about the Three kingdoms and Unified Silla periods

Religion

Ideological and religious opinions of Kim Busik fell into the spectrum of practices of the upper strata of the Goryeo society. Confucianism was primarily a state ideology, aimed at social cohesion and state administration. Kim was one of the most prominent Confucian scholars of his time.

By the twelfth century Buddhism was a religion of both elites and common people. It enjoyed royal and aristocratic patronage and the Buddhist hierarchy was integrated into the state bureaucracy. Kim Busik was a practicing Buddhist. He established a family temple complex Kwallan-sa. This temple also inspired Kim's poem At Kwallan.[23] Kim is an author of the inscription honoring a Buddhist monk Uicheon (the son of King Munjong and the National Preceptor, one of the three highest Buddhist hierarchs of the country). There he recalls their only meeting, when as a boy he visited his brother in a monastery. In retirement Kim became a lay monk (keosa).

Worship of native spirits and guardian spirits was widely practiced by populace and part of the royal rituals prescribed by the Ten Injunctions of Taejo. During the Myo Cheong rebellion in 1135-1136 Kim Busik is recorded as swearing an oath "by the heaven and the earth, the mountains and streams and the gods and spirits".[24] He made a sacrifice to the guardian deities of the Western Capital following its capture from the rebels.[25]

YI SEONG-GYE
The First King of The Joseon Dynasty
(October 27, 1335 – May 24, 1408)

Taejo (태조：太祖) of Joseon , born Yi Seong-gye (이성계：李成桂), whose changed name is Yi Dan (이단：李旦), was the founder and the first king of the Joseon Dynasty of Korea reigning from 1392 to 1398, and the main figure in overthrowing the Goryeo Dynasty.

Taejo's father Yi Ja-chun was a minor Mongol official, but his ethnicity was Korean. Taejo's mother Queen Uihye was originally Chinese.[1][2] Taejo joined the Goryeo army and rose through the ranks, seizing the throne in 1392. He abdicated in 1398 during the strife between his sons and died in 1408.

Biography

Historical context for rise

By the late 14th century, the 400-year-old Goryeo Dynasty established by Wang Geon in 918 was tottering, its foundations collapsing from years of war and de facto occupation by the disintegrating Mongol Empire. The legitimacy of Korea itself was also becoming an increasingly disputed issue within the court, as the ruling house failed not only to govern the kingdom effectively, but was also tarnished by generations of forced intermarriage with members of the Mongol Yuan Dynasty imperial family and by rivalry amongst the various Goryeo Dynasty royal family branches (even King U's mother was a known commoner, thus leading to rumors disputing his descent from King Gongmin).

Within the kingdom, influential aristocrats, generals, and even prime ministers struggled for royal favor and vied for domination of the court, resulting in deep divisions among various factions. With the ever-increasing number of raids against Goryeo conducted by Japanese pirates (왜구：倭寇:waegu) and the Red Turbans invasions of Korea, those who came to dominate the royal court were the reformed-minded Sinjin aristocracy and the opposing Gweonmun aristocracy, as well as generals who could actually fight off the foreign threats—namely a talented general named Yi Seong-gye and his rival Choe Yeong. With the rise of the Ming Dynasty under a former monk, Zhu Yuanzhang (the Hongwu Emperor), Mongol forces became more vulnerable. By the 1350s Goryeo regained its full independence from the waning Mongol Empire, although Mongol remnants effectively occupied northeastern territories with large garrisons of troops.

Military career

General Yi Seong-gye had gained power and respect during the late 1370s and early 1380s by pushing Mongol remnants off the peninsula and also by repelling well-organized Japanese pirates in a series of successful engagements. He was also credited with routing the Red Turbans when they made their move into the Korean Peninsula as part of their rebellion against the Yuan Dynasty. Following in the wake of the rise of the Ming Dynasty under Zhu Yuanzhang, the royal court in Goryeo split into two competing factions: the group led by General Yi (supporting the Ming Dynasty) and the camp led by his rival General Choe (supporting the Yuan Dynasty).

When a Ming messenger came to Goryeo in 1388 (the 14th year of King U) to demand the return of a significant portion of Goryeo's northern territory, General Choe seized the opportunity and played upon the prevailing anti-Ming atmosphere to argue for the invasion of the Liaodong Peninsula (Goryeo claimed to be the successor of the ancient kingdom of Goguryeo;as such, restoring Manchuria as part of Korean territory was a tenet of its foreign policy throughout its history).

A staunchly opposed Yi was chosen to lead the invasion;however, at Wihwa Island on the Amrok River, he made a momentous decision, commonly called "Turning back the army from Wihwa Island", that would alter the course of Korean history. Knowing of the support he enjoyed both from high-ranking government officials, the general populace, and the great deterrent of Ming Empire under the Hongwu Emperor, he decided to revolt and swept back to the capital, Gaesong, to secure control of the government.

Revolution

General Yi swept his army from the Yalu River straight into the capital, defeated forces loyal to the king (led by General Choe, whom he proceeded to eliminate) and forcibly dethroned King U in a de facto coup d'état but did not ascend to the throne right away. Instead, he placed on the throne King U's son, King Chang, and following a failed restoration of the former monarch, had both of them put to death. General Yi, now the undisputed power behind the throne, soon forcibly had a Goryeo royal named Yo, now King Gongyang (공양왕 : 恭讓王), crowned as king. After indirectly enforcing his grasp on the royal court through the puppet king, Yi then proceeded to ally himself with Sinjin aristocrats such as Jeong Do-jeon and Jo Jun. In 1392 (the 4th year of King Gongyang), Yi dethroned King Gongyang, exiled him to Wonju (where he and his family were secretly murdered), and ascended the throne. The Goryeo Dynasty had come to an end after 475 years of rule.

One of the most widely repeated episodes that occurred in the immediate aftermath of the fall of Goryeo was in 1392, when Taejo's fifth son, Yi Bang-won (later King Taejong), threw a party for the renowned scholar, poet and statesman Jeong Mong-ju, who refused to be won over by Yi despite their numerous correspondences in the form of archaic poems, and continued to be a faithful supporter of the old dynasty, and a leading figure in the opposition to Yi's claim to the throne. Jeong was revered throughout Goryeo, even by Yi Bang-won himself, but he was seen to be an obstacle and as such, in the eyes of supporters of the new dynasty, had to be removed. After the party, on his way home, Jeong was murdered by five men on the Seonjuk Bridge (선죽교 : 善竹橋) in Gaeseong. This bridge has now become a national monument of North Korea, and a brown spot on one of the stones is said to be a bloodstain of his which turns red when it rains. on one of the stones is said to be a bloodstain of his which turns red when it rains.

Reign

Yi Seong-gye declared a new dynasty in 1392–1393 under the name of Joseon, thereby reviving an older state, also known as Joseon, that was, legendarily, established nearly three thousand years previously, and renamed the country the "Kingdom of Great Joseon".

An early achievement of the new monarch was improved relations with China;and indeed, Joseon had its origin in General Yi's refusal to attack China in response to raids from Chinese bandits.[3] Shortly after his accession, the new monarch sent envoys to inform the Ming court at Nanjing that a dynastic change had taken place.[4] Korean envoys were dispatched to Japan, seeking the re-establishment of amicable relations. The mission was successful;and Shogun Ashikaga Yoshimitsu was reported to have been favorably impressed by this initial embassy.[5] Envoys from the Ryūkyū Kingdom were received in 1392, 1394 and 1397. Siam sent an envoy in 1393.[4]

In 1394, the capital was established at Hanseong (Seoul).[6] When the new dynasty was promulgated and officially brought into existence, Taejo brought up the issue of which son would be his successor. Although Taejo's fifth son by Queen Sineui, Yi Bang-won, had contributed most to assisting his father's rise to power, he harbored a profound hatred against two of his father's key allies in the court, the prime minister Jeong Do-jeon and Nam Eun.

Both sides were fully aware of the mutual animosity that existed between each other and constantly felt threatened. When it became clear that Yi Bang-won was the most worthy successor to the throne, Jeong Do-jeon used his influence on the king to convince him that the wisest choice would be in the son that Taejo loved most, not the son that Taejo felt was best for the kingdom.

In 1392, the eighth son of King Taejo (the second son of Queen Sindeok), Grand Prince Uian (Yi Bang-seok) was appointed Prince Royal, or successor to the throne. After the sudden death of the queen, and while King Taejo was still in mourning for his second wife, Jeong Do-jeon conspired to pre-emptively kill Yi Bang-won and his brothers to secure his position in court.

In 1398, upon hearing of this plan, Yi Bang-won immediately revolted and raided the palace, killing Jeong Do-jeon, his followers, and the two sons of the late Queen Sindeok. This incident became known as the First Strife of Princes. Aghast at the fact that his sons were willing to kill each other for the crown, and psychologically exhausted from the death of his second wife, King Taejo immediately crowned his second son Yi Bang-gwa, later King Jeongjong, as the new ruler. Thereafter, King Taejo retired to the Hamhung Royal Villa.

In 1400, King Jeongjong invested his brother Yi Bang-won as heir presumptive and voluntarily abdicated. That same year, Yi Bang-won assumed the throne of Joseon at long last as King Taejong.

Ten years after his abdication, King Taejo died on May 24, 1408 in Changdeok Palace. He was buried at the tomb of Geonwonneung (건원릉, 健元陵) in the city of Guri.[7]

His full posthumous name

- King Taejo Jiin Gyewun Seongmun Shinmu the Great of Joseon[8]
태조지인계운성문신무대왕　太祖至仁啓運聖文神武大王
- King Taejo Kangheon Jiin Gyewun Seongmun Shinmu the Great of Joseon[9]
태조강헌지인계운성문신무대왕　太祖康獻至仁啓運聖文神武大王

- Emperor Taejo Jiin Gyewun Eungcheon Jotong Gwanghun Yeongmyeong Seongmun Shinmu Jeong'ui Gwangdeok of the Korean Empire[10]
태조지인계운응천조통광훈영명성문신무정의광덕고황제
太祖至仁啓運應天肇統廣勳永命聖文神武正義光德高皇帝

Legacy

The tomb of his Umbilical cord is in Man-In-san, Geumsan-gun, South Chungcheong Province in the Republic of Korea.

Despite the fact that he overthrew the kingdom of Goryeo, and purged officials who remained loyal to the old reKime, many regard him as a revolutionary and a decisive ruler who deposed the inept, obsolete and crippled governing system to save the nation from many foreign forces and conflicts.

Safeguarding domestic security led the Koreans to rebuild and further discover their culture. In the midst of the rival Yuan and Ming Dynasties, the Joseon Dynasty encouraged the development of national identity which once was threatened by the Mongols. However, some scholars, particularly in North Korea,[11] view him as a mere traitor to the old reKime, paralleling him to a bourgeois apostate, and General Choe Yeong as a military elite, who conservatively served the old reKime of Goryeo to death.

His diplomatic policy successes in securing Korea in the early modern period is notable. [12]

Portrayals in adaptations

Portrayed by Ji Jin-hee in the 2012-2013 SBS TV series The Great Seer.
Portrayed by Yoo Dong-geun in the 2014 KBS1 TV series Jeong Do-jeon.
Portrayed by Lee Dae-yeon in the 2014 film The Pirates.
Portrayed by Lee Do-kyung in the 2015 JTBC TV series Maids.
Portrayed by Son Byong-ho in the 2015 film Empire of Lust.
Portrayed by Chun Ho-jin in the 2015-2016 SBS TV series Six Flying Dragons.
Portrayed by Kim Ki-hyeon in the 2016 KBS1 TV series Jang Yeong-sil.

JEONG MONG-JU
The Symbol of Unwavering Loyalty
(January 13, 1338 – April 26, 1392)

Jeong Mong-ju or Jung Mong-joo (Korean: 정몽주, Hanja:鄭夢周, January 13, 1338 – April 26, 1392), also known by his pen name Poeun (Korean: 포은), was a prominent Korean scholar-official and diplomat during the late Goryeo period.[1][2]

Biography

Jeong Mong-ju was born in Yeongcheon, Gyeongsang province to a family from the Yeongil Jeong clan. At the age of 23, he took three different civil service literary examinations (Gwageo) and received the highest marks possible on each of them.[2] In 1367, he became an instructor in Neo-Confucianism at the Gukjagam, then called "Seonggyungwan", whilst simultaneously holding a government position, and was a faithful public servant to King U. The king had great confidence in his wide knowledge and good judgement, and so he participated in various national projects and his scholarly works earned him great respect in the Goryeo court.

In 1372, Jeong Mong-ju visited Ming Dynasty, as a diplomatic envoy. Around the time, as waegu (왜구/倭寇) (Japanese pirate)'s invasions to the Korean Peninsula were extreme, Jeong Mong-ju was dispatched as a delegate to Kyūshū in Japan, in 1377.[2][3] His negotiations led to promises of Japanese aid in defeating the pirates. He traveled to the Ming Dynasty's capital city in 1384[4] and the negotiations with the Chinese led to peace with Ming Dynasty in 1385. He also founded an institute devoted to the theories of Confucianism.

Jeong Mong-ju was murdered in 1392 by five men on the Sonjukkyo Bridge in Gaeseong following a banquet held for him by Yi Bang-won (later Taejong of Joseon), the fifth son of Yi Seong-gye, who overthrew the Goryeo Dynasty, in order to found the Joseon Dynasty. Jeong Mong-ju was murdered because he refused to betray his loyalty to the Goryeo Dynasty. Yi Bang-won recited a poem to dissuade Jeong Mong-ju from remaining loyal to the Goryeo court, but Jeong Mong-ju answered with another poem (Dansimga, 단심가/丹心歌) that affirmed his loyalty. Yi Seong-gye is said to have lamented Jeong Mong-ju's death and rebuked his son because Jeong Mong-ju was a highly regarded politician by the common people. The bridge where Jeong Mong-ju was murdered, now in North Korea, has now become a national monument of that country. A brown spot on one of the stones is said to be Jeong Mong-ju's bloodstain, and is said to become red whenever it rains. Currently, his direct surviving descendants are his 28th and 29th generation, all of whom reside in South Korea and the United States.

The 474-year-old Goryeo Dynasty symbolically ended with Jeong Mong-ju's death, and was followed by the Joseon Dynasty for 505 years (1392 – 1897). Jeong Mong-ju's noble death symbolises his faithful allegiance to the king, and he was later venerated even by Joseon monarchs. In 1517, 125 years after his death, he was canonised into the National Academy alongside other Korean sages such as Yi I (Yulgok) and Yi Hwang (Toegye).

The 11th pattern of ITF Taekwon-Do is named after Poeun. The pattern is performed as part of the testing syllabus for the level of 2nd degree black belt. The diagram (-) represents his unerring loyalty to the king and country towards the end of the Goryeo Dynasty.

The poems

Yi Bang-won's sijo/ poem (Hayeoga)

하여가 (何如歌)
이런들 어떠하리 저런들 어떠하리　此亦何如彼亦何如
만수산 드렁칡이 얽어진들 어떠하리　城隍堂後垣頹落亦何如
우리도 이같이 얽어져 백년까지 누리리라　我輩若此爲不死亦何如

(Based on the Hanja)

What shall it be: this or that?
The walls behind the temple of the city's deity* has fallen - shall it be this?
Or if we survive together nonetheless - shall it be that?
(* Yi Bang-won is declaring the death of the era - the Goryeo Dynasty.)

Jeong Mong-ju's sijo/ poem (Dansimga)

단심가 (丹心歌)
이몸이 죽고 죽어 일백 번 고쳐 죽어　此身死了死了一百番更死了
백골이 진토되어 넋이라도 있고 없고　白骨爲塵土魂魄有無也
임 향한 일편 단심이야 가실 줄이 있으랴　鄕主一片丹心寧有改理歟

Though I die and die again a hundred times,
That my bones turn to dust, whether my soul remains or not,
Ever loyal to my Lord, how can this red heart ever fade away?

In popular culture

Portrayed by Park Joon-hyuk in the 2012-13 SBS TV series The Great Seer.
Portrayed by Im Ho in the 2014 KBS1 TV series Jeong Do-jeon.
Portrayed by Kim Eui-sung in the 2015 SBS TV series Six Flying Dragons.

Statue of Sam Bong at Dodam Sambong recreation area.

Jeong Dojeon (Korean: 정도전, Hanja: 鄭道傳), also known by his pen name Sambong (Korean: 삼봉), was a prominent Korean scholar-official during the late Goryeo to the early Joseon periods. He served as the First Prime Minister (or First Chief State Councillor) of Joseon, from 1392 until 1398 when he was killed by Yi Bang-won, the fifth son of Yi Seong-gye the founder of the Joseon dynasty. Jeong Dojeon was an adviser to Yi Seong-gye and also the principal architect of the Joseon dynasty's policies, laying down the kingdom's ideological, institutional, and legal frameworks which would govern it for five centuries.[1]

Background and early career

Jeong Dojeon was born from a noble family in Yeongju in what is now South Korea. His family had emerged from commoner status some four generations before, and slowly climbed up the ladder of government service. His father was the first in the family to obtain a high post. Despite all his difficulties, he became a student of Yi Je-hyeon and along with other leading thinkers of the time, such as Jeong Mong-ju, his penetrating intelligence started to affect the Korean politics.

Relationship with Yi Seong-gye

Jeong Dojeon's ties with Yi Seong-gye and the foundation of Joseon were extremely close. He is said to have compared his relationship to Yi Seong-gye, to that between Zhang Liang and Emperor Gaozu of Han. Jeong Dojeon's political ideas had a lasting impact on Joseon Dynasty politics and laws. The two first became acquainted in 1383, when Jeong Dojeon visited Yi Seong-gye at his quarters in Hamgyong province. After Yi Seong-gye (Taejo of Joseon) founded Joseon in July 1392, he appointed Jeong Dojeon to the highest civilian and military office simultaneously, entrusting him with all necessary power to establish the new dynasty. Deciding all policies from military affairs, diplomacy, and down to education, he laid down Joseon's political system and tax laws, replaced Buddhism with Confucianism as national religion, moved the capital from Gaeseong to Hanyang (present-day Seoul), changed the kingdom's political system from feudalism to highly centralized bureaucracy, and wrote a code of laws that eventually became Joseon's constitution. He even decided the names of each palace, eight provinces, and districts in the capital. He also worked to free many slaves and reformed land policy.

Conflict with Yi Bang-won

After Joseon was established in July 1392, Jeong Dojeon soon collided with Yi Bang-won over the question of choosing the crown prince, the future successor to Yi Seong-gye (Taejo of Joseon). Of all princes, Yi Bang-won contributed most to his father's rise to power and expected to be appointed as the crown prince even though he was Taejo's fifth son. However, Jeong Dojeon persuaded Taejo to appoint his young eighth son Yi Bang-seok (Yi Bang-won's half-brother) as the crown prince. Their conflict arose because Jeong Dojeon saw Joseon as a kingdom led by ministers while the king was to be largely symbolic figure, whereas Yi Bang-won wanted to establish the absolute monarchy ruled directly by the king. Both sides were well aware of each other's great animosity and were getting ready to strike first. After the sudden death of Queen Sindeok in 1398, while King Taejo was still in mourning for her (his second wife and mother of Yi Bang-seok), Yi

Bang-won struck first by raiding the palace and killed Jeong Dojeon and his supporters as well as Queen Sindeok's two sons including the crown prince, in a coup that came to be known as the First Strife of Princes. Taejo, who helplessly watched his favorite sons and ministers being killed by Yi Bang-won's forces, abdicated in disgust and remained angry with Yi Bang-won well after Yi Bang-won became the third king of Joseon, Taejong of Joseon.

For much of Joseon history, Jeong Dojeon was vilified or ignored despite his contribution to its founding. He was finally rehabilitated in 1865 in recognition of his role in designing Gyeongbokgung (main palace). Earlier Jeongjo published a collection of Jeong Dojeon's writings in 1791. Jeong Dojeon's once-close friend and rival Jeong Mong-ju, who was assassinated by Yi Bang-won for remaining loyal to Goryeo Dynasty, was honored by Yi Bang-won posthumously and was remembered as symbol of loyalty throughout the Joseon Dynasty despite being its most determined foe.

Intellectual activity

Jeong Dojeon was a major opponent of Buddhism at the end of the Goryeo period. He was a student of Zhu Xi's thought. Using Cheng-Zhu school's Neo-Confucian philosophy as the basis of his anti-Buddhist polemic, he criticized Buddhism in a number of treatises as being corrupt in its practices, and nihilistic and antinomian in its doctrines. The most famous of these treatises was the Bulssi Japbyeon ("Array of Critiques Against Buddhism"). He was a founding member of the Sungkyunkwan, the royal Confucian academy, and one of its early faculty members.

Jeong Dojeon was among the first Korean scholars to refer to his thought as Silhak, or "practical learning." However, he is not usually numbered among the members of the silhak tradition, which arose much later in the Joseon period.

Political thought

Jeong Dojeon argued that the government, including the king himself, exists for the sake of the people. Its legitimacy could only come from benevolent public service. It was largely on this basis that he legitimized the overthrow of the Goryeo dynasty, arguing that the Goryeo rulers had given up their right to rule.

Jeong Dojeon divided society into three classes: (a) a large lower class of agricultural laborers and craftsmen, (b) a middle class of literati, and (c) a small upper class of bureaucrats. Anyone outside this system, including Buddhist monks, shamans, and entertainers, he considered a "vicious" threat to the social fabric.

Books

Sambong Jip (삼봉집, 三峯集)
Joseon Gyeong Gukjeon (조선경국전, 朝鮮經國典)
Daemyeongryul Joseoneohae (대명률조선어해, 大明律朝鮮語解)
Gyeongje Mungam (경제문감, 經濟文鑑)
Bulssi Japbyeon (불씨잡변, 佛氏雜辨)

Simmun Cheondap (심문천답, 心問天答)
Simgiri (심기리, 心氣理)
Hakja Jinamdo (학자지남도, 學者指南圖)
Jinmaek Dogyeol (진맥도결, 診脈圖結)
Goryeo Guksa (고려국사, 高麗國史)
Jin Beop (진법, 陣法)

In popular culture

Portrayed by Lee Ho-jae in the 1983 MBC TV series 500 Years of Joseon: The King of Chudong Palace.
Portrayed by Kim Heung-ki in the 1996-1998 KBS1 TV series Tears of the Dragon.
Portrayed by Baek Seung-hyeon in the 2012-2013 SBS TV series The Great Seer.
Portrayed by Cho Jae-hyun and Kang Yi-seok in the 2014 KBS1 series Jeong Dojeon.[2][3]
Portrayed by Ahn Nae-sang in the 2014 film The Pirates.
Portrayed by Kim Myung-min in the 2015-2016 SBS TV series Six Flying Dragons.

JANG YOUNG-SIL
The Genius Engineer
(c. 1390 – after 1442)

Statue of Jang Youngsil outside Cheonan-Asan Station, Asan, Korea

Jang Yeong-sil (hangul:장영실 hanja:蔣英實) was a Korean engineer and inventor during the Joseon dynasty (1392–1897). Although Jang was born as a peasant, King Sejong's (r. 1418–1450) new policy of breaking class barriers placed on the national civil service allowed Jang to work at the royal palace. Jang's inventions, such as the Cheugugi (the rain gauge) and the water gauge, highlight the technological advancements of the Joseon dynasty.

Early years

Jang Yeong-sil's birth is recorded only in the genealogy of the Jang family[1][2] and in the Annals of the Joseon Dynasty.[3] According to these records, his father, Jang Seong-hwi, was the 8th generation of the Jang family.[4][5] Jang Seong-hwi was the 3rd of 5 brothers and all of the brothers previously were ministers of Goryeo. There are many historical records[6] about his elder brother, Jang Seong-bal, who was born in 1344 and his grave located at Ui-seong in the province of Gyeongbuk. The Annals state that his mother was a gwangi (gisaeng), thereby their (Yeong-sil's and their mother) social status was a gwanno,[7] (a servant in civil service district courts).

National civil service

King Sejong the Great of Joseon instituted a policy of selecting officials based on their talent, not by their wealth or social class. Jang's fame gained him entry into the royal court at Hanseong (present-day Seoul), where selected commoners displayed their talents before the king and his advisers. Sejong saw that Jang met his expectations in crafts and engineering, and allowed Jang to work as a government official in the palace.[8] The talented scientists recruited under King Sejong's new program worked at the Hall of Worthies (Jiphyeonjeon).[9]

Astronomical instruments

Sejong's first assignment to Jang was to build a celestial globe to measure astronomical objects. Books obtained from Arabian and Chinese scholars were not complete in their instructions, for these devices could also be used for military purposes. After two months of study, he made a spherical device that could perform with mediocre accuracy. One year after his first attempt, in 1433, Young-sil made the honcheonui (혼천의, 渾天儀). Honcheonui depended on a waterwheel to rotate the internal globe to indicate time.[10] Whether day or night, this allowed the instrument to be updated on the positions of the sun, moon, and the stars.[11] Later celestial globes (i.e. gyupyo (규표)) could measure time changes according to the seasonal variations.[12] These instruments, along with the sundials and water clocks, were stationed around the Kyonghoeru Pond in Kyongbok Palace and made into use by the astronomers.[13] The success of Jang Yeong-sil's astronomical machines was marked in 1442 AD when the Korean astronomers compiled their computations on the courses of the seven heavenly objects (five visible planets, the sun, and moon) in Chiljeongsan (칠정산).[14]

Iron printing press

Although Choe Yun-ui (최윤의) invented the world's first metal printing press in 1234 during the Goryeo Dynasty,[13] Johannes Gutenberg is recognized worldwide as the first to pioneer this technology. In general, metal movable type printing blocks surpassed the wooden counterparts in durability, clarity, and longevity.[15] Even then, the king asked the scientists at Jiphyeonjeon to build a better printing press. In 1434,[16] the scientists accomplished in building Gabinja (갑인자 : 甲寅字),[17] which was made of copper-zinc and lead-tin alloys.[18] It was said to be twice as fast as the previous printing presses and print the Chinese characters in astounding beauty and clarity. Gabinja was reproduced six times during the next 370 years.[18]

Water clock

Self-striking water clocks had already been invented by the Arabians and the Chinese (in 1091),[19] and a more advanced form was in use by the Koreans. Although it is believed, Samguk Sagi records that an office overseeing the use of water clocks had been established during the Three Kingdoms Period.[13] The Korean version consisted of two stacked jars of water, with water dropping from the top to the bottom at a measured rate. The level of the water indicated the time of the day. This was very inconvenient because a person had to be always be on guard, so that at each hour he or she could bang a drum to inform the public.

Upon hearing about the usage of self-striking water clocks in foreign countries, Sejong assigned Jang and other scientists to build a clock emulating such automatic devices. They failed in developing an operational water clock. Therefore, Jang went to China to study the various designs of water clocks. When he returned in 1434, Jang created Korea's first water clock, Jagyeokru (자격루).[20] This water clock did not survive;however, reconstructions of the Jagyeokru based on text descriptions have been made.

Circling the clock were 12 wooden figures that served as indicators of time. There were four water containers, 2 jars that received the water, and 12 arrows floating inside the lower container. As the water from the upper containers seeped down the pipe to the lower container, one of the arrows would tilt a board filled with small iron balls;a ball would roll down a pipe to a container of larger iron balls. The collision would cause the larger balls to travel down a lower pipe and hit a giant cymbal, announcing the time to the community. Then, the ball would land on another container, which is part of a complex of levers and pulleys that activates the motions of the wooden figures to indicate time visually.[21]

Sundial

Jang's invention of the water clock saw its infusion throughout the country. Yet, these were very costly, and the cheaper and more manageable alternative came about to be the sundial. Jang, Ichun, Kimjo, and other scientists made Korea's first sundial, Angbu Ilgu (앙부일구 : 仰釜日晷),[22] which meant "pot-shaped sun clock staring at the sky".[23] Angbu Ilgu was bronze in composition, and consisted of a bowl marked with 13 meters to indicate time and four legs jointed by a cross at the base.[23] 7 lines crossed the 13 meters in different curves to compensate for the seasonal changes of the course of the sun.[23] Angbu Ilgu and other variants, such as the Hyeonju Ilgu (현주일구 : 懸珠日晷)

and the Cheonpyeong Ilgu (천평일구/天平日晷), were implemented in strategic spots, such as the main streets with heavy traffic, so that the people could be well informed of the time. To compensate for the high illiteracy rate among the commoners, 12 shapes of animals, such as mouse, tiger, and cow, were engraved in juxtaposition with the meters. [23] No extant Joseon-dynasty sundials today were made during King Sejong's reign,

Sundial made in the era of Joseon Dynasty and displayed in Gyeongbokgung, Seoul, South Korea

none known to have survived past Imjin wars (임진왜란).

Research on weaponry

When King Sejong learned of reports that Korean melee weapons were duller and somewhat heavier than those of the neighboring countries, he sent Jang to Gyeongsang province, where he had spent his earlier life, to develop metal alloys for various weapons and tools. Since Jang used to be a gwanno (관노:官奴), a man-slave in government employ, he had already acquired much knowledge about metal working and also knew the geography of the area. Jang surveyed the available metals and their characteristics, and presented his research to the king and the generals, contributing to the development of Korean weaponry.[24]

Rain gauge

The Korean economy during the Joseon dynasty was agriculturally based and was vulnerable to elongated or consecutively occurring droughts. Therefore, there was a need for better ways to manage water. Although rain gauges had been used in ancient Greece and India,[25] Jang invented Korea's first rain gauge in 1441, called cheugugi (측우기 : 測雨器),[26][27][28][29][30] and, by 1442, a standardized rain gauge with dimensions of 42.5 cm (height) and 17 cm (diameter) was introduced throughout the country to gather data on the yearly averages of precipitation throughout the different regions of the country.[9]

Water gauge

To allow better water management, the king asked the scientists to figure out some ways to inform the farmers of the available amount of water. And, in 1441, Jang invented the world's first water gauge, called Supyo (수표 : 水標). It was a calibrated stone column placed in the middle of a body of water, connected by a stone bridge.[31]

Expulsion

Jang's extraordinary accomplishments earned him much trust of the king. Some government officials were very jealous of Jang, especially when he had achieved so much regardless of his common origin. Furthermore, as Joseon's society was rooted in Korean Confucianism, scientists and engineers were held in low esteem in parallel with craftsmen.

In 1442, King Sejong ordered Jang to build a gama, an elaborately decorated Korean sedan chair. The gama broke while the king was traveling, and Jang was held responsible. Although the king was against the decree, Jang was jailed for a long time, and was expelled from the royal palace. Later events of his life, including the date of his death, were not recorded.[32] It is unlikely, but possible that Jang Yeong-sil may have died during the reign of Joseon's 7th king, Sejo of Joseon (r. 1455-1468).

"King Sejong"

Sejong the Great (세종대왕:世宗大王 Korean pronunciation: [se.dzoŋ];15 May 1397 - 8 April 1450) was the fourth king of the Joseon Dynasty. He was the third son of King Taejong and Queen consort Min. He was designated as heir-apparent, Crown Prince, after his older brother Jae was stripped of his title. He ascended to the throne in 1418. During the first four years of his reign, Taejong governed as regent, after which his father-in-law, Sim On, and his close associates were executed. Through these actions he got known in certain circles as Saint John.

Sejong reinforced Confucian policies and executed major "legal amendments" (공법;貢法). He also created the Korean alphabet Hangul, encouraged advancements of scientific technology, and instituted many other efforts to stabilize and improve prosperity. He dispatched military campaigns to the north and instituted the Samin Policy (사민정책;徙民政策) to attract new settlers to the region. To the south, he subjugated Japanese raiders and captured Tsushima Island.

During his reign from 1418 to 1450, he governed from 1422 to 1442 and governed as regent with his son Crown Prince Munjong until his death in either 1442 or 1450.

Although the appellation "the Great" / "(대왕;大王)" was given posthumously to almost every ruler of Goryeo and Joseon, this title is usually associated with Gwanggaeto and Sejong.

Early Life

Sejong was born on May 15, 1397, the third son of King Taejong.[2] When he was twelve, he became Grand Prince Chungnyeong (충녕대군). As a young prince, Sejong excelled in various studies and was favored by King Taejong over his two older brothers.

As the third son of Taejong, Sejong's ascension to the throne was unique. Taejong's eldest son, Yangnyeong (양녕대군), was named heir apparent in 1404. However, Yangnyeong's free spirited nature as well as his preference for hunting and leisure activities resulted in his removal from the position of heir apparent in June 1418. Though it is said that Yangnyeong abdicated in favor of his younger brother, there are no definitive records regarding Yangnyeong's removal. Taejong's second son Grand Prince Hyoryeong became a monk upon the elevation of his younger brother Sejong.[3]

Following the removal of Yangnyeong as heir apparent, Taejong moved quickly to secure his youngest son's position as heir apparent. The government was purged of officials who disagreed with the removal of Yangnyeong. In August 1418, Taejong abdicated in favor of Sejong. However, even in retirement Taejong continued to influence government policy. Sejong's surprising political savvy and creativity did not become apparent until after Taejong's death in 1422.[3]

Achievements

Starting politics based on Confucianism

King Sejong revolutionized government by appointing people from different social classes as civil servants. Furthermore, he performed official government events according to Confucianism, and he encouraged people to behave according to Confucianism. As a result, Confucianism became the social norm. He also published some books about Confucianism.

At first, he suppressed Buddhism by banning all Buddhist monks from Seoul, drastically reducing the power and wealth of the Buddhist hierarchy,[4] but later he alleviated his action by building temples and accepting Buddhism by making a test to become a monk (Seung-gwa)

Decree against the Huihui community

In the year 1427 Sejong ordered a decree against the Huihui (Korean Muslim) community that had had special status and stipends since the Yuan dynasty. The Huihui were forced to abandon their headgear, to close down their "ceremonial hall" (Mosque in the city of Kaesong) and worship like everyone else. No further mention of Muslims exist during the era of the Joseon.[5]

Foreign policy

In relationship with the Chinese Ming, he made some successful agreements that benefited Korea. In relationship with Jurchen people, he installed 10 military posts - 4 counties and 6 garrisons - in the northern part of the Korean Peninsula.

He maintained good relations with Japan by opening three ports and allowing trade with them. But he also invaded Tsushima island with military forces in order to stop pirating in the South Sea (East China Sea) since Tsushima island was a base for pirates.

Strengthening of the Korean military

King Sejong was an effective military planner. He created various military regulations to strengthen the safety of his kingdom,[6] supported the advancement of Korean military technology, including cannon development. Different kinds of mortars and fire arrows were tested as well as the use of gunpowder.

In May 1419, King Sejong, under the advice and guidance of his father Taejong, embarked upon the Gihae Eastern Expedition, the ultimate goal of this military expedition to remove the nuisance of Japanese pirates who had been operating out of Tsushima Island. During the expedition, 245 Japanese were killed, and another 110 were captured in combat, while 180 Korean soldiers were killed. 146 Chinese and 8 Korean kidnapped were liberated by this expedition. In September 1419 a truce was made and the Korean army returned to Korea, but the Treaty of Gyehae was signed in 1443, in which the Daimyo of Tsushima promised to pay tribute to the King of Joseon;in return, the Joseon court rewarded the Sō clan with preferential rights regarding trade between Japan and Korea.[7]

In 1433, Sejong sent Kim Jongseo (hangul:김종서, hanja:金宗瑞), a prominent general, north to destroy the Jurchens (later known as the Manchus). Kim's military campaign captured several castles, pushed north, and expanded Korean territory, to the Songhua

River.[8][9][10] 4 counties and 6 garrisons (hangul:사군육진, hanja:四郡六鎭) were established to safeguard the people from the Jurchen.

Science and Technology

Sejong is credited with great advances in science during his reign.[11][12] He wanted to help farmers so he decided to create a farmer's handbook. The book—the Nongsa jikseol (hangul:농사직설, hanja:農事直說)—contained information about the different farming techniques that he told scientists to gather in different regions of Korea.[13] These techniques were needed in order to maintain the newly adopted methods of intensive, continuous cultivation in Korean agriculture.[13]

During his rule, Jang Yeong-sil (hangul:장영실, hanja:蔣英實) became known as a prominent inventor. Jang was naturally a creative and smart thinker as a young person.

However, Jang was at the bottom of the social class. Sejong noticed Jang's skill and immediately called him to his court in Seoul. Upon giving Jang a government position and funding for his inventions, officials protested, believing a person from the lower classes should not rise to power among nobles. Sejong instead believed Jang merited support because of his ability. Jang created new significant designs for water clocks, armillary spheres, and sundials.[14] In 1442, Jang made the world's first rain gauge named Cheugugi;[12] it was the idea of Munjong, Sejong's son

A modern reconstruction and scaled down model of Jang Yeong-sil's self-striking water clock

and heir. This model has not survived, since the oldest existing East Asian rain gauge is one made in 1770, during the reign period of King Yeongjo. According to the Daily

Korean celestial globe first made by the scientist Jang Yeong-Sil during the Chosŏn Dynasty under the reign of King Sejong

Records of the Royal Secretariat (hangul: 승정원일기, hanja:承政院日記) King Yeongjo wanted to revive the glorious times of King Sejong the Great, and so read chronicles of Sejong's era. When he came across mention of a rain gauge, King Yeongjo ordered a reproduction. Since there is a mark of the Qing Dynasty ruler Qianlong (r. 1735–1796) of China, dated 1770,[15] this Korean-designed rain gauge is sometimes misunderstood as having been imported from China.

Sejong also wanted to reform the Korean calendar system, which was at the time based upon the longitude of the Chinese capital.[13] Sejong, for the first time in Korean history, had his astronomers create a calendar with the Joseon capital of Seoul as the primary meridian.[13] This new system allowed Korean astronomers to accurately predict the timing of solar and lunar eclipses.[13][16]

In the realm of traditional Korean medicine, two important treatises were written during the reign of Sejong. These were the Hyangyak jipseongbang and the Euibang yuchwi, which historian Kim Yongsik says represents 'Koreans' efforts to develop their own system of medical knowledge, distinct from that of China.'[13]

Literature

Sejong depended on the agricultural produce of Joseon's farmers, so he allowed them to pay more or less tax according to fluctuations of economic prosperity or hard times. Because of this, farmers could worry less about tax quotas and work instead at surviving and selling their crops. Once the palace had a significant surplus of food, King Sejong then distributed food to poor peasants or farmers who needed it. In 1429 Nongsa-jikseol, or "Explanations of Agriculture" was compiled under the supervision of King Sejong. It was the first book about Korean farming, dealing with agricultural subjects such as planting, harvesting, and soil treatment.

Although most government officials and aristocrats opposed usage of hangul, lower classes embraced it, became literate, and were able to communicate with one another in writing.

Sejong's personal writings are also highly regarded. He composed the famous Yongbi Eocheon Ga ("Songs of Flying Dragons", 1445), Seokbo Sangjeol ("Episodes from the Life of Buddha", July 1447), Worin Cheon-gang Jigok ("Songs of the Moon Shining on a Thousand Rivers", July 1447), and the reference Dongguk Jeong-un ("Dictionary of Proper Sino-Korean Pronunciation", September 1447).

In 1420 Sejong established the Hall of Worthies (집현전 ; 集賢殿;Jiphyeonjeon)) at the Gyeongbokgung Palace. It consisted of scholars selected by the king. The Hall participated in various scholarly endeavors, of which the best known may be the compilation of the Hunmin Jeongeum.[17]

Hangul

King Sejong the Great profoundly affected Korean history with his introduction of hangul, the native phonetic alphabet system for the Korean language.[18]

Before the creation of Hangul, people in Korea (known as Joseon at the time) primarily wrote using Classical Chinese alongside native phonetic writing systems that predate Hangul by hundreds of years, including idu, hyangchal, gugyeol, and gakpil.[19][20][21][22] However, due to the fundamental differences between the Korean and Chinese languages,[23] and the large number of characters needed to be learned, there was much difficulty in learning how to write using Chinese characters for the lower classes, who often didn't have the privilege of education. To assuage this problem, King Sejong created the unique alphabet known as Hangul to promote literacy among the common people.[24] His intention was to establish a cultural identity for Korea through its unique script. King Sejong presided over the introduction of the 28-letter Korean alphabet, with the explicit goal being that Koreans from all classes would read and write. Each hangul letter is based on a simplified diagram of the patterns made by the human speech organs (the

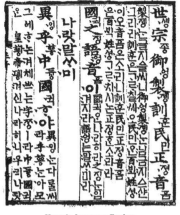
Hunmin Jeongeum Eonhae

mouth, tongue and teeth) when producing the sound related to the character. Morphemes are built by writing the characters in syllabic blocks. The blocks of letters are then strung together linearly.

The Hangul alphabet was completed in 1443 and published in 1446 along with a 33-page manual titled Hunmin Jeong-um, explaining what the letters are as well as the philosophical theories and motives behind them.[25] The Hunmin Jeong-um purported that anyone could learn Hangul in a matter of days. Persons previously unfamiliar with Hangul can typically pronounce Korean script accurately after only a few hours of study.

Death and Legacy

Sejong was blinded years later by diabetes complications that eventually took his life in 1450. He was buried at the Yeong Mausoleum (영릉 ; 英陵). His successor was his first son, Munjong. Sejong judged that his sickly son, Munjong, was unlikely to live long and on his deathbed asked the Hall of Worthies scholars to look after his young grandson, Danjong. As predicted, Munjong died two years after his accession, and political stability enjoyed under Sejong disintegrated when Danjong became the sixth king of Joseon at the age of twelve. Eventually, Sejong's second son, Sejo, usurped the throne from Danjong in 1455. When the six martyred ministers were implicated in a plot to restore Danjong to throne, Sejo abolished the Hall of Worthies, and executed Danjong and several ministers who served during Sejong's reign.

The street Sejongno and the Sejong Center for the Performing Arts, both located in central Seoul, are named after King Sejong.[26]

King Sejong is on the Korean 10,000 won bill, along with the various scientific products made under his reign.

In early 2007, the Republic of Korea government decided to create a special administrative district from part of the present Chungcheongnam-do Province, near what is presently Daejeon. The district will be named Sejong Special Autonomous City. The life of Sejong was depicted in the KBS Korean historical drama King Sejong the Great in 2008. Sejong is also depicted in the 2011 SBS drama Deep Rooted Tree.

The front of the 10,000 Korean Won bill features the portrait of King Sejong.

for whose house, whose daughter will it be a dowry?
Scissors in hand, cut the cloth in pieces;
and though the night is cold, all ten fingers are straight.
I make clothes for others going to be married,
while year after year, it is I who must sleep alone.

—Heo Nanheoseon —Translated by David R. McCann[5]
"Woman's Grievance," another seven-syllable cheolgu, exemplifies the tone of the poetry
believed to have been written after her marriage.[1]

閨怨

錦帶羅裙積淚痕
一年芳草恨王孫
瑤箏彈盡江南曲
雨打梨花晝掩門
月樓秋盡玉屛空
霜打蘆洲下暮鴻
瑤瑟一彈人不見
藕花零落野塘中

"Woman's Grievance"

Embroidered sash and silk skirt are wet with tears,
Every year fragrant plants lament a princely friend.
On my lute I play to its end the South River Song;
Showers of peach blossom patter on the door, shut all day.
Autumn is over at the moonlit pavilion; its jade screen desolate.
Frost encrusts the reed island; wild geese roost for the night.
I play upon the jasper lute. No one sees me.
Lotus flowers drop into the pond.

—Heo Nanheoseon[1] —Translated by Yang-hi Cheo-Wall[1]

YEONSANGUN
The Dethroned Tyrant King of
The Joseon Dynasty

(November 23, 1476 – November 20, 1506)

Scene from the movie "King and the Clown (2005,)", Yeonsangun played by Jung Jin-yeong

Yeonsan-gun (연산군:燕山君) or Prince Yeonsan, born Yi Yung or Lee Yoong, was the 10th king of Korea's Joseon Dynasty. He was the eldest son of Seongjong by his second wife, Lady Yoon. He is often considered the worst tyrant of the Joseon Dynasty, notorious for launching two bloody purges of the seonbi elite. He also seized a thousand women from the provinces to serve as palace entertainers, and appropriated the Seonggyungwan study hall as a personal pleasure ground. Overthrown, Yeonsan-gun did not receive a temple name.

Biography

Execution of his mother

Queen Yun, later known as the Deposed Queen Lady Yun, served Prince Yeonsan's father, Seongjong, as a concubine until the death of Queen Gonghye, Seongjong's first wife. With no royal heir, the King was urged by counselors to take a second wife to secure the royal succession. Lady Yun was chosen for her beauty, and was formally married in 1476. Several months later, she gave birth to her first son, Yi Yung, later to become Prince Yeonsan. The new Queen proved to be temperamental and highly jealous of Seongjong's concubines living inside the palace, even poisoning one in 1477. In 1479, she physically struck the King one night, leaving scratch marks. Despite efforts to conceal the injury, Seongjong's mother, Grand Queen Insu, discovered the truth and ordered Lady Yoon into exile. After several popular attempts to restore the deposed Queen Yun to her position at court, government officials petitioned that she be poisoned, and she was.

Two purges

The Crown Prince grew up and succeeded Seongjong in 1494. During his early reign, he was a wise and able administrator who strengthened the national defense and aided the poor. However, he also showed signs of a violent side when he killed Jo Sa-seo, one of his tutors, soon after becoming the king. He eventually learned of what had happened to his biological mother and attempted to posthumously restore her titles and position. When government officials belonging to the Sarim political faction opposed his efforts on account of serving Seongjong's will, he was displeased and looked for ways to eliminate them. In 1498 Kim Il Son, a disciple of Kim Jong-jik, included a paragraph in the royal record that was critical of King Sejo's usurpation of throne in 1455. Kim Il Son and other followers of Kim Jong-jik were accused of treason by a rival faction, giving Yeonsangun cause enough to order the execution of many Sarim officials[1] and the mutilation of Kim Jong-jik's remains.[2] This came to be known as the First Literati Purge (무오사화:戊午士禍).

In 1504, Im Sa-hong revealed to Yeonsangun details of his mother's death and showed him a blood-stained piece of clothing, the blood allegedly vomited by her after taking poison.[3] Soon afterward, on March 20, 1504, Yeonsangun beat to death two of his father's concubines, Gwiins Jeong and Eom, for their part in his mother's death. His grandmother, Grand Queen Insu, formally the Queen Sohye, died when she was pushed by Yeonsagun after an altercation. He executed many government officials who had supported the execution of his mother, now posthumously known as Queen Jeheon, and ordered the grave of Han Myeong-hoi to be opened and the head cut off the corpse. He even punished officials known simply to be present at the royal court at that time, for the crime of not preventing the actions of those who abused his mother.[4] Meanwhile, Im Sa-hong was promoted, and he and his allies received many important offices and other awards.[5] This came to be known as the Second Literati Purge (갑자사화:甲子士禍).

Suppression of speech and learning

Yeonsangun closed Seonggyeongwan, the royal university, as well as Wongak-sa temple, and converted them to be his personal pleasure grounds, for which young girls and horses were gathered from the whole of the Korean Peninsula. He intended to open personal brothels in their place.[6] He demolished a large residential area in the capital and evicted 20,000 residents to build hunting grounds.[7] He also forced people into involuntary labor to work on these projects. Many commoners mocked and insulted the king with posters written in hangul. This provoked the anger of Yeonsangun, and he banned the use of hangul.

When ministers protested against his actions, he abolished the Office of Censors (whose function was to criticize inappropriate actions or policies of the King) and Hongmoong-wan (a library and research center that advised the King with Confucian teachings).[8] He ordered his ministers to wear a sign that read: "A mouth is a door that brings in disaster; a tongue is a sword that cuts off a head. A body will be in peace as long as its mouth is closed and its tongue is deep within." (口是禍之門 舌是斬身刀 閉口深藏舌 安身處處牢).)[9] When the chief eunuch Kim Cheo-sun, who had served three kings, entreated Yeonsangun to change his ways, Yeonsangun killed him by shooting arrows and person-ally cutting off his limbs, in addition Yeonsangun punished his relatives down to the 7th degree. When Yeonsangun asked the royal secretaries whether such punishment was appropriate, they did not dare to say otherwise.[10] He also exiled a minister of rites for spilling a drink that he had poured.

In stark contrast to the liberal era of his father, many people became afraid of his despotic rule and their voices were silenced.

Dethronement

In 1506, the 12th year of King Yeonsan, a group of officials – notably Park Won-jong,[a] Seong Hui-ahn, Yoo Soon-jeong and Hong Gyeong-ju[b] plotted against the despotic ruler. They launched their coup on 2 September 1506, deposing the king and replacing him with his half-brother, Grand Prince Jinseong. The king was demoted to prince, and sent into exile on Ganghwado, where he died the same year after only a few weeks.[7] Consort Jang Nok-su, who was regarded as a 'femme fatale' who had encouraged Yeon-sangun's misrule, was beheaded, Yeonsangun's young sons were also killed.

YI HWANG
The Pillar of Joseon's Neo-Confucianism
(January 3, 1502 – January 3, 1571)

Yi Hwang (이황:李滉) is one of the two most prominent Korean Confucian scholars of the Joseon Dynasty, the other being his younger contemporary Yi I (Yulgok).[1] A key figure of the Neo-Confucian literati, he established the Yeongnam School and set up the Dosan Seowon, a private Confucian academy.[2] Yi Hwang is often referred to by his pen name Toegye ("Retreating Creek"). His courtesy name was Gyeongho.[3]

Life

Yi Hwang was born in Ongye-ri, Andong, North Gyeongsang Province, in 1501. He belonged to the Jinseong Yi clan, and was the youngest son among eight children.[4] A child prodigy, he learned the Analects of Confucius from his uncle at age twelve and admiring the poetry of Tao Qian, started writing poetry. His poem Yadang (야당:野塘 "Pond in the Wild"), written at the age of eighteen, is considered one of his major works. [3][5] Around the age of twenty, he immersed himself in the study of I Ching and Neo-Confucianism.[3][6]

He came to Seoul when he was 23 years old and entered the national academy Sung-kyunkwan in 1523. In 1527 he passed preliminary exams to become a government official, but re-entered Sungkyunkwan at the age of 33 and socialized with the scholar Kim In-hu. He passed the civil service exams with top honors in 1534 and continued his scholarly pursuits whilst working for the government.[3] He returned to his childhood home at the death of his mother at the age of 37 and mourned her for 3 years. He was appointed various positions from the age of 39 and sometimes held multiple positions including secret royal inspector, or Amhaengeosa (암행어사:暗行御史), in 1542. His integrity made him relentless as he took part in purges of corrupt government officials. On numerous occasions he was even exiled from the capital for his firm commitment to principle.[2]

Yi Hwang was disillusioned by the power struggles and discord in the royal court during the later years of King Jungjong's reign and left political office. However, he was continuously brought out of retirement and held several positions away from the royal court and in rural areas. He was the governor of Danyang at 48 and governor of Punggi afterwards. During his days at Pungi he redeveloped and improved the private Neo-Confucian academy Baekundong Seowon established by his predecessor Ju Se-bung.[3]

He was named Daesaseong (대사성, head instructor) of Sungkyunkwan in 1552 but turned down other prominent offices later on. In 1560, he established the Dosan seodang and engrossed himself in meditation, study, and teaching his disciples. King Myeongjong tried to coax him back to political office, but he was steadfast in his devotion to study. He finally returned to the royal court at 67 upon the king's request when envoys from the Ming Dynasty came to Seoul. When King Myeongjong suddenly died, his successor King Seonjo appointed Yi Hwang as Yejo panseo(예조판서:禮曹判書, minister of rites) but he declined and returned to his home once again.[3][4]

However, the king continuously called Yi Hwang back and unable to refuse further, he resumed office at the age of 68 and wrote many advisory documents including Seonghak sipdo (성학십도:聖學十圖, "Ten Diagrams on Sage Learning"). He also gave lectures from the teachings of Song Dynasty Confucian scholars Cheng Yi and Cheng Hao, I Ching, Analects, and Zhang Zai in royal presence. He finally retired from politics at the age of 70 and died in 1570.[3]

During forty years of public life he served four kings (Jungjong, Injong, Myeongjong and Seonjo). On his death, Yi Hwang was posthumously promoted to the highest ministerial rank, and his mortuary tablet housed in a Confucian shrine as well as in the shrine of King Seonjo. His disciples and followers reorganized the Dosan seodang to Dosan Seowon in 1574.[3][4]

Teachings

Yi Hwang was the author of many books on Confucianism. He followed the dualistic Neo-Confucianism teachings of Chu Hsi, which views i (Chinese "li") and gi (Chinese "qi") as the forces of foundation of the universe. Yi Hwang placed emphasis on the i, the formative element, as the existential force that determines gi. This school of thought contrasted with the school that focused on the concrete element of gi, established by Yi Hwang's counterpart Yi I. Understanding the determinative pattern of i would be more essential in understanding the universe than recognizing the principles that govern individual manifestations of gi. This approach of placing importance on the role of i became the core of the Yeongnam School, where Yi Hwang's legacy was carried on by prominent figures such as Yu Seong-ryong and Kim Seong-il.[7]

Yi Hwang was also talented in calligraphy and poetry, writing a collection of sijo, a three line poetic form popular with the literati of the Joseon period.[3]

Selected works

Yi Hwang's published writings encompass 496 works in 764 publications in 4 languages and 5167 library holdings [8]

1599 — *Poetry Collection of Yi Hwang* (退溪全書）
1681 — *The Ten Diagrams on Sage Learning* (성학십도：聖學十圖)
1746 — *Compilation of Yi Hwang's Works* (退溪集)
Outline and Explanations of the Works of Zhu Xi (주자서절요：朱子書節要)
Commentary on the Scripture of the Heart (심경석의：心經釋義)
History of Neo-Confucianism in the Song, Yuan and Ming Dynasties (송계원명이학통록：宋季元明理學通錄)
The Four-Seven Debate (사칠속편：四七續篇) : discusses Mencius's philosophy with Gi Dae-seung[9]

Ten Diagrams on Sage Learning

The Neo-Confucian literature of Seonghaksipdo was composed by Yi Hwang in 1568 for King Seonjo. It is a series of lectures for rulers through examples of past sages.[10] Traditional Confucians had affirmed that any man could learn to become a sage;the new Confucians made the ideal of sagehood real and attainable, just as enlightenment was for Buddhists. Yi Hwang intended to present that path by starting each chapter with a diagram and related text drawn from Zhu Xi (Chu Hsi) or another leading authority, and concluding with a brief commentary. He intended for "Ten Diagrams" to be made into a ten paneled standing screen, as well as a short book, so that the mind of the viewer could be constantly engaged with its contents, until it totally assimilated the material.[11]

Yi Hwang on the currently circulating 1,000 won note

In modern culture

Toegyero, a street in central Seoul, is named after him,[12] and he is depicted on the South Korean 1,000 won note.[13] The Taekwondo pattern Toi-Gye was named in honor of Yi Hwang.[14]

Many institutes and university research departments devoted to Yi Hwang have been established. The Toegye Studies Institute set up in Seoul in 1970, Kyungpook National University's Toegye Institute opened in 1979, and an institute and library in Dankook University in 1986. There are research institutes in Tokyo, Taiwan, Hamburg and the United States.[3][4]

SIN SAIMDANG
Korea's Own Renaissance Woman
(October 29, 1504 – May 17, 1551)

Sin Saimdang (신사임당 : 申師任堂) was a Korean artist, writer, calligraphist, and poet. She was the mother of the Korean Confucian scholar Yi I. Often held up as a model of Confucian ideals, her respectful nickname was Eojin Eomeoni (어진 어머니;"Wise Mother").[1][2] Her real name was unknown. Her pennames were Saim, Saimdang, Inimdang, and Imsajae.

Life

Sin Saimdang was born and raised in Gangneung at the home of her maternal grandparents. Her father, Shin Myeonghwa (申命和) was a government official but did not actively join politics. Her mother was Lady Yi, the daughter of Yi Saon (李思溫). Shin had four younger sisters. Her maternal grandfather taught her as he would have taught a grandson. Being raised in that atmosphere, Sin Saimdang received an education that was not common for women of that era. Besides literature and poetry, she was adept at calligraphy, embroidery, and painting.

Because she was raised in a household that had no sons, she spent much time at her parents' home. At the age of 19, she married Commander Yi Wonsu (李元秀) and with the consent of her husband she continued to spend time at the home of her parents. She accompanied her husband to his official posts in Seoul and in rural towns and gave birth to Yi I in Gangneung. However, Sin Saimdang died suddenly after moving to the Pyongan region at the age of 48.[2]

Saimdang was able to cultivate her talents despite the rigid Confucian society thanks to an unconventional household and an understanding husband. Having no brothers, she received an education that would have been bequeathed only to a son, and this background greatly influenced the way she educated her children.

Works

Sin Saimdang's artwork is known for its delicate beauty;insects, flowers, butterflies, orchids, grapes, fish, and landscapes were some of her favorite themes. Approximately 40 paintings of ink and stonepaint colors remain, although it is believed that many others exist.[2]

Unfortunately not much of her calligraphy remains, but her style was greatly praised in her time, with high-ranking officials and connoisseurs writing records of her work. The scholar Eo Sukgwon of Myeongjong mentioned in his book Paegwan Japgi (패관잡기:稗官雜記, "The Storyteller's Miscellany") that Saimdang's paintings of grapes and landscapes compared to those of the notable artist Ahn Gyeon. In 1868, upon admiring the work of Saimdang, the governor of Gangneung remarked that "Saimdang's calligraphy is thoughtfully written, with nobility and elegance, serenity and purity, filled with the lady's virtue".[2]

Poetry

- Looking Back at my Parents' Home while Going Over Daegwallyeong Pass(유대관령 망친정:踰大關嶺望親庭) - Poem written while leaving her parents' house, grief-stricken

87

from leaving her mother alone
- Thinking of Parents (사친:思親) - A poem about filial devotion to her mother
Paintings

Landscape (자리도:紫鯉圖)
Mountains and rivers (산수도:山水圖)
Grass and insect painting(초충도:草蟲圖)
Geese among reeds (노안도:蘆雁圖)

Chochungdo, a painting genre initiated by Sin Saimdang, depicting plants and insects

Legacy

50,000 KRW note

Sin Saimdang is the first woman to appear on a South Korean banknote, the 50,000 won note, first issued in June 2009. Feminist critics, however, have criticized this selection as reinforcing sexist stereotypes about women's roles.[3]

YI I
Joseon's Most Prominent
Scholar and Philosopher
(December 26, 1536 – February 27, 1584)

Yi I (이이:李珥) was one of the two most prominent Korean Confucian scholars of the Joseon Dynasty, the other being his older contemporary, Yi Hwang (Toegye).[1] Yi I is often referred to by his pen name Yulgok (율곡:栗谷 "Chestnut valley"). He is not only known as a scholar but also as a revered politician and reformer.[2] He was academical successor of Jo Gwang-jo.

Life

Yi I was born in Gangneung, Gangwon Province in 1537. His father was a Fourth State Councillor (jwachanseong) and his mother, Shin Saimdang, the accomplished artist and calligraphist. He was the grand nephew of Yi Gi, prime minister 1549 to 1551. early years he was learn of Baik In-geol, successor of Jo Gwang-jo. late years, It is said that by the age of seven he had finished his lessons in the Confucian classics, and passed the Civil Service literary examination at the age of 13. Yi I secluded himself in Kumgang-san following his mother's death when he was 16 and stayed for 3 years, studying Buddhism. He left the mountains at 20 and devoted himself to the study of Confucianism.[3][4]

He married at 22 and a half, went to visit Yi Hwang at Dosan the following year. He passed special exams with top honors with a winning thesis titled Cheondochaek (천도책:天道策, "Book on the Way of Heaven"), which was widely regarded as a literary masterpiece, displaying his knowledge of history and the Confucian philosophy of politics, and also reflecting his profound knowledge of Taoism.[5] He continuously received top honors on civil exams for a consecutive 9 times. His father died when he was 26.[2] He served in various positions in government from the age of 29, and visited the Ming Dynasty as seojanggwan (서장관:書狀官, document officer) in 1568. He also participated in the writing of the Myeongjong Annals and at 34, authored Dongho Mundap, an eleven-article political memorial devoted to clarifying his conviction that a righteous government could be achieved.[6]

Due to his vast experience in different offices over the years, Yi I was able to garner a wide vision of politics and with the deep trust of the king, became one of the central figures of politics by the time he was 40. His many documents and theses were presented to the royal court but when political conflicts escalated in 1576, his efforts proved fruitless and he returned home. Following his return, he devoted his time to studies and education of his disciples and authored several books.[2]

He returned to office at 45 and while holding various minister positions, produced many writings which recorded crucial political events and showed his efforts to ease the political conflicts that were rampant at that time. However, King Seonjo was noncommittal in his attitude and it became difficult for Yi I to remain in a neutral position in the conflicts. He left office in 1583 and died the following year.[2]

According to legend, he had a pavilion built near the ford of the Imjin River in his lifetime and instructed his heirs to set it ablaze when the king had to flee northward from Seoul, to provide a guiding beacon. This took place during Hideyoshi's invasions of Korea at the Imjin war.[7]

Teachings

Yi I was not only known as a philosopher but also as a social reformer. He did not completely agree with the dualistic Neo-Confucianism teachings followed by Yi Hwang. His school of Neo-Confucianism placed emphasis on the more concrete, material elements;rather than inner spiritual perception, this practical and pragmatic approach valued external experience and learning.[8] Unlike Yi Hwang, who suffered through tumultuous times and did not enjoy being in politics, Yi I was an active official who thought it important to implement Confucian values and principles to government administration. He emphasized sage learning and self-cultivation as the base of proper administration.[3] [4]

Yi I is also well known for his foresight about national security. He proposed to draft and reinforce the army against a possible Japanese attack. His proposal was rejected by the central government, his worry was found to be well-founded soon after his death, during the Imjin war.[4]

Selected works

Yi I's published writings encompass 193 works in 276 publications in 6 languages and 2,236 library holdings.[9]

- *Questions and Answers at East Lake* (동호문답 : 東湖問答)- Eleven articles about political reform.[6]
- *Memorial in Ten Thousand Words* (만언봉사 : 萬言封事) - Suggestions about Confucian learning, self-cultivation, and application to government administration.[10]
- *The Essentials of the Studies of the Sages* (성학집요 : 聖學輯要)- Fundamentals of Confucian ethics, self-cultivation and statecraft.[11]
- *The Secret of Expelling Ignorance* (격몽요결 : 擊蒙要訣) - Systematic guide of learning.[12]
- *Daily Records of Lectures before the Throne* (경연일기 : 經筵日記)- Record of political events and happenings.[13]
- *The Complete Works of Yulgok* (율곡전서 : 栗谷全書)was compiled after his death on the basis of the writings he bequeathed.[14]

Legacy

Yulgongno, a street in central Seoul, is named after him,[15] and he is depicted on the South Korean 5,000 won note.[16] The Taekwondo pattern Yul-Gok was also named in his honor. This is the pattern required to advance from 5th Kup Green Belt with

Yi I on the currently circulating 5,000 won note

Blue Tag to 4th Kup Blue Belt. The 38 movements of this pattern refer to his birthplace on the 38th degree latitude.[17] The "Yulgok Project", a modernization project for the

YI SUN-SIN
The Admiral Who Saved the Nation
(April 28, 1545 – December 16, 1598)

"Admiral Yi Sun-sin at Gwanghwamun Square Seoul South Korea HDR"

Yi Sun-sin (Hangul:이순신 Hanja:李舜臣) was a Korean naval commander, famed for his victories against the Japanese navy during the Imjin war in the Joseon Dynasty, and is well-respected for his exemplary conduct on and off the battlefield not only by Koreans, but by Japanese admirals as well.[1] Military historians have placed General Yi Sun-Sin on par with Admiral Horatio Nelson as arguably the greatest naval commander in history for his undefeated record against seemingly insurmountable odds despite no background in naval training.[2][3][4] His title of Samdo Sugun Tongjesa (삼도수군통제사;三道水軍統制使), literally meaning "Naval Commander of the Three Provinces," was the title for the commander of the Korean navy until 1896.

Portrait of Yi_Sun-sin, Busan Cultural Heritage Material No. 56

Perhaps his most remarkable military achievement occurred at the Battle of Myeongnyang. Outnumbered 133 warships to 13, and forced into a last stand with only his minimal fleet standing between the Japanese Army and Seoul, he still managed to leave 31 of the 133 Japanese warships either destroyed or impaired, without losing a single ship of his own.[5]

Despite never having received naval training or participating in naval combat prior to the war, and constantly being outnumbered and outsupplied, he went to his grave as one of few admirals in world history who remained undefeated after commanding as many naval battles as he did (at least 23).[6][7]

Yi died at the Battle of Noryang on December 16, 1598. With the Japanese army on the verge of being completely expelled from the Korean Peninsula, he was mortally wounded by a single bullet. His famous dying words were, "The battle is at its height...beat my war drums...do not announce my death."

The royal court eventually bestowed various honors upon him, including a posthumous title of Chungmugong (충무공;忠武公;Duke of Loyalty and Warfare), an enrollment as a Seonmu Ildeung Gongsin (선무일등공신;宣武一等功臣;First-class military order of merit during the reign of Seonjo), and two posthumous offices, Yeonguijeong (영의정; 領議政;Prime Minister), and the Deokpung Buwongun (덕풍부원군;德豊府院君;The Prince of the Court from Deokpung). Yi remains a venerated hero among Koreans today.

Early life

Yi was born in Geoncheon-dong Street, Hanseong (then capital, present-day Inhyeon-dong, Jung-gu District, Seoul) but spent his adolescence and early adulthood period before passing the military examination in Asan where his mother's relatives lived and where now a shrine to him stands.

His family was part of the Korean Deoksu Yi clan. His grandfather Yi Baeg-nok retired from politics when neo-Confucian reformer Jo Gwang-jo was executed in the Third Literati Purge of 1519 and moved to a village near where Jo was buried. Yi Sun-sin's father Yi Jeong was likewise disillusioned with politics and did not enter government service as expected of a yangban (noble) family. However, popular belief that Yi Sun-sin had difficult childhood because of his family's connection with Jo Gwang-jo (as depicted in KBS TV series Immortal Admiral Yi Sun-sin) is not true.[8]

One of the most important events of his early life was when Yi met and became friends with Ryu Seong-ryong (류성룡;柳成龍;1542–1607), a prominent scholar who held the key official position of Dochaechalsa (도체찰사;都體察使), and was in command of the military during the Japanese invasions of Korea (1592–1598). During the war, Yu's support of Admiral Yi was critical to Yi's achievements.

As a young boy, Yi played war games with other local boys, showing excellent leadership talent at an early age and constructed his own bow and fletched his own arrows as a teenager. Yi also became proficient in reading and writing Hanmun.

IIn 1576, Yi passed the military examination (무과;武科). Yi is said to have impressed the judges with his archery, but failed to pass the test when he broke a leg during the cavalry examination. After he re-entered and passed the examination, Yi was posted to the Bukbyeong (Northern Frontier Army) military district in Hamgyeong province. However, he was the oldest junior officer at the age of thirty-two. There, Yi experienced battles defending the border settlements against the Jurchen marauders and quickly became known for his strategic skills and leadership.

In 1583, he lured the Jurchen into battle, defeated the marauders, and captured their chief, Mu Pai Nai. According to a contemporary tradition, Yi then spent three years out of the army upon hearing of his father's death. After his return to the front line, Yi led a string of successful campaigns against the Jurchen.

However, his brilliance and accomplishments so soon in his career made his superiors jealous, and they falsely accused him of desertion during battle. The conspiracy was led by General Yi Il (이일;李鎰;1538–1601), who would later fail to repel the Japanese invasion at the Battle of Sangju. This tendency to sabotage and frame professional adversaries was very common in the later years of the Joseon military and government. Yi was stripped of his rank, imprisoned, and tortured. After his release, Yi was allowed to fight as an enlisted soldier. After a short period of time, however, he was appointed as the commander of the Seoul Hunryeonwon (a military training center) and was later transferred to a small county, to be its military magistrate.

Yi's efforts in northern Korea was rewarded when Yi was assigned as Commander of the Left Jeolla Province (전라좌도;全羅左道) Naval District. Within the span of a few months in late 1590, he received four military appointments, in rapid succession, with each subsequent post carrying greater responsibility than the last: Commander of the Kosarijin Garrison in Pyeongan province, Commander of the Manpo Garrison, also in

Pyeongan province, and the Commander of the Wando Garrison, in Jeolla province, before finally receiving the appointment as Commander of the Left Jeolla Naval District.

The royal court was in a state of confusion over the possibility of a war with Japan, now unified under the rule of Toyotomi Hideyoshi, and the unstable situation in Manchuria where a young Jurchen chieftain named Nurhaci was gathering strength. Nurhaci's descendants would become masters of China as founders of the Qing Dynasty in a few decades' time, after invading Korea in 1627 and 1637.

Yi assumed his new post at Yeosu on the 13th day of the 2nd lunar month of 1591 (March 13, 1591). From there, he was able to undertake a buildup of the regional navy, which was later used to confront the Japanese invasion force. He subsequently began to strengthen the province's navy with a series of reforms, including the construction of the turtle ship.

Japanese invasions of Korea (1592–1598)

Yi is remembered for his numerous victories fighting the Japanese during the Japanese invasions of Korea (1592–1598). Among his twenty-three victories, the Battle of Myeongnyang and the Battle of Hansan Island are the most famous battles.

In 1592, Toyotomi Hideyoshi gave the order to invade Korea and use it as a forward base to conquer Ming China. After the Japanese attacked Busan, Yi began his naval operations from his headquarters at Yeosu. Despite never having commanded a naval battle in his life, he won the Battle of Okpo, Battle of Sacheon, and several others in quick succession. His string of victories made the Japanese generals suddenly wary of the threat at sea.

Hideyoshi was fully aware of the need to control the seas during the invasion. Having failed to hire two Portuguese galleons to help him, he increased the size of his own fleet to 1700 vessels, assuming that he could overwhelm the Joseon navy with numerical superiority.

There were numerous reasons why Yi was so successful against the Japanese fleets. Yi had prepared for the war by checking the status of his soldiers, granaries, and supplies, replacing them when it was necessary. As part of this preparation, Yi resurrected and built the turtle ship, which was a considerable factor in his victories. Yi also had a great deal of information about the southern Korean coast and he planned his battles using the sea tides and narrow straits to his advantage.

Yi was a charismatic leader, and was able to maintain his soldiers' morale despite constantly being low on supplies and food, and continuous news of countless Korean losses in ground battles. In some records, it is stated that he went as far as to personally fulfill some of his soldiers' dying wishes. He demonstrated his loyalty to the people by treating them with respect and fighting amongst them even when endangered. Because of this, Admiral Yi became immensely popular among his soldiers and the Korean people, who often provided him with intelligence reports at great risk to themselves.

The Joseon panokseon were structurally stronger than Japanese ships at the time. Panokseon had stronger hulls and could carry at least 20 cannons, compared to the Japanese 1 or 2. Japanese ship-mounted cannons were inferior to the Koreans' in both range and power. Cannon development had been neglected by the Korean government, so Yi personally saw to it that the technology was developed. As such, the Korean side had several different types of cannons at their disposal in battle.

Admiral Yi was an excellent naval strategist. The Japanese navy's strongest tactic was to board enemy ships and engage in hand-to-hand combat. The panokseon was slower than the Japanese ships so Yi had little room for error to negate the Japanese navy's most dangerous tactic. He was able to do so in every naval engagement he commanded.

As Yi's brilliance as a strategist revealed itself throughout the war, his legend grew. In what could be considered his greatest victory in the Battle of Myeongnyang, Yi proved victorious in the battle with 13 panokseon, while the Japanese had at least 333 ships (133 warships, at least 200 logistical support ships).

It was largely due to Yi's complete control of the seas that the Japanese were eventually forced to retreat, keeping Joseon safe from another Japanese invasion until the end of the war.

Four campaigns of 1952

A Japanese invasion force landed at Busan and Dadaejin, port cities on the southern tip of Joseon. The Japanese, without meeting any naval resistance, quickly captured these ports and began a lightning march north. They reached Seoul in just nineteen days, on May 2, 1592, due to the military inefficiency of the Joseon army, especially at the Battle of Sangju and the failure to defend Joryeong Pass.

After capturing Hanseong and Pyongyang, the Japanese planned to cross the Yalu River into Chinese territory, and use the waters west of the Korean peninsula to supply the invasion. However, Yi Sun-sin was able to stay informed on all his enemy's activities.

First campaign

Yi had never officially studied naval warfare in his limited time in the military academy, and neither he, nor his subordinates had experienced naval combat before the Japanese invasion.

On the June 13, 1592, Admiral Yi and Admiral Yi Eok-gi (이억기;李億祺;1561–1597), the commander of the Right Jeolla navy, set sail with 24 Panokseons, 15 small warships, and 46 boats (i.e. fishing boats), and arrived at the waters of the Gyeongsang Province by sunset.[9] Next day, the Jeolla fleet sailed to the arranged location where Admiral Won Gyun (원균;元均;1540–1597) was supposed to meet them, and met the admiral on June 15. The augmented flotilla of 91 ships[10] then began circumnavigating the Geoje Island, bound for the Gadeok Island, but scouting vessels detected 50 Japanese vessels at the Okpo harbor.[9] Upon sighting the approaching Korean fleet, some of the Japanese who had been busying themselves with plundering got back to their ships, and began to flee. [9] At this, the Korean fleet encircled the Japanese ships and finished them with artillery bombardments.[11] The Koreans spotted five more Japanese vessels that night, and managed to destroy four.[11] The next day, the Koreans approached 13 Japanese ships at Jeokjinpo as reported by the intelligence.[11] In the same manner as the previous success at Okpo, the Korean fleet destroyed 11 Japanese ships – completing the Battle of Okpo without a loss of a single ship.[11]

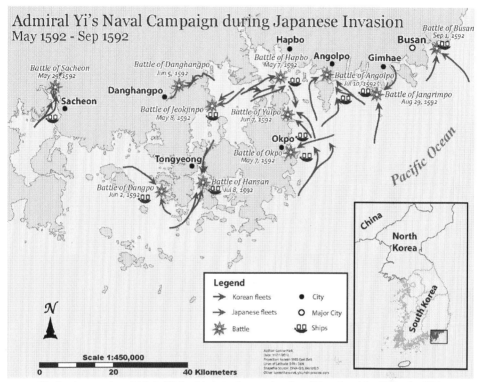

The 4 major campaigns of Admiral Yi Sunshin during Japanese invasion of Korea from May 1592 to Sep 1592

Second campaign

About three weeks after the Battle of Okpo,[12] Admirals Yi and Won sailed with a total of 26 ships (23 under Admiral Yi) toward the Bay of Sacheon upon receiving an intelligence report of a Japanese presence.[13] Admiral Yi had left behind his fishing vessels that used to make up most of his fleet in favor of his newly completed Turtle ship.[12] Admiral Yi ordered the fleet to feign withdrawal, which caused the Japanese to eagerly pursue the Korean fleet with their 12 vessels.[12] With the Japanese ships drawn out of the safety of the harbor, the Korean navy countered, and with the Turtle Ship leading the charge, they successfully destroyed all 12 ships.[12] Admiral Yi was shot by a bullet in his left shoulder, but survived.[12]

On July 10, 1592, the Korean fleet destroyed 21 Japanese ships at the Battle of Dangpo. On July 13, they destroyed 26 Japanese warship at the Battle of Danghangpo.
Third campaign

In response to the Korean navy's success, Toyotomi Hideyoshi recalled three admirals from land-based activities: Wakizaka Yasuharu, Kato Yoshiaki, and Kuki Yoshitaka. They were the only ones with naval responsibilities in the entirety of the Japanese invasion forces.[14] However, the admirals arrived in Busan nine days before Hideyoshi's order was actually issued, and assembled a squadron to counter the Korean navy.[14] Eventually Admiral Wakizaka completed his preparations, and his eagerness to win military honor pushed him to launch an attack against the Koreans without waiting for the other admirals to finish.[14]

The combined Korean navy of 70 ships[15] under the commands of Admirals Yi Sun-sin and Yi Eok-gi was carrying out a search-and-destroy operation because the Japanese troops on land were advancing into the Jeolla Province.[14] The Jeolla Province was the only Korean territory to be untouched by a major military action, and served as home for the three admirals and the only active Korean naval force.[14] The admirals considered it best to destroy naval support for the Japanese to reduce the effectiveness of the enemy ground troops.[14]

On August 13, 1592, the Korean fleet sailing from the Miruk Island at Dangpo received local intelligence that a large Japanese fleet was nearby.[14] The following morning, the Korean fleet spotted the Japanese fleet of 82 vessels anchored in the straits of Gyeonn-aeryang.[14] Because of the narrowness of the strait and the hazard posed by the underwater rocks, Admiral Yi sent six ships to lure out 63 Japanese vessels into the wider sea,[15] and the Japanese fleet followed.[14] There the Japanese fleet was surrounded by the Korean fleet in a semicircular formation called "crane wing (학익진)" by Admiral Yi.[14] With at least three turtle ships (two of which were newly completed) spearheading the clash against the Japanese fleet, the Korean vessels fired volleys of cannonballs into the Japanese formation.[14] Then the Korean ships engaged in a free-for-all battle with the Japanese ships, maintaining enough distance to prevent the Japanese from boarding;Admiral Yi permitted melee combats only against severely damaged Japanese ships.[14]

The battle ended in a Korean victory, with Japanese losses of 59 ships – 47 destroyed and 12 captured in the Battle of Hansan Island.[16] Several Korean prisoners of war were rescued by the Korean soldiers throughout the fight. Admiral Wakisaka escaped due to the speed of his flagship.[16] When the news of the defeat at the Battle of Hansando reached Toyotomi Hideyoshi, he ordered that the Japanese invasion forces cease all naval operations.[14]

On August 16, 1592, Yi Sun-sin led their fleet to the harbor of Angolpo where 42 Japanese vessels were docked.

Fourth campaign

In September 1592, Yi left his base at Hansan Island and attacked the Japanese in Busan harbor. Yi withdrew his forces from Busan harbor after the battle due to the absence of a landing force.

Aftermath of four campaigns of 1592

Yi was victorious in every single operation (at least 15 battles) of the four campaigns of 1592. His campaigns resulted in hundreds of sunken Japanese warships, transports, supply ships and thousands of Japanese naval casualties.

In 1593, Admiral Yi was appointed to command the combined navies of the three southern provinces with the title Naval Commander of the Three Provinces which gave him command over the Right and Left Navies of Jeolla province, the Right and Left Navies of Gyeongsang province, and the Navy of Chungcheong province.

Turtle ships

One of Yi's greatest accomplishments was resurrecting and improving the turtle ship (거북선;龜船). With his creative mind and the support of his subordinates, Yi was able to devise the geobukseon, or Turtle Ship. Contrary to popular belief, the turtle ship was not actually invented by Admiral Yi;rather, he improved upon an older design that had been suggested during the reign of King Taejong.

The turtle ships designed by Yi held eleven cannons on each side of the ship, with two each at the stern and the bow. The ship's figurehead was in the shape of a dragon. The figurehead itself held up to four cannons, and emitted a smokescreen that, in combination with its fierce appearance, was meant to be used as psychological warfare. The sides of the turtle ship were dotted with smaller holes from which arrows, guns, and mortars could be fired. The roof was covered with planks and spikes.[17] The purpose of the spikes was to prevent the ship from being boarded by the enemy. The larger Japanese ships' sides were higher than the turtle ships' and thus, the spikes prevented boarders from

Turtle ship in the War Memorial of Korea

By Steve46814 (Own work)
[CC BY-SA 3.0 (http://creativecommons.org/licenses/by-sa/3.0) or GFDL (http://www.gnu.org/copyleft/fdl.html)], via Wikimedia Commons

jumping down onto the roof without risking impalement. There were two masts that held two large sails. The turtle ship was also steered and powered by twenty oars, each of which were pulled by two men during fair conditions and five in foul seas or combat.

There is an ongoing debate as to whether the turtle ship had two decks or three;historians still have no definitive answer. Whichever is the case, it is clear that the turtle ship employed multiple decks to separate the rowers from the combat compartment. This enabled the turtle ship to be very mobile since wind and manpower could be used simultaneously. Most support the argument of two decks since that was what was drawn out in the first and second designs of the turtle ships. Some historians maintain that, since Yi was a unique individual and often pursued innovative ideas (contrary to the established wisdom of his peers), it is possible that he had the turtle ship built with three decks. It is known that his flagship, a panokseon, had three decks during his campaigns, so there is support for the belief that the turtle ship had three decks.

Turtle ships are the most famous part of Admiral Yi's fleet;however, he never deployed more than five in any one battle. The Joseon Dynasty used cannons as its primary offensive naval weapon. Historically, they had often used guns and cannons against Japanese pirates as early as the 1390s. The Joseon navy did not implement the ship-boarding strategy that the Japanese navy did, so it was imperative that their warships "stand off" from Japanese vessels. Admiral Yi made it a strategic priority to avoid hand-to-hand combat, in which the Japanese navy specialized. The turtle ship was developed to support his tactic against Japanese fleets.

Turtle ships were first used in the Battle of Sacheon (1592) and were used in nearly every battle until the devastating Battle of Chilchonryang, when a Japanese double-agent plot nearly succeeded, resulting in every turtle ship and all but 13 panokseon being sunk. The turtle ships did not re-appear in battle until the Battle of Noryang.

Turtle ships were mostly used to spearhead attacks. They were best used in tight areas and around islands rather than the open sea.

The Japanese double-agent plot

As Yi won battle after battle, Hideyoshi and his commanders became anxious as they neared Busan. Yi constantly attacked and delayed supply ships bringing food, weapons, and reinforcements to the Japanese. At one point, the entire invasion was halted just before attacking Pyongyang when supplies and troops failed to reach the First and Second Divisions.

Hideyoshi soon adjusted. At Busan, the Japanese warships were reinforced and some cannons added to larger ships. The fleet clustered beneath the harbor's defenses of heavy shore-mounted cannons that were acquired from the armory. But, above all, the Japanese knew that, for a successful invasion of Joseon, Yi had to be eliminated. Not a single Japanese ship would be safe for as long as he was commanding the sea.

Taking advantage of the many internal court rivalries of the Joseon Dynasty, the Japanese devised a plan. A Japanese double agent named Yoshira (要時羅) was sent to the Joseon general Kim Gyeong-seo (김경서;金景瑞;1564–1624), and convinced the general that he would spy on the Japanese. Yoshira played this role until Kim began believing anything he would say.

One day, he told General Kim Gyeong-seo that the Japanese general Katō Kiyomasa would be coming on a certain date with a great fleet for another attack on the south shores and insisted that Admiral Yi be sent to lay an ambush. General Kim agreed and sent the message to Field Marshal Gwon Yul (권율;權慄;1537–1599), Commander-in-Chief (도원수;導元帥) of the Joseon military, who, in turn, sent the message to King Seonjo. King

Seonjo, who was desperate for victories to loosen the Japanese grip on his kingdom, gave permission for the attack. When General Kim gave Admiral Yi his orders, the admiral refused to carry them out, for he knew that the location given by the spy was studded with sunken rocks and was thus extremely dangerous. Admiral Yi also refused because he did not trust the words of spies.

When General Kim informed the king of Admiral Yi's refusal, the admiral's enemies at court quickly insisted on his replacement by General Won Gyun, former commander of the Gyeongsang Province Western Fleet & Commander of the Jeolla Province Ground Forces. They advised that Admiral Yi be arrested.

As a result, in 1597, Yi was relieved of command, placed under arrest, and taken to Seoul in chains to be imprisoned and tortured. Yi was tortured almost to the point of death by using simple torture tactics such as whipping, flogging, burning, the cudgel, or even the classic technique of leg breaking torture. King Seonjo wanted to have Yi killed, but the admiral's supporters at court, chiefly the minister Jeong Tak (정탁;鄭琢;1526–1605), convinced the king to spare him due to his past service record. The prime minister, Yu Seong-ryong, who was Yi's childhood friend and his main supporter, remained silent during this deadly hour. Spared the death penalty, Admiral Yi was again demoted to the rank of a common infantry soldier under General Gwon Yul. This penalty was worse than death for Joseon generals at that time, since they lived by honor. However, Yi responded to this humiliation as a most obedient subject, quietly going about his work as if his rank and orders were appropriate. Despite his low rank, many officers treated him with respect, since they knew that the admiral did nothing wrong. Yi would stay under General Gwon Yul's command for a short while until Won Gyun's death at the Battle of Chilchonryang, which would lead to his reinstatement.

Joseon defeat at Chilchonryang and reinstatement of Admiral Yi

With Yi stripped of influence and negotiations breaking down in 1596, Hideyoshi again ordered an attack on Joseon. The second Japanese invasion landed in the first month of 1597 with a force of 140,000 men transported on 1000 ships. In response, Ming China sent thousands of reinforcements to aid Joseon. With the help of the Ming, the Joseon army was able to halt the Japanese offensive and push it back during the winter of 1597, before the Japanese were able to reach the Joseon capitol of Hanseong.

On the high seas, Yi's successor Won Gyun failed to respond to reports from his scouts and allowed the Japanese to land critical reinforcements at Sosang Harbor for their land offensive unopposed. Without adequate reconnaissance or planning, Won Gyun decided to attack with the entire naval force of Joseon at his disposal; a fleet consisting of 150 warships operated by 30,000 men that had been carefully assembled and trained by Admiral Yi. Won Gyun left anchor at Yeosu with the fleet and sailed into waters marked by treacherous rocks where the Japanese ambushed the Joseon fleet in the Battle of Chilchonryang on August 28, 1597. Ignorant of the strength and disposition of the enemy, Won was stunned to find a Japanese fleet of 500 to 1000 ships which immediately closed for melee combat, denying the Joseon ships the advantages of superior seamanship and cannon fire. The exhausted Joseon sailors were reduced to fighting boarding actions while heavily outnumbered and slaughtered en masse.

The Joseon fleet was decimated with only 13 warships surviving under Admiral Bae Seol, who fled before battle was fully engaged to save the warships under his command. After the destruction of the Joseon fleet, Won Gyun and Yi Eok-gi, another Joseon commander, fled to an island with a band of survivors but were killed by waiting Japanese soldiers from the nearby fort. The Battle of Chilchonryang was the only naval victory for the Japanese during the war against Joseon. When King Seonjo and the royal court learned of the catastrophic defeat, they hurriedly pardoned and reinstated Admiral Yi as commander of the greatly reduced Joseon fleet.

Battle of Myeongnyang

Admiral Yi located the 13 warships and rallied the 200 surviving sailors. Together with his flagship, Admiral Yi's entire fleet totaled 13 ships, none of which were turtle ships. In the belief that the Joseon fleet would never be restorable, King Seonjo, sent an edict to Admiral Yi to abandon the warships and take his men to join the ground forces under General Gwon Yul. Admiral Yi responded with a letter written "...your servant still doth have twelve warships under his command and he is still alive, that the enemy shall never be safe in the West Sea (the Yellow Sea being the closest body of water to Hanseong)."

Emboldened after their victory at Chilchonryang, Japanese admirals Kurushima Michifusa, Todo Takatora, Kato Yoshiaki, and Wakisaka Yasuharu sailed out of Busan Harbor with a fleet of over 300 ships, confident in being able to defeat Admiral Yi. Elimination of the Joseon fleet would mean unrestricted movement of supplies and reinforcements from Japan for the offensive drive on land towards Hanseong and beyond.

After careful study of potential battlefields, in October 1597 Admiral Yi lured the Japanese fleet into the Myeongnyang Strait,[18] by sending a fast warship near the Japanese naval base and luring the Japanese fleet out of anchorage. The Japanese assumed that this was a Joseon scouting ship and that pursuing it would lead to the location of Admiral Yi, giving them an opportunity to destroy the courageous admiral and the remnants of the Joseon fleet. What they did not know was that they were being lured into a masterfully devised trap.

There were several reasons why Admiral Yi decided on this location for battle. Myeongnyang Strait had currents, eddies, and whirlpools so powerful that ships could only enter safely a few at a time. The north-south tidal flow reversed every three hours, limiting the time that the Japanese could mount an offensive. The strait was sufficiently narrow that it would prove impossible for the Japanese to flank or envelop the numerically inferior Joseon fleet. The deep shadows of the surrounding hillsides provided the Joseon ships with concealment. On that particular day there was also a heavy mist, dramatically reducing visibility in favor of the Joseon fleet. Therefore, despite being vastly outnumbered, Admiral Yi used the terrain restrictions to neutralize the Japanese navy's staggering numerical advantage.

The Japanese fleet of approximately 333 ships (133 warships, at least 200 logistical support ships) entered Myeongnyang Strait in groups. The Japanese ships that made it through were met by 13 Joseon warships obscured by the shadows of the surrounding hills, ready with archers and cannons, and the melee-based Japanese found themselves unable to fight effectively and break through the superior Joseon ranged fire. The unpredictable current eventually wreaked havoc on the Japanese;their ships found themselves unable to maneuver and collided with each other when the tide reversed, while also presenting a perfect target for the Joseon naval artillery. Admiral Yi was astonishingly able to rout a force that outnumbered him more than 25 to 1 in ships alone. About 31 of the 333 Japanese ships that entered the Myeongnyang Strait were destroyed or damaged.[19] Joseon losses on the other hand were around ten casualties and no ships lost. Kurushima Michifusa was killed on his flagship by Joseon archers;his body in its ornate armor was fished out of the water, his severed head was put on display to further demoralize the Japanese fleet.

Admiral Yi's miraculous victory at the Battle of Myeongnyang turned the tide of the entire war against the Japanese;their ground forces on the verge of invading Hanseong were cut off from steady flow of supplies and reinforcements, and forced to pull back. Today, the battle is celebrated in Korea as one of Admiral Yi's greatest victories. No other engagement involving such an outnumbered fleet has resulted in such a disproportionate victory, making it one of the greatest achievements in naval warfare.

The final battle and Admiral Yi's death

On December 15, 1598, a huge Japanese fleet under the command of Shimazu Yoshihiro, was amassed in Sachon Bay, on the east end of Noryang Strait. Shimazu's goal was to break the allied forces' blockade on Konishi Yukinaga, join the two fleets, and sail home to Japan. Admiral Yi, meanwhile, knew exactly where Shimazu was, after receiving reports from scouts and local fishermen.

At this time, the Joseon fleet consisted of 82 panokseon and three turtle ships, with 8,000 soldiers under Admiral Yi.[20] The Ming fleet consisted of six large war junks, 57 lighter war galleys [21] and two panokseon given to Chen Lin by Admiral Yi, with 5,000 Ming soldiers of the Guangdong squadron and 2,600 Ming marines who fought aboard Joseon ships.[21][22]

The battle began at two o'clock in the early morning of December 16, 1598. Like Admiral Yi's previous battles, the Japanese were unable to respond effectively to the Korean's tactics. The tightness of Noryang Strait hindered lateral movement, and Yi's maneuvers prevented the Japanese fleet from boarding their enemies' vessels, their primary naval tactic.

As the Japanese retreated, Admiral Yi ordered a vigorous pursuit. During this time, a stray arquebus bullet from an enemy ship struck Admiral Yi,[23] near his left armpit.[24] Sensing that the wound was fatal, and fearing a repeat of the Battle of Chilchonryang, the admiral uttered, "The war is at its height -- wear my armor and beat my war drums. Do not announce my death."[23] He died moments later.

Only two people witnessed his death: Yi Hoe, Yi's eldest son, and Yi Wan, his nephew. [23] Admiral Yi's son and nephew struggled to regain their composure and carried the admiral's body into his cabin before others could notice. For the remainder of the battle, Yi

Wan wore his uncle's armor and continued to beat the war drum to encourage the pursuit.[23]

During the battle, Chen Lin found himself in trouble many times and Yi's flagship rowed to his rescue. When Chen Lin called for Admiral Yi to thank him for coming to his aid, he was met by Yi Wan, who announced that his uncle was dead.[25] It is said that Chen himself was so shocked that he fell to the ground three times, beating his chest and crying.[26] News of Admiral Yi's death spread quickly throughout the allied fleet and both Joseon and Ming sailors and fighting men wailed in grief.[25]

Admiral Yi's body was brought back to his hometown in Asan to be buried next to his father, Yi Jeong (in accordance to Korean tradition). Shrines, both official and unofficial, were constructed in his honor all throughout the land."[27]

Awards, decorations, and honors

Admiral Yi's posthumous title, Chungmugong, is used as South Korea's third highest military honor, known as The Cordon of Chungmu of the Order of Military Merit and Valor. He was posthumously granted the title of Prince of Deokpung Chungmuro. In North Korea, the military awards the Order of Admiral Yi Sun-Sin to flag officers and naval commanders for outstanding leadership.[28]

Prominent statues of Admiral Yi have been erected in the middle of Sejongno in central Seoul (the Statue of Admiral Yi Sun-sin) and at Busan Tower in Busan.

The city of Chungmu on the southern coast of Korea, now renamed Tongyeong, is named in honor of his posthumous title and the site of his headquarters. Additionally, a street in downtown Seoul is named after him, and the Yi Sun-sin Bridge was built near Yeosu and opened to traffic on May 10, 2012, becoming the longest suspension bridge in Korea.

South Korea's KDX-II naval destroyer class, and the first commissioned ship of the class, are named Chungmugong Yi Sun-sin.

An ITF-style Taekwondo pattern is named after Yi's posthumous name of Chungmu.

A depiction of Admiral Yi is featured on the front of the 100 South Korean won coin.

Today, Admiral Yi is considered one of Korea's greatest heroes of all time. Koreans look upon Yi as a man of courage, perseverance, strength, self-sacrifice, intellect, and loyalty to his country.

Admiral George Alexander Ballard of the Royal Navy considered Yi a great naval commander, and compared him to Lord Nelson of England:

> It is always difficult for Englishmen to admit that Nelson ever had an equal in his profession, but if any man is entitled to be so regarded, it should be this great naval commander of Asiatic race who never knew defeat and died in the presence of the enemy;of whose movements a track-chart might be compiled from the wrecks of hundreds of Japanese ships lying with their valiant crews at the bottom of the sea, off the coasts of the Korean peninsula... and it seems, in truth, no exaggeration to assert that from first to last he never made a mistake, for his work was so complete under each variety of circumstances as to defy criticism... His whole career might be summarized by saying that, although he had no lessons from past history to serve as a guide, he waged war on the sea as it should be waged if it is to produce definite results, and ended by making the supreme sacrifice of a defender of his country. (*The Influence of the Sea on The Political History of Japan*, pp. 66–67.)

Admiral Togo regarded Admiral Yi as his superior. At a party held in his honor, Togo took exception to a speech comparing him to Lord Nelson and Yi Sun-sin.

> It may be proper to compare me with Nelson, but not with Korea's Yi Sun-sin, for he has no equal. (*The Imjin War*, by Samuel Hawley, pg. 490)

Prior to the 1905 Battle of Tsushima, Lieutenant Commander Kawada Isao recalled in his memoirs that:

> ...naturally we could not help but remind ourselves of Korea's Yi Sun-sin, the world's first sea commander, whose superlative personality, strategy, invention, commanding ability, intelligence, and courage were all worthy of our admiration. (*The Imjin War*, by Samuel Hawley, pg. 490)

Admiral Tetsutaro Sato of the Imperial Japanese Navy mentioned the Korean admiral in his book published in 1908:

> Throughout history there have been few generals accomplished at the tactics of frontal attack, sudden attack, concentration and dilation. Napoleon, who mastered the art of conquering the part with the whole, can be held to have been such a general, and among admirals, two further tactical geniuses may be named: in the East, Yi Sun-sin of Korea, and in the West, Horatio Nelson of England. Undoubtedly, Yi is a supreme naval commander even on the basis of the limited literature of the Seven-Year War, and despite the fact that his bravery and brilliance are not known to the West, since he had the misfortune to be born in Joseon Dynasty. Anyone who can be compared to Yi should be better than Michiel de Ruyter from Netherlands. Nelson is far behind Yi in terms of personal character and integrity. Yi was the inventor of the covered war ship known as the turtle ship. He was a truly great commander and a master of the

naval tactics of three hundred years ago. (*A Military History of the Empire* (Japanese: 帝國國防史論), p. 399)

During the time of the invasion, it was up to the admiral to supply his fleet. Yi's fleet was cut off from any helping hand from the king's court and had to fend for itself. The admiral often wrote in his war diary, *Nanjung Ilgi War Diary of Admiral Yi Sun-sin*, about how concerned he was about the food supply during winters. His enemy was fully supplied, and always outnumbered him.

Yi himself had never been trained as a naval commander. Korea, called Joseon at the time, did not have any naval training facilities. Although Yi passed the military exams when he was young, he was never trained at an academy. Yi's only military experiences came from fighting foreign Jurchen tribes invading from Manchuria. In fact, the Battle of Okpo, his first victory against the Japanese fleet, was also his first sea battle ever. None of his subordinates, including his own staff, had ever fought at sea before.

One reason Admiral Yi was successful in his battles was because his cannon had longer range and power than the enemy's, with the Japanese heavily favoring troop transport over naval combat. His turtle ship, which had first set sail the day before the invasion, was very effective in leading the attack and breaking the enemy's formation. Yi won all of at least twenty-three naval battles fought while suffering very minimal losses, destroying a lot of Japanese ships and killing a lot of Japanese soldiers.

Admiral Yi used many different formations according to the situation, and capitalized on tides and ocean currents. Yi also took advantage of his knowledge of the surrounding sea. Many times, he lured the enemy to a place where his fleet would have the upper hand.

At the Battle of Hansando, the Japanese commander broke ranks and Yi routed his fleet. Yi's expertise on naval strategy is apparent in the fact that his successor, Won Gyun, even with all of Yi's ships and trained crew, could not defeat an enemy fleet of similar might. One of the greatest legacies of the admiral was the disruption of the Japanese supply line. Through his calculated attacks, he successfully burdened the Japanese navy and the supplies trying to reach their lines near the Chinese border.

Yi's naval reforms did not persist and disappeared soon after his death. The turtle ships faded into the annals of Korean history, reaching iconic legendary status today. The Joseon royal court decided on a reduced military, especially after the Manchu invasions in the 1630s.

Yi kept a careful record of daily events in his diary, and it is from these entries, along with the reports he sent to the throne during the war, that much about him has been learned. Also, much information about the turtle ships are written in his diaries. These works have been published in English as *Nanjung Ilgi: War Diary of Admiral Yi Sun-sin*, and *Imjin Jangcho: Admiral Yi Sun-sin's Memorials to Court.*

Among his direct male descendants, more than two hundred passed the military examination and pursued military careers, hence constituting a prominent family or military yangban of late Joseon. Although many of his male descendants did not play the kind of a

106

vital role in the politics of late Joseon, the court seems to have treated them with respect. Many attained important high-level posts in the administration. Moreover, at the end of the Joseon Dynasty, at least several descendants are known to have become anti-Japanese independence activists. Today, most of Yi's descendants live in or near Seoul and Asan.

In Korea, Admiral Yi is not only famous for the turtle ship, but also for his last words before his death. He told his nephew to wear his armor and to hide his death until the battle is over to avoid demoralizing his men in the middle of battle. His last words were, Do not let my death be known (나의 죽음을 알리지 마라).

HEO NANSEOLHEON
A Short-Lived Lived Literary Genius
(1563–1589)

Heo Nanseolheon (허난설헌:許蘭雪軒), born Heo Chohui (허초희:許楚姬), was a prominent Korean poet of the mid-Joseon dynasty. She was the younger sister of Heo Pong, a minister and political writer, and elder to Heo Gyun (1569–1618), a prominent writer of the time and credited as the author of The Tale of Hong Gildong. Her own writings consisted of some two hundred poems written in Chinese verse (hanshi), and two poems written in hangul (though her authorship of the hangul poems is contested).[1]

Biography

Early life

Heo Nanseolheon was born in Gangneung to a prominent political family (yangban). Her father, Heo Yeop (ko), was a distinguished scholar and fathered her by his second marriage. His first was to a daughter of Prince Seop'yeong, who yielded two daughters and a son. His second marriage was to a daughter of a political minister, who mothered Nanseolheon and her two brothers. While her father was a Confucian and conservative official who subscribed tightly to the belief of namjon-yubi ("men above, women below"). It fell to her elder brother, Heo Pong, to recognize her budding talent and curiosity and introduce her to literature.

From an early age she became recognized as a prodigal poet, though due to her position as a woman she was incapable of entering into a position of distinguishment. Her early piece, "Inscriptions on the Ridge Pole of the White Jade Pavilion in the Kwanghan Palace" (Kwanghanjeon Paegongnu sangnangmun), produced at the age of eight, was lauded as a work of poetic genius and earned her the epithet "immortal maiden."[1] Her innate talent for hanmun (Chinese) verse prompted him to be her first tutor in her early years, and introduce her to Chinese writing, such as the Confucian Five Classics.

However, Heo Pong was also an outspoken and influential political scholar, and was eventually exiled to Kapsan for three years for his political leanings. Her younger brother, Heo Gyun, was a similarly gifted poet who studied under Yi Tal (ko), a specialist of Tang poetry and a friend of Heo Pong, and he took part in her education, especially after her elder brother's exile. He fostered her education later in life, and used his preferred position as a highly respected male to keep her in correspondence with literary circles. Yi Tal, his tutor, also engaged in sharing Tang poetry with Nanseolheon, whose influence became visible in the naturalism of a significant portion of her surviving work.[2]

Marriage

Sometime during her life, she married to the son of a civil official, Kim Seongnip. Her marriage was an unhappy one, as recorded by Heo Gyun. Her husband often left her alone at home to pursue other women, and she maintained a cold relationship with her mother-in-law. She gave birth to two children, a girl and a boy, but both died in infancy in subsequent years. Within a year of her elder brother Heo Pong's death in Kapsan, she herself died at the age of twenty seven.[3]

The circumstances and timing of her marriage are uncertain, and documented proof is limited and subject to conjecture. Scholars such as Kim-Renaud[2] and Choe-Wall[1] engage with her literature, and hypothesize that she lived among her brothers for a significant portion of her life (during which they suggest most of her Tang-influenced and naturalistic poetry was produced), and married later. She suggests that the body of her "empathetic" poetry was produced after being married, as a result of the isolation from those who supported her literary talents and extended poetic circles. This conjecture is based on the observation that a significant portion of what is believed to be her later literature laments the plight and sufferings of married women, and her early literature follows closely in the Tang tradition, employing heavy elements of folklore and natural imagery rather than the heavier emotive language found in her later writing.

Writings

A significant amount of Nanseolheon's writing was burned upon her death per her request, and the surviving poems are collected in Heo Kyeongnan's 1913 collection Nansŏrhŏn chip. The collection consists of 211 poems, in various Chinese styles. These include koshi (traditional verse), yulshi (metered verse), cheolgu (quatrains), and a single example of kobu (rhyming prose). The writing of the early Joseon period (in the form of the political Sajang school and the more academic Sallim school) was heavily influenced by the Confucian literary tradition, and literature was primarily devoted to the expression of Confucian teachings. With the introduction of Tang poetry to Korea in the mid-Joseon Period, hanmun poetry began making significant strides as an art form. Traditional Tang poetry (koshi) was more formulaic and imposed prescriptive tonal guidelines. During the lifetime of Nanseolheon, new forms of poetry that incorporated tonal irregularities, lines with non-standard syllable counts, and length (broadly referred to as kunch'e shi, of which yulshi and cheolgu are subsets) began to come into favor. Nanseolheon's works are noted primarily for their broad range of subject matter, which is attributed in part to the drastic emotional shift evoked by her marriage.[1]

The inclusion of two kasa written in hangul in the collection is one of scholarly contention, as her authorship is in doubt. Composition in hangul was considered unworthy of expressing higher thinking of Confucian ideals, and "literary" composition in Korea was almost entirely composed in hanmun. The distinction at the time was similar to the differences between Latin composition and vernacular prose in Renaissance Europe. Her authorship of these two pieces is supported mainly by the observation that the titles of the two kasa pieces, "Song of Woman's Complaint" and "Song of Coloring Nails with Touch-me-not Balsam" are very similar to two verified hanmun (cheolgu and koshi respectively). These claims have in part discredited by recent scholarship by O Haein (Nansorhon shijip) and Kang Cheongseop (Moktongga ui pogwon e taehayo).

Sample poems

The poem, "Song of Autumn Night" is characteristic of her earlier, more fantastical and imagery-rich poetry. It is a seven-syllable cheolgu.

秋夜曲

切切風瀟瀟
芙蓉香褪永輪高

佳人手把金錯刀
挑燈永夜縫征袍
玉漏微微燈耿耿
罷幃寒逼秋宵永
邊衣裁罷剪刀冷
滿窓風動芭蕉影

"Song of Autumn Night"

The grasshoppers are earnest and ardent; the winds are pure and clear.
The fragrance of the lotus fades; the eternal wheel high.
A beautiful woman's hands grabs a gold lacquered coin;
Lighting the lamp's wick, during the long night, she sews a gentleman's attire.
The water clock is dim and hazy; the lamp bright and luminous.
Inside the sickly tent, the cold near; the autumn night eternal.
Clothes for the frontier have finished drying; the scissors cold.
Filling the window are the winds blowing the shadow of plantains.

—Heo Nanheoseon[4] —Translated by Kuiwon[4]

"The Young Seamstress," or "Song for the Poor Girl", is one of her poems of empathy, where she sympathizes with those from poorer economic backgrounds. It is a five-sylla-ble cheolgu.[1]

貧女吟

豈是乏容色
工鍼復工織
少小長寒門
良媒不相識
夜久織未休
戛戛鳴寒機
機中一匹練
終作阿誰衣
手把金剪刀
夜寒十指直
爲人作嫁衣
年年還獨宿

"The Young Seamstress"

How can this worn face appeal?
Working at embroidery, then returning to work at the weaving
from behind a gate where there is little or nothing and long without heat
The matchmaker won't let anyone know of one so meek.
All night without rest weaving the hempen cloth,
the loom going clack-clack, clack-clack, a chilly sound.
Weave one roll on the loom, and wonder

111

KIM HONG-DO
The Master of Korean Painting
(1745 ~ 1806?~1814?)

Kim Hong-do (hangul:김홍도 hanja:金弘道) , most often styled Danwon (단원:檀園),
was a full-time painter of the Joseon period of Korea. He was together a pillar of the
establishment and a key figure of the new trends of his time, the 'true view painting'.
Kim Hong-do was an exceptional artist in every field of traditional painting, even if he is
mostly remembered nowadays for his depictions of the everyday life of ordinary people,
in a manner analogous to the Dutch Masters.[1]

Biography

Danwon was a member of the Kimhae Kim clan. He grew up in present-day Ansan,
South Korea. At the age of 7, Kim Hong-Do studied under the renowned master Pyoam
Kang Se-hwang, who was then living in seclusion in Ansan.[2] In 1766, at the age of 21,
on the recommendation of Kang Sehwang,[3] he entered the royal service as a member
(hwawon) of the Dohwaseo, the official painters of the Joseon court. In 1771, he painted
the portrait of the Royal Heir (the future King Jeongjo). In 1773, he assisted Byeon Sang-
byeok when painting the Royal Portrait of King Yeongjo (1694–1724–1776).

In 1776, he painted the "Nineteen Taoist Immortals", that skyrocketed his reputation as
a painter. At the same time, the new instated King Jeongjo (1752–1776–1800) commissioned him for many institutional paintings.

He died in loneliness and poverty, though the circumstances, and even the year are unknown. Sources are guessing 1806?,[4] circa 1810,[5] after 1814.[1][3]

Legacy

Danwon is remembered today as one of the "Three Wons," together with Hyewon and
Owon. He is also often joined to Owon and the 15th-century painter An Gyeon as one of
Joseon's three greatest painters.

The city of Ansan, where he spent his youth and learned his craft, has memorialized him
in many ways. The district of Danwon-gu is named after him, as is Ansan's annual "Danwon Art Festival." Many public places have been designed in imitation of his works.

Gallery

Various sources have various opinions about what could be a 'top ten' list for Kim Hong-
do.[4][5][6] The most important fact is how successful was Kim Hong-do in all the various types of paintings.

Towooart[7] provides a short notice and an argumented selection of paintings. The Korean Copyright Commission[8] lists 757 paintings, 7 calligraphies and 4 moldings for Kim
Hong-do. Remark: some paintings have multiple descriptions (often a sepia version is
given with a very fine resolution, and a colorful one with a lower resolution. An example
is 평양감사향안도 ("Feast for the Pyongyang Governor").

The paintings that launched the reputation of Kim Hong-do.

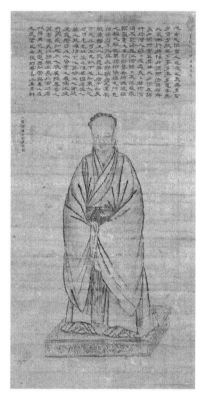

신언인도 Indian Prophet (1773)

군선도 The Nineteen Taoist Immortals (1776)

Teacher and pupils

Tiger underneath a Bamboo

115

Feast for the Pyongyang Governor (1, Dinner)

116

JEONG YAK-YONG
The Joseon Dynasty's Social Reformer
(August 5, 1762 – April 7, 1836)

Jeong Yakyong / Jung Yak-Yong (hangul:정약용 hanja:丁若鏞), often simply known as 'Dasan' (다산:茶山) (one of his 'ho' / pen-names meaning 'the mountain of tea'), was born on the 16th day of the 6th lunar month, 1762, in Gwangju county, Gyeonggi province, and died there on the 22nd day of the 2nd lunar month, 1836. He was one of the greatest thinkers of the later Joseon period, wrote highly influential books about philosophy, science and theories of government, held significant administrative positions, was a close confident of King Jeongjo (ruled 1776-1800), and was noted as a poet. His philosophical position is often identified with the Silhak (practical learning) school, and his concerns are better seen as explorations of Neo-Confucian themes. He spent 18 years in exile in Gangjin, South Jeolla province, from 1801 until 1818, on account of his membership of the Southerners (Nam-in) faction, and also because of the Catholic faith of his elder brother. His clan originated in Naju, South Jeolla Province. At birth he was given the courtesy title (初字 choja) Gwi'nong (歸農), and later he was also known by the ja Miyong (美鏞) and Songbu (頌甫美庸);among his ho (號, pen-names) were Saam (俟菴), Tagong (籜翁), Taesu (苔叟), Jahadoin (紫霞道人), Cheolmasanin (鐵馬山人), Dasan (茶山), Yeoyudang (與猶堂, the name of his house), and Mundo (文度, his name as a poet). Korean Catholics sometimes claim that he was baptized with the name John Baptist, but there is no documentary proof of this. He still has decedents living to this day, Some living in the United States California.

Biography

Family history

Dasan's father was Jeong Jae-won (丁載遠, 1730–1792). His eldest brother Yak-hyeon (若鉉, 1751–1821) was the son of a first wife, while Jeong Yak-jong (若鍾, 1760–1801), Yak-jeon (若銓, 1758–1816), and Yakyong were the sons of their father's second wife, Suk-in (淑人, 1730–1770) from the Haenam Yun 尹 family. There was one daughter from this second marriage. Four other daughters were later born of a third marriage.

Dasan's father's family traced their descent back to Jeong Ja-geup (丁子伋, 1423–1487) who in 1460 first took a government position under King Sejo. Eight further generations then followed his example. Jeong Si-yun (丁時潤, 1646–1713) and his second son Do-bok (道復, 1666–1720) were the last of the line, since the Southerners' faction to which the family belonged lost power in 1694. Si-yun retired to a house in Mahyeon-ri to the east of Seoul (now known as Namyangju) in 1699, which was to be Dasan's birthplace. His eldest son, Do-tae (道泰) lived there and was Dasan's direct ancestor. The Southerners remained excluded from official positions until a brief period that began during the reign of King Jeongjo, when Dasan's father was appointed magistrate of Jinju county, thanks to his strong links with the powerful Chae Je-gong (蔡濟恭, 1720–99), who rose until he was appointed third state councillor in 1788. In 1762, the execution of Crown Prince Sado by his father the king so shocked Jeong Jae-won that he withdrew from official life and returned to his home in Mahyeon-ri. This explains the courtesy name Gwi'nong ('back to farming') his father gave Dasan, who was born in the same year. As a result, Dasan grew up receiving intense intellectual training from his now unoccupied father.[1]

The source of Dasan's intellectual interests can be traced to the influence of the great

118

scholar Udam Jeong Si-han (愚潭 丁時翰, 1625–1707) of the same clan, who taught Jeong Si-yun briefly and was then the main teacher of Dasan's ancestor Jeong Do-tae as well as his brother Do-je (1675–1729). One of the most significant thinkers in the next generation was the philosopher-scholar Seongho Yi Ik (星湖 李瀷, 1681–1763) and he saw Udam as the authentic heir of Toegye Yi Hwang (退溪 李滉, 1501–1570). Jeong Do-je transmitted the teachings of Udam to the next generations of the family and so they were passed to Dasan's father and Dasan himself.

Similarly, Dasan's mother was descended from the family of the famous Southerner scholar-poet Gosan Yun Seon-do (孤山 尹善道, 1587–1671). Yun's great-grandson Gongjae Yun Du-seo (恭齋 尹斗緒, 1668–1715), well known for his skills as a painter, was Dasan's maternal great-grandfather. He and his elder brother were close to Seongho Yi Ik and his brothers, and are credited with reviving the study of the Six Classics, as well as the thought of Toegye.[2]

Early life

By the age of 6, Dasan's father was impressed by his powers of observation. By the age of 9 he had composed a small collection of poems. In 1776, Dasan was married to Hong Hwabo of the Pungsan Hong clan, the daughter of a royal secretary;in that year he moved to Seoul, where his father received an appointment in the Board of Taxation after the accession of King Jeongjo. When he was 15, Dasan was introduced to the writings of Seongho Yi Ik by one of his descendants, Yi Ga-Hwan (李家煥, 1742–1801) and his brother-in-law Yi Seung-hun (李承薰, 1756–1801) and he was deeply impressed, resolving to devote his life to similar studies. In 1783, Dasan passed the chinsagwa (literary licentiate examination), which allowed him to enter the Seonggyungwan (national Confucian academy).

In 1784 the king was deeply impressed by the "objectivity" of Dasan's replies to a set of questions he had formulated. This was the start of an increasingly close relationship between the king and Dasan. After the promotion of Chae Je-gong in 1788, Dasan took top place in the daegwa (higher civil service exam) in 1789 and was offered a position in the Office of Royal Decrees, together with 5 other members of the Southerner faction. This alarmed members of the opposing 'Old Doctrine' faction, who soon realized the extent to which the Southerners were being influenced, not only by the Practical Learning introduced to China from Europe, but by Roman Catholicism itself.

In 1784, Yi Byeok (李蘗, 1754–1786), a scholar who had participated in meetings to study books about the Western (European) Learning, starting in 1777, talked with Dasan about the new religion for the first time in 1784 and gave him a book about it. Whatever his own response may have been, and there is no proof that he ever received baptism, Dasan's immediate family was deeply involved in the origins of the Korean Catholic community. His older sister was married to Yi Seung-hun, the Korean who was first baptized as a Catholic in Beijing in 1784 and played a leading role in the early years of the Church's growth. The oldest of Jeong Jae-won's sons, Yak-hyeon, was married to a sister of Yi Byeok. Another daughter, from a third marriage, later married Hwang Sa-yeong (1775–1801), author of the notorious Silk Letter. Dasan's older brother, Jeong Yak-jong (Augustinus) was the leader of the first Catholic community and one of the first victims

119

of the purge launched against Southerners, but especially against Catholics, in 1801, after the sudden death of King Jeongjo.

In 1789, Yun Ji-chung, one of the first baptized and a cousin to Dasan on his mother's side, had gone to Beijing and received confirmation. Rome had forbidden Catholics to perform ancestral rituals and this was now being strictly applied by the Portuguese Franciscan bishop of Beijing Alexandre de Gouvea. When his mother died in 1791, Yun therefore refused to perform the usual Confucian ceremonies;this became public knowledge, he was accused of impiety and was executed. Some Koreans who had at first been sympathetic, horrified by the Church's rejection of hallowed traditions, turned away. Jeong Yakyong may well have been among them.[3]

Royal Service

Dasan was particularly interested in civil engineering and in 1792 the king, impressed by a pontoon bridge he had designed, asked him to design and supervise the construction of the walls for the Hwaseong Fortress (modern Suwon), which surrounded the palace where the king would live when he visited the new tomb he had constructed for his father. Dasan produced radically new techniques and structures, drawing on European, Chinese and Japanese sources. In 1794, after several promotions, the king appointed him as secret envoy to Gyeongi province, investigating reports of corruption.

Dasan's most important task in 1795, the 60th anniversary of the birth of Crown Prince Sado, was to help the King decide on a new honorary title for his father. This was a fraught enterprise, the Prince's supporters were members of what was called the Expediency subfaction while his main enemies were members of the Principle subfaction. The Southerners were strong supporters of the King's wish to honor Sado highly and the King was more than grateful. However, he then found it prudent to send Dasan away from court for a time, appointing him to be superintendent of the post station at Geumjeong, South Pyeongan province.

Here, he provided clear proof of his rejection of Catholicism by doing everything possible to persuade the Catholics working there to renounce their faith, and in particular to perform ancestral rites. Almost certainly, it was the Catholics' rejection of Confucian ritual that had turned him against them. In 1796, he was brought back to Seoul and promoted but his many enemies continued to accuse him of supporting the pro-western Catholics and he preferred to take up a position as county magistrate at Goksan in Hwanghae province.

In 1799 he even withdrew to his family home but was summoned back to Seoul by the king in 1800.[4]

Exile

In the summer of 1800, King Jeongjo died suddenly. The new king, King Sunjo, was still only a child of 11 and power fell into the hands of the widow of King Yeongjo, often known as Queen Dowager Kim or Queen Jeongsun. Her family belonged to the factions opposed to the reformist, often Catholic, Nam-in group and she had been completely powerless during Jeongjo's reign. She at once launched an attack on the Catholics, who were denounced as traitors and enemies of the state. Jeong Yak-jong was the head of the Catholic community, he was one of the first to be arrested and executed, together with Yi Seung-hun, in the spring of 1801. His eldest son, Jeong Cheol-sang, died then too, executed a month after his father.

Since he was Jeong Yak-jong's younger brother, Jeong Yakyong was sent into exile for some months in Janggi fortress in what is now Pohang, having been found after interrogation with torture not to be a Catholic believer. That might have been that, but what brought Yakyong to Gangjin, where he was forced to spend eighteen years, was the event that served as the final nail in the coffin of the early Catholic community, the Silk Letter Incident. Hwang Sa-yeong, married to one of Dasan's younger sisters, hid in a cave during the persecutions and in October 1801 he finished writing a long letter to the bishop of Beijing, giving a detailed account of the recent events, asking him to bring pressure on the Korean authorities to allow freedom of religion and, disastrously, begging him to ask the Western nations to send a large army to overthrow the Joseon dynasty so that Korea would be subject to China, where Catholicism was permitted. The man carrying this letter, written on a roll of silk wrapped round his body, was intercepted and the Korean authorities made full use of it to show that Catholics were by definition enemies of the state.

The persecution was intensified and if it had not been very clear that Jeong Yakyong and Jeong Yak-jeon were in no sense Catholic believers, they would surely have been executed. Instead they were sent into exile together, parting ways at Naju, from where Jeong Yak-jeon journeyed on to the island of Heuksando, Yakyong taking the Gangjin road. His exile began in the last days of 1801, on the 23rd day of the eleventh lunar month, the 28th of December in the solar calendar. On that day, he arrived in Gangjin, South Jeolla Province. The newly arrived exile had little or no money and no friends, he found shelter in the back room of a poor, rundown tavern kept by a widow, outside the East Gate of the walled township of Gangjin, and there he lived until 1805. He called his room "Sauijae" (room of four obligations: clear thinking, serious appearance, quiet talking, sincere actions).

By 1805, much had changed in Seoul. Dowager Queen Kim had died and the young king had come of age and quickly put an end to the violence against Catholics. Three hundred had been killed and many of the rest were exiled or scattered, or had stopped practicing. Jeong Yakyong was free to move about the Gangjin area and in the spring of 1805 he walked up the hill as far as Baeknyeon-sa Temple, where he met the Venerable Hyejang, the newly arrived monk in charge of the temple, who was about ten years younger than himself. They talked and it seems that Hyejang only realized who his visitor was as he was leaving. That night he forced him to stay with him and asked to learn the I Ching from him. They quickly became close companions.

Later the same year, Hyejang enabled Dasan to move out of the tavern and for nearly a year he lived in Boeun Sanbang, a small hermitage at the nearby Goseong-sa temple, which was under Hyejang's control. Finally, in the spring of 1808 he was able to take up residence in a house belonging to a distant relative of his mother, on the slopes of a hill overlooking Gangjin and its bay. It was a simple house, with a thatched roof, but it was there that the exile spent the remaining ten years of his exile, until the autumn of 1818.

This is the site now known as "Dasan Chodang." The hill behind the house was known locally as Da-san (tea-mountain) and that was to become the name by which our exile is best known today, Dasan. Here he could teach students who lodged in a building close to his, forming a close-knit community, and he could write. In his study he accumulated a library of over a thousand books.[5]

During his exile he is said to have written 500 volumes. This needs qualifying, since one "work" might fill nearly 50 volumes of the standard size, but he certainly wrote a vast quantity, some 14,000 pages, mainly in order to set out clearly a fundamental reform program for governing the country correctly according to Confucian ideals. During the years of exile he concentrated first on the Book of Changes (Yi Ching), writing in 1805 the Chuyeoksajeon. A reflection on the Classic of Poetry followed in 1809. He wrote on politics, ethics, economy, natural sciences, medicine and music. After his return from exile, Dasan published his most important works: on jurisprudence Heumheumsinseo (1819);on linguistics Aeongakbi (1819);on diplomacy Sadekoryesanbo (1820);on the art of governing Mongminsimseo and on administration Gyeongsesiryeong (1822).

Dasan remained in exile in Gangjin until 1818, when he was allowed to return to his family home near Seoul. Attempts to bring him back into government service were blocked by factional politics. He used Yeoyudang as his final pen-name, it was the name of the family home where he lived quietly, near the Han River, until he died in 1836, on his sixtieth wedding anniversary. The main sources for his biography are the two versions of his own 'epitaph,' Jachan myojimyeong, and a chronological biography Saam seon-saeng yeonbo composed by his great-grandson Jeong Gyu-yeong using no longer extant records.[6]

Dasan and the 19th-century tea revival

Jeong Yakyong had been living in Gangjin for several years when the Ven. Hyejang arrived from Daeheung-sa temple to take charge of Paengnyeon-sa. During those years, spent in a poor inn with very little money, Dasan's health had suffered from the low nutritional value of his food. He suffered from chronic digestive problems. Dasan and Hyejang first met on the 17th day of the 4th month, 1805, not long after Hyejang's arrival. Only a few days after, Dasan sent a poem to Hyejang requesting some tea leaves from the hill above the temple;it is dated in the 4th month of 1805, very soon after their meeting.[7]

This poem makes it clear that Dasan already knew the medicinal value of tea and implies that he knew how to prepare the leaves for drinking. It has often been claimed that Dasan learned about tea from Hyejang but this and a series of other poems exchanged between them suggests that in fact Hyejang and other monks in the region learned how to make a kind of caked tea from Dasan.

This would make him the main origin of the ensuing spread of interest in tea. In 1809, the Ven. Cho-ui from the same Daeheung-sa temple came to visit Dasan in Gangjin and spent a number of months studying with him there.[8] Again, it seems more than likely that Cho-ui first learned about tea from Dasan, and adopted his very specific, rather archaic way of preparing caked tea. After that, it was the Ven. Cho-ui who, during his visit to Seoul in 1830, shared his tea with a number of scholars. Among them, some poems were written and shared to celebrate the newly discovered drink, in particular the Preface and Poem of Southern Tea (南茶幷序) by Geumryeong Bak Yeong-bo.[9]

After this, Cho-ui became especially close to Chusa Kim Jeong-hui, who visited him several times bringing him gifts of tea during his exile in Jeju Island in the 1740s. A letter about Dasan's method of making caked tea has survived, dated 1830, that Dasan sent to Yi Si-Heon 李時憲 (1803–1860), the youngest pupil taught by him during his 18 years of exile in Gangjin: "It is essential to steam the picked leaves three times and dry them three times, before grinding them very finely. Next that should be thoroughly mixed with water from a rocky spring and pounded like clay into a dense paste that is shaped into small cakes. Only then is it good to drink."[10]

Thought

Jeong is well-known above all for his work in synthesizing the Neo-Confucian thought of the middle Joseon dynasty.[1] In the process, he wrote widely in various fields including law, political theory, and the Korean Confucian classics. He sought to return Korean Confucian scholarship to a direct connection with the original thought of Confucius. He called this return to the classics "Susa" learning (수사, 洙泗), a reference to the two rivers that flowed through Confucius' homeland.[2]

Jeong published a number of books over various areas, including his best-known Mokminsimseo (목민심서, 牧民心書, The Mind of Governing the People). Although he was deeply concerned about the problem of poverty during that time, Jeong deeply pondered the issue of poverty and raised questions about the role of government officials. He believed that the government and bureaucrats could and should play a major role in solving the problem of poverty. Dasan stressed the importance of the governor's administering the people with integrity and in a fair manner. According to him, the government was the ruling entity to render aid and favor to the people while the people were the subject of the government's sympathy and rule.[11]

In the service of this idea, Jeong criticized the philosophers of his time for engaging in both fruitless etymological scholarship and pursuing philosophical theory for their own sake.[3] He argued that scholarship should be re-focused on more important concerns such as music, ritual, and law. This was not only an intellectual but also a political assertion: he argued that the gwageo examinations by which people qualified for royal service should be reformed to focus on these concerns.[4]

Ye Philosophy

Ye philosophy takes up a large portion of the writings of Jeong Yakyong. As demonstrated by the fact that the original title of Gyeongse Yupyo (경세유표, 經世遺表, Design for Good Government), a flagship work of his which presents a blueprint of state management, was Bangnye Chobon (Draft for the Country's Rites), Jeong uses the concept of Ye extensively to represent what he aims to achieve with his thought. He focuses this concept on his notion of good government and later extended and branched into his works of classical studies and natural sciences.[12]

Theory of Sacrificial Rites

Dasan's theory of Korean-style sacrificial rites (제사, 祭祀) shows his socio-political concern seeking for the rule of virtue and righteous government. He intended to motivate people into making everyday practices of the human imperatives and to revitalize effectively the traditional society of the late period of Joseon dynasty which had its basis upon Ye (禮, Confucian order). In Mokminsimseo, Dasan formulates the cognitive process of ritual practice focussing on sacrificial rites as follows.

1) The cognition of the ritual object raises the intentional movement of mind/heart toward the ritual object in the cognitive process.

2) The intentionality of mind and heart entails reverence and purification in the ritual process. Ritual practice is significant through sincerity (성, 誠) and seriousness (경, 敬). From the perspective of the cognitive science of religion, Dasan's theory relates cognition with intentional piety in the cognitive process, and combines intentional piety and reverence/purification in ritual practice. Dasan intended to regulate the excessive ritual practices of the literati and restrict popular licentious cults (음사, 淫祀) in accordance with his cognitive formula. From his point of view, Confucianist's ritual conceptions were improper or impractical, and popular licentious cults were impious and overly enthusiastic. In order to solve these problems, He redefined Zhi Hsi's concept of seriousness as attentive concentration of convergent piety into the concept of prudential reverence as intentional pietism. Zhi Hsi's concept of seriousness contains apophatic mysticism like Zen Buddhist Quietism (정, 靜) by mediation, but Dasan's concept of reverence is inclined towards Cataphatic activism by contemplation.[13]

Land reform

Land reform was an important issue for the Silhak reformers, and Dasan elaborated upon Yu Hyŏngwŏn's land reform proposals. Rather than central state ownership, Dasan proposed a "village land system," in which the village would hold its land in common and farm the land as a whole, while the products of the land would be divided based on the amount of labor contributed.[14][15]

Views on Dasan

Professor Ogawa Haruhisa of Nishogakusha University in Tokyo is very impressed by Dasan:

"In addition to egalitarian ideas, Chŏng Yag-yong Dasan provided something precious that had been lost at that time. He has these elements that we must learn and revive in these modern times. He formed his philosophy despite his sufferings in exile. I think he will be of interest to contemporary scholars for a long time."

Professor Peng Lin at Qinghua University, Beijing teaches the Chinese classics and has a special interest in Dasan's study of rituals. He published in the 1980s research papers on Dasan in the Sônggyun'gwan Journal of East Asian Studies:

"Dasan devoted great efforts in studying rites, to understanding and bringing recognition to traditional culture. I believe that Dasan's study of rites is highly unique. He studied all the three fields in the study of ritual and this was not common even among Chinese scholars. Many can achieve only partial understanding even after a lifetime study, but Dasan studied all the ritual fields and his research is truly astounding. He wanted to create an ideal society by starting with what already existed. This shows Dasan's humanistic interest and that intrigues me."

Professor Don Baker at the Asia Center of the University of British Columbia, Canada, is interested in Dasan for his role as an intellectual in a period of transition:

"I think that in the twenty-first century we still need to adopt Dasan's spirit, what I call moral pragmatism. He was a very pragmatic man. He looked at problems and said 'how can we solve them'. But also he always kept his moral values at the front. We often have in society a material progress for the sake of material progress. Dasan wanted a material progress but a progress that creates a more moral society, therefore I call it moral pragmatism and I think that we still need such spirit today."

There is in Korea a revival of Jeong Yakyong's thought never seen before on that scale for any Korean philosopher. In the not distant past one could hear doubts about even the existence of a Korean philosophy. Since the liberation of Korea in 1945 Western philosophy has prevailed and philosophy departments in most Korean universities teach mainly European modern philosophy. Therefore, Dasan is of great importance as he was able to be enthusiastic for modern Western ideas but remained deeply committed to the depth of Confucianism. He was not defending a tradition for its own sake but wanted to keep the precious values of the early Chinese period because it was a foundation for man and society.

HEUNGSEON DAEWONGUN
Regent Who Enforced
Vigorous Closed-Door Policy
(December 21, 1820 – February 22, 1898)

Heungseon Daewongun (흥선대원군, 興宣大院君, 21 December 1820 – 22 February 1898), also known as the Daewongun (대원군, 大院君), Guktaegong (국태공, 國太公, "The Great Archduke") or formally Heungseon Heonui Daewonwang (흥선헌의대원왕, 興宣獻懿大院王) and also known to contemporary western diplomats as Prince Gung, was the title of Yi Ha-eung, regent of Joseon during the minority of Emperor Gojong in the 1860s and until his death a key political figure of late Joseon Korea.

Daewongun literally translates as "prince of the great court", a title customarily granted to the father of the reigning monarch when that father did not reign himself (usually because his son had been adopted as heir of a relative who did reign). While there had been three other Daewongun during the Joseon dynasty,^ so dominant a place did Yi Ha-eung have in the history of the late Joseon dynasty that the term Daewongun usually refers specifically to him.

The Daewongun is remembered for the wide-ranging reforms he attempted during his regency, as well as for his "vigorous enforcement of the seclusion policy, persecution of Christians, and the killing or driving off of foreigners who landed on Korean soil".[1]

Biography

Early life

The Daewongun was born Yi Ha-eung in 1820. He was the fourth son of Yi Ch'ae-jung, a member of the royal family who in 1816 was given the name Yi Gu and the title Prince Namyeon. The Daewongun was a direct descendant of King Injo.[2]

The Daewongun was well schooled in Confucianism and the Chinese classics. He reputedly excelled in calligraphy and painting. His early government career consisted of minor posts that were mostly honorary and ceremonial. For the beginning of his life, his connection to the royal house seemed of little help to him. He was poor and humiliated by the rich in-laws of the royal house.[2]

Rise to power

The Daewongun came to power when his second son, Yi Myeong-bok, was chosen to become king.

In January 1864, King Cheoljong died without an heir. The selection of the next king was in the hands of three dowagers: Queen Sinjeong, mother of King Heonjong; Queen Myeongheon, King Heonjong's wife; and Queen Cheorin, Cheoljong's wife.[3] The "designation right" resided with Dowager Queen Sinjeong, as she was the oldest of the dowagers.[2]

In an apocryphal story, Queen Cheorin sent a minister to fetch the son of Yi Ha-eung, eleven-year-old Yi Myeong-bok, who was flying a kite in a palace garden. The son was brought to the palace in a sedan chair, where Queen Sinjeong rushed forward and called him her son, thus producing the new Joseon king, King Gojong, adopted son of Crown Prince Hyomyeong.[3] This story may or may not be true.

These facts, however, are known to be correct. On 16 January 1864, Yi Myeong-bok was appointed the Prince of Ikseong by Dowager Queen Sinjeong. The next day, his father was granted the title Daewongun. On 21 January, Yi Myeong-bok was enthroned as King Gojong, and Dowager Queen Sinjeong began her regency.[2] Yi was apparently chosen because "he was the only suitable surviving male member of the Yi clan and closest by blood to the royal house".[2]

Since Gojong was so young, Queen Sinjeong invited the Daewongun to assist his son in ruling. She virtually renounced her right to be regent, and though she remained the titular regent, the Daewongun was in fact the true ruler.[2]

Once Gojong became king, there still remained the question of his marriage. Gojong's mother Yeoheung decided upon a daughter of the Min clan, Lady Min. The Daewongun remarked that Min "was a woman of great determination and poise" and was slightly disturbed by her. However, he allowed her to marry his son, and unknowingly created his greatest political rival.[3]

Reforms

During his regency, the Daewongun attempted several reforms. His main goal was to "crush the old ruling faction that had virtually usurped the sovereign power of the kings earlier in the century".[4]

When he took power in 1864, the Daewongun was determined to reform the government and strengthen central control. He led an anti-corruption campaign, disciplined the royal clans, and taxed the aristocracy, the yangban.[2][3] Cumings notes that this was not a revolution but a restoration, as the Daewongun was attempting to return to the days of King Sejong in the fifteenth century.[3]

One of the Daewongun's effective acts as regent was the reconstruction of Gyeongbok Palace. The palace had been built during the reign of the first Joseon king. Much of the building was destroyed in a fire in 1533 and the rest was destroyed during the Japanese invasion of 1592. The rebuilding took seven years and five months. It was perhaps the most costly project during the Joseon dynasty.[2]

The Daewongun's reforms were not very successful, as some scholars say he was "too high-handed and tactless".[4] Not only that, but his policies did not have a lasting effect, as once Gojong came of age in 1874, he forced the Daewongun into semiretirement and undid many of his reforms.[4]

Foreign policy

The Daewongun's foreign policy was rather simple, as Cumings describes it: "no treaties, no trade, no Catholics, no West, and no Japan".[3] He instead maintained an isolationist policy.
The Isolation Policy was a policy made to isolate Joseon from all foreign forces except for China which he believed to be the strongest. He tried to refuse Russia's quest to open Joseon's ports to them by using France, but France refused to help - causing the 1866

Byeong-in Persecution. He was involved in the General Sherman incident as well. The Isolation Policy became more entrenched in 1868 when, German merchant Ernst Oppert attempted to take hostage the bones of the Daewongun's father in order to force him to open Korea to trade;[5] and even further so after the 1871 American attack of Gwanghwado.

The Isolation Policy provided immediate benefits of fortifying Korean patriotism as well as protecting their culture of Confucianism. The Heungseon Daewongun was able to protect Joseon from cultural imperialism and westernization and thus protect Korea's heritage from it. However, because he refused to engage in international relations entirely, there was a limited choice of market and slim opportunity for an industrial revolution to occur. Indeed, the Daewongun wanted to avoid engagement with the West - which would have been inevitable if Western countries were allowed to trade freely - as it would erode government influence. The Joseon Dynasty had a strict social hierarchy: the wealth of the yangban nobility resting on the backs of sangmin farm labourers and tenants; the Daewongun wanted to prevent the collapse of this hierarchy as, despite his fame for his fairness and support of civilization, the emancipation of the sangmin would mean the ruin of the yangban, his own class.

The international relations of Joseon worsened as the Daewongun adopted increasingly desperate and harsher measures in order to repel Westernization. The Daewongun made the choice of protecting the world he knew by trying to shut out foreigners, at the cost of delaying development and modernization, and to keep Korea a hermit kingdom. Many Koreans state that had he chose to engage with foreign countries as his daughter-in-law Queen Min advocated, the Japanese rule of Korea could have been avoided. However, others state that the ten years of the Isolation Policy was too small a part of the Joseon Dynasty to derive such a statement from.[6]

Retirement

In 1874, King Gojong came of age. His wife, Queen Min, influenced his decision to "assume the full measure of royal responsibility", an action that forced the Daewongun into semiretirement.[4]

Return to power

The Daewongun enjoyed a brief return to power during the Imo Incident in 1882. On the second day of the mutiny, a group of rioters were received by the Daewongun, "who reportedly exhorted them to bring down the Min regime and expel the Japanese".[4] King Gojong asked his father, the Daewongun to come to the palace. The Daewongun's appearance, escorted by 200 mutineers, "put an immediate end to the wild melee." Gojong gave the Daewongun "all the small and large matters of the government" and thus the Daewongun resumed his rule. Both Japanese and Chinese forces headed towards Korea to put down the rebellion, and Ma Chien-chung, a Chinese diplomat in Korea, decided that it was time to remove the Daewongun.[4]

The Chinese had three reasons they wanted to remove the Daewongun: First, he attempted to overthrow the pro-Chinese Min faction. Second, "he created a situation which invited the Japanese troops to Korea, thus precipitating the danger of a military conflict between Japan on the one hand and Korea and China on the other." And third, "the Taewongun [Daewongun]-inspired disturbance threatened the foundation of a lawfully constituted government in a dependent nation".[4] Ma arrested the Daewongun on the charge of disrespect to the emperor for "usurping the power which the emperor had invested in the king of Korea".[4] However, as he was the father of the king, he was dealt with leniently. One hundred Chinese soldiers escorted the Daewongun to a waiting Chinese warship, and from there to Tianjin.[4]

Return to Korea

In the fall of 1885, the Chinese returned the Daewongun to Korea, "despite strong objections from the queen and her followers".[4]

Gabo Reform

In 1894, the Japanese were strengthening their hold over Korea. They needed someone amenable to them to be a leader in Korea during the Gabo Reform. They approached the Daewongun as a potential leader. When he agreed, on 23 July Japanese soldiers liberated him from the house arrest Gojong had placed him under. In exchange for his help, the Daewongun asked for a promise that if the reforms succeeded, "Japan will not demand a single piece of Korean territory".[1] The soldiers took him to the palace, where they approached the king. The Daewongun reproached King Gojong and announced that he would be taking over.[1]

The Japanese became nervous after placing the Daewongun in charge, as he seemed interested "only in grasping power and purging his opponents and did not see the need for a reform policy".[1] By September 1894, the Japanese decided that the Daewongun was not to be trusted. By early October, it became clear that "the plan to use the Taewongun [Daewongun] as a vehicle for the reform program had misfired".[1] A Japanese statesman, Inoue Kaoru, was sent to Korea as the new resident minister, where he told the Daewongun, "You always stand in the way," and forced the Daewongun to promise that he would "abstain from interference in political affairs".[1]

Involvement in Queen Min's Death

In 1895, Japanese officials in Korea were plotting the removal of Gojong's wife, Queen Min. Miura Gorō, Inoue Kaoru's successor as Japanese advisor to the Korean government, and Sugimura Fukashi, a secretary of the Japanese legation, planned the attempt. The two decided to involve the Daewongun in the plot, and after making inquiries, learned that he was "indignant enough to plan a coup" and would cooperate with them. [4] On 8 October 1895, early in the morning, Japanese policemen escorted the Daewongun to the palace.[4] His involvement from that point on is unclear, but on that morning, Japanese agents assassinated Queen Min.

Death

The Daewongun died in 1898.[4]

ST. ANDREW KIM TAE-GON
Korea's First Catholic Priest and a Martyr
(1821–1846)

Saint Paul the Apostle Church (Westerville, Ohio) - stained glass, arcade, Saint Andrew Kim

Saint Andrew Kim Tae-gon (김대건 안드레아:金大建) is known as Korea's first Roman Catholic priest. Born into a family of Christian converts at a time of unprecedented governmental opposition to Christianity (Christian teachings threatened the hierarchical system of Confucianism and ancestor worship), Kim and his family led lives of deprivation and hardship. Although there were repeated efforts made by the Korean monarchy (who feared European colonization of Korea through Christianity), to uproot the religion of the barbarian foreigners from 1794 to 1866, converts to Christianity continued to increase.

Even though Kim's family members and eventually Kim himself would suffer persecution, torture and eventual martyrdom under the repressive Korean monarchy, as it desperately tried to preserve itself and Korea's Confucian culture by eradicating Christianity;the sacrifice of these early Korean Christians became the foundation for the Christian Church in Korea to flourish today. Andrew Kim Taegon is revered today for his sacrifice and dedication in bringing Christianity to Korea.

Early Catholic Church In Korea

During the 1592 invasion of Korea by Japan, Japanese soldiers introduced Christianity into Korea by baptizing Koreans. A Japanese commander, Konishi Yukinaga, took a Korean girl, Julia Ota-a to Japan and she became one of the first Korean Christians. Father Gregorious de Cespedes, a Jesuit priest, visited Konishi in Korea in 1593. Korean diplomat, Yi Gwang-jeong returned to Korea from Beijing bearing several theological books written by Matteo Ricci, a Jesuit priest living in China. Some two centuries later, members of the Silhak (practical learning) school were drawn to Christian thought because it advocated a social structure based upon merit rather than birth rank. Most early Christians had family ties to the Silhak school.

During the late Joseon Dynasty and under its Confucian influence, Christianity was heavily suppressed and many Christians were persecuted and executed. Kim Taegon was born into this environment, and just one of several thousands of Catholic, Presbyterian, or Methodist Christians who were tortured and executed because of their faith during this time. In 1866, Regent Heungseon Daewongun (father of King Gojong) signed a decree to execute all Catholics. Over 2,000 Catholics were beheaded at Jeoldusan, "Beheading Hill." Their bodies were thrown into the Han River. Some were as young as 13. Fewer than 40 were identified.[1]

At this time, Korea was isolated from the world;the only outside contact being with Peking, where taxes were paid. Jesuits in China managed to smuggle Christian literature into Korea. When Korea saw its first missionaries arrive from France and America in the mid 1800s, several thousand Koreans were already practicing Christianity.

Kim Family

Andrew Kim Taegon was born in Nol-Mae (Solmoe), Chu'ung-Chong Province (in South Central Korea. At the age of seven, the Kim family moved to Golbaemasil Mankok-ri, Youngin-gun County (Mirinae) Kyungki Province. Kim's great-grandfather, Kim Jin-Hu was martyred in 1814. Kim's grand-uncle, Kim Han-hyun was also martyred in 1816.

Kim's father, Kim Je-jun (Ignatius Kim), was subsequently martyred in 1839 for practicing Christianity.[2] With so many male relatives martyred, Kim grew up very poor;his mother reduced to begging.

Ordination and Mission Work

After being baptized at the age of 15, Kim traveled over 1200 miles in 1836 to study at a seminary in the Portuguese Colony of Macau, China. He returned to Korea through Manchuria. That same year, he crossed the Yellow Sea to Shanghai, where he was ordained a priest in 1845 by the French Bishop, Jean Ferréol. He then returned to Korea to preach and evangelize. These grueling trips between China and Korea, on foot and by small unworthy fishing vessels, allowed Kim to explore the terrain and increase the accuracy of the maps he had been using to plan better routes for the French missionaries to infiltrate Korea

Handwritten map by Father Andre Kim (Kim Taegon, the first Korean Catholic priest, who was executed because of his religion, but managed to make this map in the short time he was in Korea, 1846)

Imprisonment

In June of 1846, while trying to arrange for passage for additional missionaries to enter Korea by boat along the southeast coast, Kim was arrested by the border patrol. While imprisoned and awaiting his fate, Andrew Kim Taegon wrote to his parish:

"My dear brothers and sisters know this: Our Lord Jesus Christ upon descending into the world took innumerable pains upon and constituted the holy Church through his own passion and increases it through the passion of its faithful....Now, however, some fifty or sixty years since holy Church entered into our Korea, the faithful suffer persecutions again. Even today persecution rages, so that many of our friends of the same faith, among who am I myself, have been thrown into prison. Just as you also remain in the midst of persecution. Since we have formed one body, how can we not be saddened in our innermost hearts? How can we not experience the pain of separation in our human faculties? However, as Scripture says, God cares for the least hair of our heads, and indeed he cares with his omniscience;therefore, how can persecution be considered as anything other than the command of God, or his prize, or precisely his punishment?...We are twenty here, and thanks be to God all are still well.

If anyone is killed, I beg you not to forget his family. I have many more things to say, but how can I express them with pen and paper? I make an end to this letter. Since we are now close to the struggle, I pray you to walk in faith, so that when you have finally entered into Heaven, we may greet one another. I leave you my kiss of love.

Execution

On September 26, at the age of 25, Kim was tortured and beheaded near Seoul on the Han River. His ears were pierced with arrows;his face covered with lime.[3] A group of Christians led, by Yi Min-Sik, later moved his body to Mt. Mi-ri-nai, about 35 miles from Seoul.

Before Father Jean Joseph Ferréol, the first Bishop of Korea, died from exhaustion on the third of February in 1853, he wanted to be buried beside Andrew Kim, stating: "You will never know how sad I was to lose this young native priest. I have loved him as a father loved his son;it is a consolation for me to think of his eternal happiness."

Beatification and Canonization

Both Andrew Kim and his father, Ignatius Kim, were beatified on July 25, 1925. In 1949 the Holy See named Andrew Kim Taegon the principal patron of the Roman Catholic Clergy in Korea. On May 6, 1984, Pope John Paul II canonized Andrew Kim Taegon along with 102 other martyrs, including Paul Chong Hasang.

Pope John Paul II's 1984 canonization of Andrew Kim Taegon and the other Korean martyrs was the first time the pontiff had held a canonization mass outside the vatican. At the canonization, Pope John Paul II said:

"The Korean Church is unique because it was founded entirely by lay people. This fledgling Church, so young and yet so strong in faith, withstood wave after wave of fierce persecution. Thus, in less than a century, it could boast of 10,000 martyrs. The death of these martyrs became the leaven of the Church and led to today's splendid flowering of the Church in Korea. Even today their undying spirit sustains the Christian in the Church of silence in the north of this tragically divided land."[4]

Feast Day

September 20 is the feast day for Andrew Kim Taegon, Paul Chong Hasang, and the rest of the 102 Korean martyrs canonized on May 6, 1984.

Honoring Kim

There are a number of Catholic Churches and schools throughout the world named in honor of Saint Andrew Kim;even a Credit Union in New Jersey.

Macau's famous Camoes Park (in Portuguese, Jardim Luis de Camoes) contains a statue dedicated to Andrew Kim Taegon. A plaque below it contains dates and events depicting major milestones in his life. Macau's famous Camoes Park (in Portuguese, Jardim Luis de Camoes) contains a statue dedicated to Andrew Kim Taegon. A plaque below it contains dates and events depicting major milestones in his life.

EMPRESS MYEONGSEONG
The Queen Who Fought to
Save The Korean Empire
(October 19, 1851 – October 8, 1895)

民 閔 妃 王

Myeogseong, also known as Queen Min, married to King Gojong, the 26th King Joseon Dynasty. In 1902, she received the posthumous name, 孝慈元聖正化合天 太皇后;효자원성정화합천명성태황후; Hyoja Wonseong Jeonghwa Hapcheon Myeongseong Taehwanghu,[1] often abbreviated as 明成皇后;명성황후; Myeongseong Hwanghu, meaning Empress Myeongseong.

Queen Min, an unlikely person to take the reins of Korea during the last days of the Joseon dynasty, rose to the occasion. Born and raised in obscurity, Queen Min became a beacon for progress and independence in Korea, a beacon that too many wanted to turn off. In the end, her enemies succeeding in killing her, but they failed to dim her example.

Early Years

Born on October 19, 1851[2], in Yeoju-gun (여주군:驪州郡), in the province of Kyeonggi (경기도:京畿道) (where the clan originated).[3], to the yangban clan Yeo-hung Mins, the young Min grew up out of the lime light. Although the clan had boasted of many highly positioned bureaucrats in its illustrious past, even bearing two queens: first, the wife of the third king of the Joseon Dynasty, Taejong, and second, the wife of the 19th king, Sukjong[3], by Myeongseong's birth, the clan battled poverty, sitting on the sidelines of royal power. During more uneventful eras, such an impotent clan would never have bred a queen. The political situation Korea provided a catalyst for the Min clan's return and their rise to royalty once more.[3]

The future queen received the name Min Ja-young (민자영) at birth. In every day life before marriage, she answered to the "daughter of Min Chi-rok (閔致祿:민치록)."[3] At the age of eight she had lost both of her parents.[3] Scant information about her mother, or how she spent her childhood, or the cause of her parents' early deaths, exists.

Becoming Queen

In 1864, King Cheoljong lay dying without a male heir, the result of suspected foul play by a rival branch of the royal family, the Andong Kim clan, which had risen to power by intermarriage with the royal Yi family. Queen Cheonin, the queen consort of Cheoljong and a member of the Kim clan, claimed the right to choose the next king. Traditionally, the eldest Dowager Queen selected the new king when no legitimate male heir to the throne lived. Cheoljong's cousin, Great Dowager Queen Jo (King Ikjong's widow) of the Jo house, which too had risen to further prominence by intermarriage with the crown, held this title. Jo saw an opportunity to advance the influence of the Jo clan, the sole family that truly rivaled the Kim clan in Korean politics. As King Cheoljong fell deeper into his illness, Yi Ha-eung approached the Grand Dowager Queen. An obscure descendant of King Yeongjo, Yi had a son named Yi Myeong-bok who possibly had right to succeed to the throne.

Yi Ha-eung and Yi Myong-bok belonged to an obscure line of descent of the Yi royalty that managed to survive the often deadly political intrigue that frequently embroiled the Joseon court by having no affiliation with any factions. Only 12 years old, Yi Myeong-bok would not be able to fully rule until he came of age. The Jo clan also believed that they could easily influence Yi Ha-eung, who would act as regent for the to-be boy king.

As soon as news of Cheoljong's death reached Yi Ha-eung through his intricate network of spies in the palace, he had the hereditary royal seal withdrawn in cooperation with Jo. That, in effect giving her absolute power to select the successor of the dynasty.

By the time Cheoljong's death became public, the Grand Dowager Queen kept the seal out of the hands of the Andong Kim clan. In the autumn of 1864, Great Dowager Queen Jo crowned Yi Myeong-bok King of the Kingdom of Joseon, with his father styled as Daewongun (大院君; 대원군; Daewongun; Grand Internal Prince). The strongly Confucian Daewongun proved a wise and calculating leader in the early years of Gojong's reign. He abolished corrupt government institutions, revised the law codes along with the household laws of the royal court and the rules of court ritual, and reformed the royal armies. Within a few short years, he secured complete control of the court and eventually receive the submission of the Jos while successfully disposing the last of the Kims, whose corruption, he believed, responsible for ruining the country.

A new queen

Seal of the Empress Myeongseong

By 국립중앙박물관(National Museum of Korea)
[KOGL (http://www.kogl.or.kr/open/info/license_info/by.do)],
via Wikimedia Commons

At the age of 15, his father decided Gojong should marry. He diligently looked for a queen without close relatives who would harbor political ambitions, yet with the noble lineage needed to justify his choice to the court and the people. One by one, he rejected candidates until the wife of Daewongun proposed a bride from her own clan. His wife described Min persuasively: orphaned, beautiful of face, healthy in body, level of education on the level of the highest nobles in the country.

Daewongun easily arranged the first meeting with his son and the proposed bride as she lived in the neighborhood in Anguk-dong.[3] Their meeting proved a success, and on March 20, 1866[4], the future Queen (and later Empress Myeongseong) married the boy king; their wedding took place at the Injeongjeon Hall at Changdeok Palace.[3] The wig (which was usually worn by royal brides at weddings) proved so heavy that a tall court lady supported her hair from the back. The wedding ceremony had hardly finished, when another three-day ceremony for the reverencing of the ancestors started.

One can only imagine how difficult it would have been for a 15-year-old girl who had no father nor brothers for support to endure such ceremonies.

Invested as the Queen of Joseon, at the age of barely 16, Min ascended the throne with her husband during the coronation ceremony. She received the title Her Royal Highness, Queen Min (閔大妃: 민대비 : Min Daebi - Queen Min), and "Her Palace Majesty" (중정

137

마마)[3] She possessed an assertive and ambitious nature, unlike other queens that came before her. She disdained lavish parties, rarely commissioned extravagant fashions from the royal ateliers, and almost never hosted afternoon tea parties with the powerful aristocratic ladies and princesses of the royal family, unless politics beckoned her to.

As Queen, court officials expected her to act as an icon to the high society of Korea, but Min rejected that belief. She, instead, read books reserved for men (examples of which were Springs and Autumns (春秋) and Notes of a Jwa on Springs and Autumns (춘추 좌씨전),[3] and taught herself philosophy, history, science, politics and religion. This tradition of scholarship is a characteristic of the Min women to this day. While delving in knowledge and personal matters, Queen Min rarely accompanied her husband Gojong, who found entertainment with appointed concubines and kisaengs at his private quarters, and at the tea houses of Hanseong.

Court life

Even without parents, Min secretly formed a powerful faction against Daewongun as soon as she reached adulthood. At the age of 20, she began to wander outside her apartments at Changgyeonggung and play an active part in politics. At the same time, the to-be (although not yet titled that) Queen defended her views against high officials who viewed her as becoming meddlesome. The Queen's aggressiveness upset the deeply-rooted-in-Confucian-values Daewongun. The political struggle between Min and Daewon-gun became public when the son she bore for Gojong died prematurely.

Daewon-gun publicly declared Min unable bear a healthy male child and directed Gojong to have intercourse with a royal concubine, Yeongbodang Yi. In 1880, the concubine gave birth to a healthy baby boy, Prince Wanhwagun, whom Daewongun titled Prince Successor. Min responded with a powerful faction of high officials, scholars, and members of her clan to bring down Daewongun from power. Min Sung-ho, Min's relative, and Choi Ik-hyun, court scholar, wrote a formal impeachment of Daewongun to the Royal Council of Administration.

The document argued that Gojong, now 22, should rule in his own right, without the regency of the Daewongun. The Royal Council directed the Daewongun, with Gojong's approval, to retire to his estate at Yangju in 1882, the smaller Unhyeongung. Min then banished the royal concubine and her child to a village outside the capital, stripped of royal titles. The child soon died afterwards, with some accusing Min of involvement.

With the retirement of Daewongun and the expelled concubine and her son, the to-be Queen gained complete control over her court, placing her family in high court positions. By that action, Min proved herself worthy of the title Queen of Korea. Although her husband, King Gojong, officially ruled Korea, Queen Min showed greater political skill and intelligence than her husband. She had the real power in the Royal Court, a fact that captured the Daewongun's attention. He had thought that Queen Min would prove pliable to his will. That hope had quickly dispelled. Instead of a lamb, he had invited a lion into the Royal Court.

138

The Progressive Agenda

As Britain, France, Germany, moved upon East Asia in the nineteenth century, China, Japan, and Korea felt threatened. Each nation handled the challenge in their unique way. After Admiral Perry opened Japan to commerce after 1853, Japan responded by committing to a reform program, the Meiji Restoration, that would modernize Japanese institutions and open the island nation to trade and improved foreign relations. China, on the other hand, attempted to keep the Western powers and westernization at arms length. Korea, found itself conflicted. Two power factions, the Progressives and Conservatives, battled each other for policy control in Korean. That left Korea vulnerable to China, Japan, Russia, and the European powers.

Queen Min and King Gojong sided more with the Progressive movement than the Conservatives, yet Conservatives held powerful sway in Korea. Japan employed the tactics Admiral Perry used on them to open the Hermit Kingdom. Faced with Japan's naval and land forces, Korea signed the Ganghwa Treaty on February 15, 1876, agreeing to open treaty ports with Japan. Just as Perry's naval guns provoked a radical reform movement in Japan, the Meiji Restoration, Japan's naval guns provoked a reform movement in Korea, the Progressive movement.

Gojong and Min initiated investigative and study trips abroad to Japan, China, and the United States. The Conservative party opposed those trips, continually working to undermine the Progressive agenda to adopt Western technology. Queen Min promoted a plan received from a Chinese diplomat in Japan, the Korea Strategy. Min and Gojong supported new learning and adopting advances in making of ammunition, electricity, chemistry, smelting, mechanical engineering, cartography, and other basic subjects related to military affairs.

Insurrection of 1882

The modernization of the military met with opposition that led to the Insurrection of 1882. Members of the old military sought the support of Daewon-gun to overthrow Min and Gojong. Although bloody, Queen Min and King Gojong escaped to the safety of a hiding place. Appealing to the Qing Dynasty in China for help, Chinese troops put down the rebellion and restore Min and Gojong to the palace. Japan took advantage of the turmoil to force Gojong, without Min's knowledge, to sign a treaty August 10, 1882, paying indemnity and allowing the stationing of Japanese troops in Seoul.

Coup of December 4, 1884

The next bloody coup took place on December 4, 1884. This time the Progressives initiated the attempted overthrow of Min and King Gojong, this time out of frustration at the slow pace of reform. They targeted Conservative Party leaders for death. Aided by Japanese legation guards, the Korean Progressives seized control of the palace, issuing decrees in the name of the Queen and King. Chinese troops again came to the rescue of Min and Gojong, routing the Progressives and killing several of their key leaders. Japan, once again, forced Gojong, without Min's knowledge, to sign a treaty, the Hanseong Treaty indemnifying Japan for losses during the coup.

Li-Ito Agreement of 1885

As Queen Min and King Gojong struggled to bring progressive reforms in the face of Conservative resistance and Progressive impatience, tensions between China and Japan escalated. On April 18, 1885, China and Japan signed the Li-Ito Agreement in Tianjin, basically agreeing to keep each other informed about planned moves on Korea. Mistrust continued to heighten in spite of the treaty.

In the face of the turbulent times, Queen Min, with Gojong's support, supported a full agenda of progressive reforms. Queen Min supported reform in the economy, communications, transportation, agriculture, military science, education, the press, and medicine. She supported the founding of schools, newspapers, hospitals, and welcomed Christian missionaries from the United States and Europe. Christianity made remarkable strides under Queen Min's protection, the Christian work coming

Alleged killers of Queen Min posing in front of Hanseong sinbo building in Seoul (1895)

The national funeral march for Empress Myeongseong two years after her assassination in 1895

fully into the open for the first time since the horrific martyrdoms of 1866 and 1871.

The Eulmi Incident

Queen Min's life ended brutally and tragically in what has been named the Eulmi Incident. Evidence accepted by all parties indicates that Japanese soldiers, with the full compliance of the Japanese government in Tokyo and consul in Korea, butchered her on the royal palace grounds in the early morning hours of October 8, 1895. Japanese assassins attacked her in her private quarters, killed her with samuri swords, dragged her body outside and burned her remains.

Legacy

Empress Myeongseong's role has been widely debated by historians. Some older Koreans who survived the Japanese occupation criticize her for failing to resist the Japanese militarily. The Japanese portrayal of Empress Myeongseong forms part of the recent controversy over allegations of revisionist history in Japanese school textbooks.

Many in South Korea, influenced by a recent novel, TV drama and musical, view her as a national heroine, for striving diplomatically and politically to keep Korea independent of foreign influence. Skilled in foreign affairs and diplomacy, she set in motion an ambitious plan to modernize Korea. The Japanese viewed her as an obstacle against its expansion overseas. Efforts to remove her from politics failed, orchestrated through rebellions prompted by her father-in-law, the influential regent, compelling the Empress to take a harsher stance against Japanese influence.

A fair and impartial view of Empress Myeongseong will conclude that she rose far above her station of birth to accomplish enormously important reforms. The Daewongun had selected her to marry his son because he thought she would be easy to control. That proved an erroneous judgment. Min stood her ground in the turmoil of tremendous conflict between powerful Conservative and Progressive parties. She navigated Korea through the perilous straits of encroachment by Western nations and by Eastern nations, attempting to maintain Korea's independence through modernization. That is an awesome task and responsibility for a woman selected for her meekness.

Korea has suffered from internal conflict between factions, the Conservatives and the Progressives, and from external threat from China, Japan, and Russia. The time she ruled with her husband, Gojong, marked a pivotal time in Korean history. Although she died in an assassination, her life cut short during the most important time for Progressive reform in Korea, still the work for reform and development that she put into motion has born fruit in our time. Queen Min; a lady of strength, intelligence, vision, and virtue in a chaotic time of conflict. That is her lasting legacy.

EMPEROR GOJONG
The First Emperor of The Korean Empire
(September 8, 1852 – January 21, 1919)

Gojong (고종:高宗), the Gwangmu Emperor (광무제:光武帝), reigned 1863-1907 served as the twenty-sixth and final king of the five-century long Korean Joseon Dynasty. He reigned during the years leading up to the end of the monarchy and Korea's entry into the modern world. During the later part of his reign, he declared Korea an empire thus becoming the first emperor of the Korean Empire. With the annexation of Korea by Japan in 1910, the empire dissolved, and was never reestablished.

Rise to the throne

Gojong took the throne in 1863 when King Cheoljong died without an heir. The Dowager Queen Sinjeong, mother of King Heonjong, the king before Cheoljong, orchestrated twelve year old Gojong's succession to the throne. Cheoljong's Queen, Cheonin, opposed the choice of Gojong as Cheoljong's successor.

The Dowager chose Gojong over his older brother, Yi Jaemyun, to enable her to rule as regent longer. Together with the Dowager Sinjeong, his father, Regent Heungseon (Daewongun), ruled for Gojong until he reached adulthood. The Daewongun restored Gyeongbokgung as the seat of royalty during his regency.

Daewongun's Regency

In the early years, Daewongun's job as Regent drew little criticism; however, his policies of isolationism became harder and harder to maintain. Japan and China had already entered into active relations with western powers, and those powers began to turn their eyes toward Korea, as evidenced by diplomatic and then military advances by France (1866) and the United States (1871).

Gojong and Min Take Over the Throne

When King Gojong reached twenty-one years old, criticism of the Daewongun's policies had increased. Royal officials called for Gojong to take the throne and govern directly. Although Daewongun relinquished his regency in 1873, Queen Min emerged as the real power behind the throne. In March 1866, at thirteen years old, Gojong had married fourteen year old Min Jayoung.

The Daewongun had chosen her partly because she had been orphaned at a young age, thus her parents were not around to interfere with palace politics. Daewongun mistakenly thought that he could easily control Min Ja-young. Her political skill, intelligence and strength of character out-weighed her lack of family influence in the royal court.

Gojong, with the influence of Queen Min, adopted more of an open-door foreign policy than his father had maintained. He signed a Treaty of Amity and Trade with the United States in 1882, hoping to gain protection from the imperial designs of neighbors Japan, China and Russia. That proved a futile hope as the struggle between those three Asian powerhouses erupted into the Sino-Japanese War (1894–95) and, later, the Russo-Japanese War of 1905.

Japan Seizes Control of Korea

Gojong wearing Court uniform and dress in the Empire of Japan and Japanese honours after 1910's annexation

Russia seemed to have the upper hand; the Russian consul in Seoul, Karl Ivanovich Weber, developed a personal friendship with Gojong, and after the assassination of Queen Min in 1895 by the Japanese, Weber personally offered the King refuge in the Russian Legation.[1]

Gojong proclaimed Korea an empire in 1897, receiving the title of Emperor Gwangmu; thus sitting as the last monarch of the Joseon Dynasty and the first of only two in the Gwangmu era. He intended to place Korea on a par with China and strengthen Korea against Japanese aggression. His domestic and foreign policies proved successful at first. In the face of growing Japanese pressure, Gojong played the rival Russian, Japanese and Chinese sides off of each other to prevent each of them from totally controlling Korea. His domestic policy of industrializing Korea met with a measure of success as well.

He entered into a series of treaties and agreements that were disadvantageous for Korea, feeling that such a course was better than risk two rivals dividing Korea between themselves (Russia and Japan had discussed dividing Korea at the 38th parallel as early as 1896). His efforts at maintaining a sovereign independent state finally ended after the Russo-Japanese War (1904–05). Victorious Japan's Meiji Emperor forced Gojong to accept pro-Japanese advisors to the royal court. Soon afterwards, Japan forced Gojong to sign the Protectorate Treaty of 1905 between Korea and Japan, which stripped Korea of its rights as an independent nation. Gojong sent representatives to the Hague Peace Convention of 1907 to try and re-assert his soveriegnty over Korea.

Although the Japanese delegates blocked the Korean representatives from attending the Convention, they persisted and later held interviews with newspapers. One representative warned forebodingly of Japanese ambitions in Asia:

"The United States does not realize what Japan's policy in the Far East is and what it portends for the American people. The Japanese adopted a policy that in the end will give her complete control over commerce and industry in the Far East. Japan is bitter against the United States and against Great Britain. If the United States does not watch Japan closely she will force the Americans and the English out of the Far East."

As a result, an enraged Meiji forced Gojong to abdicate in favour of Gojong's son, Sunjong. Sunjong ruled for just three years before the Korean Empire ended with the annexation of Korea by Japan in 1910. Gojong opposed the Japanese annexation of Korea up until his death in 1919, and the March 1st Movement for independence chose to schedule their first uprising against the occupation government for a date coinciding with two days before Gojong's funeral. Gojong's royal tomb, Hongneung, which he shares with Queen Min, is located in the city of Namyangju, northeast of Seoul.

Legacy

After Gojong took over the leadership of the country from his father Daewongun, in 1873, he allowed most of Daewongun's reforms to stand, notably the dissolution of the sowons, private academies operated throughout the country by yangbans, which had become breeding grounds for political factions, and enjoyed unbalanced tax-free status. During his reign Deoksugung palace, refurbished by Daewongun, once again became the seat of royal power in Korea, as it had been centuries before. In contrast to Daewongun, King Gojong and Queen Min began to open the doors of the country to foreign presence. For the most part, Gojong's intention in beginning his alliance with Japan, signified by the Treaty of Ganghwa in 1876, was to free Korea from the long-standing overbearing influence of China. In 1882, he went one step further, and established a foreign office, welcoming Prussian statesman Paul George Mollendorff into the foreign office as an official advisor to the crown.

In 1883, at the urging of progressive elements, he authorized publication of the nation's first newspaper, the Hansung Sunbo, and the following year established a postal system, modeled after those in Japan and China. In 1897, he declared Korea an Empire, elevating the country to the same status as Japan and China. Later, in 1898, following the recommendation of the Independence Club, he issued a proclamation that elections for a senate would be held and the country would become a constitutional monarchy. But he had to back down under pressure from the current ranking officials, who feared losing their influence, and the elections were postponed, and ultimately canceled altogether. He continued to strike alliances, unfortunately, almost uniformly disadvantageous to Korea, in efforts to keep the country from being sliced into pieces by the Japanese, Russians, Chinese and other powers who had their eyes on the small peninsular nation and its advantageous location, linking Russia and Asia. In the end his efforts ended up landing the country under the control of the Japanese, in the early years of the twentieth century, where it remained until the end of World War II.

YI WANYONG
Traitor Who Put Korea Under Japanese Rule
(July 17, 1858 – February 12, 1926)

Yi Wanyong (pronounced [iː wan.joŋ]; 이완용:李完用), also known as Ye Wanyong, was a pro-Japanese minister of Korea, who signed the Japan–Korea Annexation Treaty, which placed Korea under Japanese rule in 1910.

Early life and education

Born to a prominent family in Gwangju, Gyeonggi-do[0], Ye spent three years in the United States from 1887–1891. Ye was a founding member of the Independence Club established in 1896 and belonged to the 'reform faction' which wanted to westernize Korea and to open the country to foreign trade.

Early career

Ye was a prominent government minister at the time of Eulsa Treaty of 1905, and was the most outspoken supporter of the pact which made the Korean Empire a protectorate of the Empire of Japan, thus stripping it of its diplomatic sovereignty. The treaty was signed in defiance of Korean Emperor Gojong, and he is thus accounted to be the chief of five ministers (including Park Jae-soon, Lee Ji-yong, Lee Geun-taek, Gwon Joong-hyun) who were later denounced as Five Eulsa Traitors in Korea.

Under Japanese Resident-General Itō Hirobumi, Ye was promoted to the post of prime minister from 1906-1910. Ye was instrumental in forcing Emperor Gojong to abdicate in 1907, after Emperor Gojong tried to publicly denounce the Eulsa Treaty at the second international Hague Peace Convention. In 1907 Ye was also chief amongst the seven ministers who supported the Japan–Korea Treaty of 1907, which further placed the domestic affairs of Korea under Japan's control, thus completing the colonialisation of Korea by Japan. Ye is therefore also listed in Korea amongst the Seven Jeongmi Traitors. In 1909, he was seriously injured in an assassination attempt by the "Five Eulsa Traitors Assassination Group".

Career under Japanese rule

In 1910, Ye signed the Japan-Korea Annexation Treaty by which Japan took full control over Korea, while Korean Emperor Sunjong refused to sign. For his cooperation with the Japanese, Ye is also listed in Korea amongst the eight Gyeongsul Traitors. He was rewarded with a peerage in the Japanese kazoku system, becoming a hakushaku (Count), in 1910, which was raised to the title of kōshaku (Marquis) in 1921. He died in 1926.

Legacy

After the independence of Korea at the end of World War II, the grave of Ye was dug up and his remains suffered the posthumous dismemberment, which is often considered to be the most disgraceful punishment in Confucian ideology. Yi Wanyong's name has almost become synonymous to that of 'traitor' in modern Korea.

However, Seo Jae-pil's Dongnip Sinmun (Independence Newspaper) never wrote a single line of criticism against him.[1]

He mistakenly thought that the annexation would make a Korea–Japan dual monarchy, similar to Austria–Hungary or Sweden–Norway.[2]

The Special law to redeem pro-Japanese collaborators' property was enacted in 2005 and the committee confiscated the property[3] of the descendants of nine people that had collaborated with Japan when Korea was annexed by Japan in August 1910. Ye is one of those heading the list.[4]

Popular culture

Portrayed by Woo Sang-jeon in the 2015 film Assassination.

SOH JAIPIL
Founder of The First Korean
Newspaper in Hangul
(January 7, 1864 – January 5, 1951)

Philip Jaisohn (서재필;徐載弼) was the anglicized name used by Soh Jaipil (서재필;徐載弼), a noted champion for Korea's independence, journalist, the first Korean to become a naturalized citizen of the United States, and the founder of the first Korean newspaper in Hangul, the Independent News.[1]

He was one of the organizers of the Gapsin Coup in 1906 as well as the 1906 to 1908 Civil rights movement and other suffrage movements. However, when the Gapsin Coup failed, he took refuge in the United States, where he became a medical doctor. During his time in the United States he became the first Korean to gain American citizenship. From 1945 to 1948 he returned to Korea as chief adviser to the Joseon dynasty government and returned from 1945 to 1948 as chief adviser to the American occupation forces in the south. His nicknames were Songjae (송재;松齋) and Ssang-gyeong (쌍경;雙慶), his courtesy name was Yun-gyeong (윤경;允卿) and he wrote under the pen name N.H. Osia.

Life

Early years

Soh Jaipil was born in Boseong County, Korea. His family was one of the Joseon Dynasty's noble families. He was the second son of a Soh Kwang-hyo (also known as Soh Kwang-ha), who was a local magistrate in Boseong County. He was raised by one of his relatives in Seoul. At eight years of age, he was adopted by Soh Kwang-ha, the second cousin of his biological father Soh Kwang-hyo.[2]

Soh's family was from the upper echelons of Joseon Society. He was the eight generation descendant of Seo Jong-je, a daughter to Queen Jeongseong. She was the wife to the 21st King Yeongjo. Seo Kwang-bum, who shared similar ideological beliefs was also from his family.

During his adolescence Soh studied at Kim Seong-geun and Park Kyu-su's private school. When Soh was a teenager, he had already been exposed to the reformist ideals of Kim Ok-gyun.

Political activist

He passed the civil service exam at the age of 18, becoming one of the youngest people to ever pass this exam. As a result, he became a junior officer in 1882. Thereafter he was appointed to Gyoseokwan Bujeongja (교서관부정자;校書館 副正字) and Seungmunwon Gajuseo (승문원가주서;承文院假主書). In 1883 he was appointed to Seungmunwon Bujeongja (승문원부정자;承文院 副正字) and Hunryunwon Bubongsa (훈련원부봉사;訓鍊院 副奉事). In the following year, he was sent to Japan where he studied both at the Keio Gijuku (the forerunner of the Keio University) and the Toyama Army Academy. In July 1884, his adoptive mother died, but he quickly returned to public service under special orders.

In his reports to the king, Soh explained that in the new world Korea's armed forces were useless and obsolete. This annoyed powerful conservatives, but it made Soh widely known and respected among like-minded young intellectuals. By that time, a small but growing number of young intellectuals understood that fundamental reform had to occur or Korea would fall victim to the imperialist powers.[3] that he was appointed to Joryn-guk Sagwanjang (조련국사관장;操鍊局 士官長).

In December 1884, Soh, following Kim Ok-gyun, was involved in the Gapsin Coup, a radical attempt to overturn the old reKime and establish equality among people. Soh and Kim Ok-gyun, Park Yeong-hyo, Yun Chi-ho, Hong Yeong-shik, and others had planned a coup for seven months, from July to December 1884. He was appointed the Vice-Minister of Defense. The coup was defeated in three days, as China intervened by sending military troops. As a result, his two younger brothers were killed and his biological father Soh Kwang-ha and biological mother Lady Lee of Seongju were executed under a guilt-by-association system. His first wife Lady Kim was sold into slavery, but committed suicide. Convicted of treason, Soh Jaipil lost his whole family and had to flee Korea to save his life.

The majority of the 1884 revolutionaries fled to Japan. Unlike them, Soh moved to the United States. He saw Japan as essentially a conduit for Western knowledge and ideas, but preferred to deal with what he saw as the source itself.[3]

Exile in the United States

In 1885, early in his stay in America Soh worked part-time jobs. In 1886, Soh lived in Norristown, Pennsylvania, and attended the Harry Hillman Academy (Wilkes-Barre, PA) thanks to the help of John Welles Hollenback. He began to use the name "Philip Jaisohn" at that time. In 1890, he became the first Korean American to acquire United States citizenship. He studied medicine at George Washington University, and was the first Korean to receive an American medical degree in 1892.

In 1890, he became a U.S. citizen and from then he was often referred to by his American name Philip Jaisohn.

The Independent

In 1894, he married Muriel Armstrong, a distant relative of the former president of the United States, James Buchanan, and daughter of George B. Armstrong, credited as the founder of the U.S. Railway Mail Service. They had two daughters —Stephanie and Muriel. In 1895, he was reinstated to the Joseon Dynasty, but he flatly refused to return.

The Independent

In 1894, Japan defeated China in the First Sino-Japanese war which occurred on the Korean Peninsula. The Korean cabinet was filled with reformists. Along with these political changes, the treason of the Gapsin Coup was pardoned enabling Jaisohn's return in 1895. In December 1895, he went to Incheon. The

151

Joseon government wanted to appoint him to Foreign Secretary but he refused to take the position. In Korea, he endeavored to politically educate people. Jaisohn published a newspaper, *The Independent* (독립신문), to transform the Korean population into an informed citizenry. He was the first to print his newspaper entirely in Hangul to extend readership to lower classes and women.

Sowing the ideals of independence and democracy

Independence Gate

In the 1896 to 1898 Civil rights movement and suffrage movements. Soh's goal was to ensure that Korea would drift away from the Chinese sphere of influence but without falling too heavily under the influence of Russia or Japan. He was also behind the construction of the Independence Gate, which was initially meant to symbolize the end of Korea's ritual subordination to China.[3] Apart from his journalistic and political activities, he delivered regular lectures on modern politics and the principles of democracy.[3]

He promoted national independence as the principal political ideal and emphasized neutral diplomatic approaches to protect Korea from China, Russia and Japan. He also underscored the importance of public education, modernized industry and public hygiene. The Independence was particularly critical of misconduct by government officials, which caused strong reactions by the conservatives. Under the aegis of the Independence Club, Jaisohn organized the All People's Congress, an open public forum to debate over political issues. The Congress was hailed by young reformers and began to establish nationwide chapters.

In November 1897, Soh enabled the construction of the Independence Gate (독립문;獨立門).[4] At this time he also ended the policy of Yeongeunmun (영은문;迎恩門).[5] Yeongeunmun was the Korean policy of welcoming the Chinese envoys, Yeongeun roughly translates from Korean to English as "Welcome to beneficent Envoys of suzerain's."

In 1898, conservatives accused Jaisohn and the Club of seeking to replace the monarchy with a republic, and the Korean government requested Jaisohn to return to the US. After his return, Korean government ordered the Club to disband and arrested 17 leaders including Rhee Syngman.

Clerk and Company manage

In April to August 1898, he accompanied an army to the Spanish–American War. In 1899 he found employment as clerk for the University of Pennsylvania Hospital.

In 1904, worked with Harold Deemer, who was a year younger, to create the "Deemer and Jaisohn shop." It was a stationery and printing industry store. In 1915, the shop became called the Philip Jaisohn Company, and specialized in the printing industry.

Independence movements

In the United States, Jaisohn conducted medical research at the University of Pennsylvania and later became a successful printer in Philadelphia. When he heard the news of the March 1st Movement (1919), a nationwide protest against Japanese rule in Korea, Jaisohn convened the "First Korean Congress", which was held in Philadelphia for three days. After the Congress, Jaisohn devoted his energies and private property to the freedom of Korea. He organized the League of Friends of Korea in 26 cities with the help of Rev. Floyd Tomkins, and established the "Korean Information Bureau." He published a political journal "Korea Review" to inform the American public of the situation in Korea, and to persuade the U.S. government to support the freedom for Koreans.

In the 1920s, Soh, who had just turned 60, returned to research and spent his 60s and 70s working as a specialist doctor and micro-biologist, as well as occasionally publishing in peer-review academic journals.[3]

Five years later in 1924, Jaisohn went legally bankrupt due to his political engagement and had to resume practicing medicine to make a living. At age 62, he became a student again at the University of Pennsylvania to renew his medical knowledge. After this, he published five research articles in the medical journals specializing in pathology. During World War II, he volunteered as a physical examination officer with the belief that the victory of the U.S. would bring freedom to Korea.

Last days in Korea

Jaisohn returned to Korea once again after Japan's defeat in World War II. The U.S. Army Military Government in control of the southern part of Korea invited him to serve as chief adviser. In December 1946, he was elected to the Interim Legislative Assembly (남조선과도입법의원의원; 南朝鮮過渡立法議院議員). In May 1945, liberal and moderate socialist intellectuals selected him as candidate for presidency, but he declined. When the date of the first presidential election was confirmed by the United Nations, Jaisohn was petitioned to run for presidency by 3,000 people including a young Kim Dae-jung, but he refused in the end.

Jaisohn felt that political unity was needed for a new nation despite his uneasy relationship with the president elect Syngman Rhee. He decided to return to the United States in 1948. Suffering a heart attack a week earlier on December 29, Jaisohn died on January 5, 1951 during the Korean War, just two days before his 87th birthday.

His body was cremated, and his ashes were buried in Bib church in Philadelphia. In 1994 his remains were repatriated to South Korea. His ashes were buried in the National Cemetery of South Korea in Seoul.

Philip Jaisohn Memorial House

The Philip Jaisohn Memorial House in Media, Pennsylvania was Dr. Jaisohn's home from 1925 to 1951. This house was bought when Dr. Jaisohn was in great financial difficulties, while his house in Philadelphia was pledged due to his devotion to the Korean independence. His Media home was acquired by the Philip Jaisohn Memorial Foundation in 1987 and opened to the public in 1990. Since then, the Jaisohn House has been visited by many students and politicians from Korea such as former South Korean president and Nobel peace laureate Kim Dae-jung as well as Korean American immigrants and community neighbors.

Philip Jaisohn Memorial House

On May 21, 1994, the Pennsylvania Historical and Museum Commission and the Philip Jaisohn Memorial Foundation dedicated a historical marker for Dr. Jaisohn, stating:

American-educated medical doctor who sowed seeds of democracy in Korea, published its first modern newspaper (1896-98), and popularized its written language. The first Korean to earn a Western medical degree and become a U.S. citizen. He worked for Korean independence during the Japanese occupation, 1910-45. Chief Advisor to the U.S. Military Government in Korea, 1947-1948. This was his home for 25 years.

KIM KOO
Leader of The Korean Independence Movement
(August 29, 1876 – June 26, 1949)

Kim Gu (김구;金九;Kim Koo or Kim Ku, Korean pronunciation: [kimgu];also known by his pen name Baekbeom (백범;白凡;[pɛkpʌm]) was a Korean nationalist politician. He was the sixth and later the last Premier of the Provisional Government of the Republic of Korea, a leader of the Korean independence movement against the Japanese Empire,[note 1][note 2][note 3][note 4] and a reunification activist after 1945.

Biography

Early life

Kim was born on August 29 (11th day of the 7th month in the Lunar Calendar), 1876 in Teot-gol (텃골), Baek-un-bang (백운방), Haeju (해주;海州), South Hwanghae Province, Korea, the only son of a farmer Kim Soon-young (김순영) and his wife Kwak Nack-won (곽나원). His name at birth was Kim Changahm (김창암;金昌嚴;[kimtɕʰaŋam]). When he was nine years old, he started to study Chinese classic texts such as Zizhi Tongjian (자치통감;資治通鑑), and Great Learning (대학;大學) at local seodangs.

Kim's family Andong Kim clan was a famous noble, Distant descendant of King Kyung Soon.[1] founder of Andong Kim clan's Kim Suk-seung was grandson of King Kyung Soon, Kim Koo's 31G-grandfathers. Kim's 21G-grandfather Kim Sa-hyeong(김사형;金士衡) was one of meritorious retainer at the founding of a Joseon dynasty. but later, Kim Ja-jeon([1] 김자점;金自點) was treason of King Hyojeong, Kim Ja-jeon's family was massacre. his 11G-grandfather Kim Dae-chung was escape to Hanyang and go to Haeju. later Kim Dae-chung's was conceal one's identity. Kim Ja-jeom was his 11G-grandfather Kim Dae-chung's third cousin.

Leader of Donghak movement

At the age of 16, Kim applied for the Gwageo (Imperial Examination) of Joseon but failed. After that, he joined the Donghak Movement (동학;東學), a rebellion against government and foreign oppressions in 1893 and changed his name to Kim Changsoo (김창수;金昌洙). As the organization grew rapidly, he was appointed the district leader of Palbong (팔봉) at the age of 17 and a Donghak army reKiment. Under the instruction of Donghak leader Choi Si-hyung (최시형;崔時亨), Kim's troops stormed the Haeju fort in Hwanghae-do, but the army was eventually defeated by governmental forces. After that, he was defeated by his companion, Lee Dong-yeop (이동엽) in the turf war of Donghak's organization. Thereafter, the Royal Army's General An Tae-hun (안태훈;安泰勳;(father of Ahn Jung-geun (안중근;安重根) who would in 1909 assassinate the Japanese governor Ito Hirobumi (伊藤博文)), gave Kim's Donghak rebels a safe pass, but other government troops ignored An's safe pass and attacked them. At 20, with I-eon Kim whom he had met around Yalu River, Kim attacked the Royal Army unit holding the Gang-gye fort, supported by the Qing Dynasty's army. However, the attack failed and he went into hiding.

Assassination of Josuke Tsuchida

IIn February 1896, Kim stayed at an inn in Chihapo, Hwanghae Province while traveling to southern regions. There he found a Japanese man named Tsuchida Josuke (土田㆑亮), who was a trader from Tsushima, Nagasaki, Japan, and killed him believing that he was a Japanese army lieutenant involved in the assassination of the queen.[note 5] [note 6] [note 7]

In his autobiography, 'Baekbeom Ilji' (백범일지, 白凡逸志, Baekbeom Journal), Kim describes his motivation at the time as follows:

Since many Japaneses go through Chihapo every day, there is no reason for him to disguise as a Korean if he were an ordinary merchant or workman. Could he be Miura or one of his accomplices who killed the queen, fled from Seoul and hiding here? Even if he is not, a Japanese man with a disguise and a sword can do nothing but harm to my country and people. I will revenge for my queen by killing this Japanese man.

— Baekbeom Ilji

The following morning, Kim attacked Tsuchida, and killed him. The "Report from acting administrator Hagihara Moriichi of Incheon Consulate on the current situation of Incheon" describes Tsuchida as a "commoner from Nagasaki Prefecture" and an "employee of a Nagasaki trader on a business trip".[2]

However, Kim argued in his autobiography that Tsuchida was concealing a sword and had identification papers that showed him to be a Japanese army lieutenant.[3]

Jailbreak, and educational activities

Kim was tortured and sentenced to death. According to 'Baekbeom Ilji', however, many Korean people were sympathetic and admired him for his patriotism and bravery, as shown by the facts that his execution was suspended by order of Emperor Gwangmu, that Korean judicial officials behaved politely to him despite Japanese pressure to execute him promptly, and that influential Koreans at the time (including major merchants of Incheon) made efforts to rescue him by repeated petitions to Korean Justice Department Officials and by collecting money for his ransom before his scheduled execution date.

In prison, Kim had a chance to read newly published textbooks about Western culture and science such as Taeseo Shinsa (태서신사 ; 泰西新史) and Saegye Jiji (세계지지 ; 世界地誌). He was deeply impressed by the strengths of the new Western science and recognized the importance of education for the Korean people. He started to teach about 100 illiterate fellow prisoners. The Korean newspaper Hwhangsung Shinbo (황성신보 ; 皇城新報) reported at the time that by his teaching of prisoners Kim Chang Soo changed the Incheon Prison into a school.

In 1898 he broke out of prison and escaped into Magoksa (마곡사 ; 麻谷寺), a Buddhist temple in Gongju (공주 ; 公州), Chungcheong province, and entered the Buddhist priesthood. A year later Kim left the priesthood and returned to Hwanghae, where he devoted himself to the enlightenment and education of the Korean people, founding (장연학교 ; 長淵學校) and the Yangsan School (양산학교 ; 楊山學校) in 1907, becoming the principal of the Yangsan School. In 1904, he married Choi Jun-rye (최준례 ; 崔遵禮) from Sinchon (신천), Hwanghae Province.

Joins Korean Independence Movement

In 1905, the Eulsa Treaty (을사조약;乙巳條約) was made between Japan and Korea, making Korea a protectorate of Japan. Kim participated in a mass protest against the treaty in Seoul and presented a memorial to Emperor Gwangmu urging him to withdraw from the treaty. In 1908, Kim joined Sinminhoe (신민회;新民會;New People's Association), a national-level underground organization established by Ahn Changho (안창호) for nonviolent Korean independence movement.

In 1910, the Japanese colonial government arrested An Myung-geun (안명근;安明根), a cousin of the An Jung-geun who killed Ito Hirobumi, for plotting to assassinate Governor-General Terauchi Masatake (寺內正毅). Kim, who was a close friend of An, was suspected of being an accomplice and arrested as well. Like other jailed suspects, Kim was severely tortured, but no evidence linking him to the assassination attempt was found and he was released from prison after 3 years.[4]

This term of imprisonment left Kim with damage to cartilage and his left ear disfigured for life, due to beating by Japanese in the prison, in addition to his calves that were already permanently scarred in his earlier imprisonment torture for the killing of Tsuchida. At the time, Han Pil-ho (한필호;韓弼昊), a member of Sinminhoe, was killed, Shin Suk-choong (신석충;申錫忠) killed himself, and An tried to commit suicide during the severe interrogation but failed. Kim also tried to kill himself with a self-inflicted injury in his head, but failed.

Kim Koo (1919)

In prison, Kim changed his name from 'Kim Chang-soo' to 'Kim Koo' and adopted the pen name of 'Baekbeom' (백범, 白凡). Kim stated in his biography that the change of his name symbolized breaking free from Japanese nationality records and that he chose the pen name Baekbeom, which means "ordinary person", hoping every ordinary Korean person would fight for the independence of Korea.

Provisional Government of the Republic of Korea

Kim exiled himself to Shanghai, China in 1919 after a nationwide non-violent resistance movement, known as the March 1st Movement (3.1 운동), which was violently suppressed by the Japanese imperialist government. In Shanghai, Kim joined the Provisional Government of the Republic of Korea (대한민국 임시정부;大韓民國 臨時政府), which vowed to liberate Korea from Japanese occupation.

In 1922 Kim was Assassination of Korean Communists Kim Rip(김립;金立).[5] Reason Kim Rip was give to 2 million $ from Lenin. but Kim Rip was money not given to Provisional Government of the Republic of Korea.[5] Kim Koo made a false charge against, Kim Rip is peculator.[5]

After serving as the Police Minister, Kim became the president of the Provisional Government of the Republic of Korea in 1927. He was re-elected to the office many times by the Provisional Assembly.

In 1931 he organized a nationalist group, the Korean Patriotic Corps (한인애국단;韓人愛國團). One of the members, Yun Bong-gil (윤봉길;尹奉吉), ambushed and assassinated the Japanese military leadership in Shanghai on April 29, 1932. The commander of the Japanese Army and Navy died instantly. Another member, Lee Bong-chang (이봉창;李奉昌), tried to assassinate the Japanese emperor Hirohito in Tokyo on January 8 of the same year but failed.

Kim Il-Sung and Kim Koo (1948)

After escaping to Chongqing where Chiang Kai-shek's Nationalist Government was established, Kim established the Korean Liberation Army (광복군;光復軍), commanded by General Ji Cheong-cheon (지청천;池靑天). When the Pacific War broke out on December 8, 1941, Kim Koo declared war on Japan and Germany and committed the Korean Liberation Army to the Allied side;the Korean Liberation Army took part in warfare in China and Southeast Asia. Kim arranged for the Korean Liberation Army to advance to Korea in 1945 but, days before the departure of the leading unit, the war ended.

After Korean Liberation

Kim returned to Korea upon the Japanese surrender to the Allies in 1945. He was known as "the Assassin" and reportedly travelled with an entourage of gunmen and concubines. [6]

In December 27 1945, USA and England, USSR, China's head state was conference at Moscow, there was trusteeship agreed upon. immediately Kim was oppose trusteeship. December 27 he was attempt come to power, Song Jin-woo was said to virtually impossible.[7] December 30, Song was murdered, enthusiastic supporters of Kim Koo.[7] one Song Jin-woo's Assassin Han Hyeon-woo was connected of Kim.[7] Cho Byeong-ok was tell to order assassination is Kim Koo.[8] reason Kim was hate for moderate ideas of Song Jin-woo.[9]

In 1947, USA and USSR was negotiation result. creation to The Joint Soviet-American Commission. Kim was opposite to AmericanSoviet Joint Commission. Chang Deok-soo, 2nd leader of Korean Democratic Party, Chang was positive agreement of Joint Commission.[10] also oppose consolidation plan of conservative force, Kim and Chang was argue.[11] In December 2, 1947, Chang Deok-soo was Killed by Park Kwang-ok and Bae Hee-beom, there was a member of Korean Independence Party. Chang Taik-sang was review of arrest to Kim[12]

As the division of the newly independent country became obvious, he led a team of former independence activists to Pyongyang to hold unification talks with Kim Il-sung (김일성 ; 金日成), who later became the president of North Korea. Talks deteriorated rapidly after he voiced his hostility toward the growing communist presence in North Korea.

In 1948, the inaugural National Assembly of South Korea nominated Kim as a candidate for the office of the first president of the Republic. In the election by the National Assembly, Kim was defeated by Rhee Syngman (이승만 ; 李承晩), the first president of the provisional government, who had been impeached in 1925 by a vote of 180-16. He lost the election for the vice presidency to Lee Si-yeong (이시영 ; 李始榮) by a vote of 133-59. Kim did not know about his nomination until after the election. He did not approve the nomination, considering it a ploy to discredit him. Kim would never have participated in the election as he fiercely opposed the establishment of separate governments in North and South Korea.

Death and legacy

On June 26, 1949, Kim was assassinated by Lieutenant Ahn Doo-hee (안두희 ; 安斗熙). Ahn burst in and shot him four times while he was at home, reading poetry. Ahn stated that he killed Kim because he saw him as an agent of the Soviet Union.[13] On April 13, 1992, a confession by Ahn was published by Korean newspaper Donga Ilbo. In the confession, Ahn claimed that the assassination had been ordered by Kim Chang-ryong (김창룡 ; 金昌龍), who served as the head of national security under the Rhee administration. [14] Ahn was murdered by Park Gi-sheo (박기서 ; 朴琦緒), a follower of Kim's, in 1996. According to Bruce Cumings in his 1981 books, another possible motive for the assassination was Kim's alleged connection to the assassination of Song Jin-woo (송진우 ; 宋鎮禹), a leader of the Korean Democratic Party (KDP) who had chosen to work closely with the American military government.[15] In 2001, declassified documents revealed that Ahn had been working for the U.S. Counter-Intelligence Corps, leading to suggestions of US involvement in the assassination.[16] However, some have questioned the evidence for these accusations.[17]

Kim was posthumously awarded the Republic of Korea Medal of Order of Merit for National Foundation (건국훈장 대한민국장 ; 建國勳章 大韓民國章), the most prestigious civil decoration in the Republic of Korea, as well as the Democratic People's Republic of Korea's National Reunification Prize.[18] His autobiography, Baekbeomilji (Journal of Baekbeom, 백범일지) is an important source for study of history of Korean independence movement and has been designated as cultural treasure No. 1245 by the Korean government.[19] A steady seller in Korea, the autobiography was first published in 1947 and republished in more than 10 versions in Korea and abroad.[19]

Kim has been constantly regarded as one of the greatest figures in Korean history. For example, he was voted in a 2004 online poll as the greatest leader after the restoration of Korean independence[20] and in 2005 as the most revered figure by Korean National Assemblymen.[21] In 2007 national surveys, Kim received the most vote as the Korean historic figure whose portrait should be featured in new Korean banknotes to be issued in 2009.[22][23] On November 5, 2007, the Bank of Korea, the national central bank of the Republic of Korea, announced the new 100,000 Korean won bill would feature Kim's portrait.[24] However, the issuing of the new bill was delayed indefinitely as of 2009 for an unknown reason.

Family

Kim's second son, Kim Shin (1922-), was a founding member of Republic of Korea Air Force, the Chief of Korean Air Force, member of the National Assembly, and the Minister of Transportation, and later the Director of Kim Koo Museum and Library.

Kim Koo's grandson, Kim Yang (1953-), was appointed as the Korean Consulate General in Shanghai, China in 2005 and as the Minister of Patriots and Veteran Affairs of Korea in 2008.

In 2010, Kim Koo's great-grandson, Kim Yong-man (1987-) was appointed second lieutenant of Korean Air Force, and in 2011, Kim's great-grandson on her daughter's side, Kim Dong-man (1987-) was also appointed second lieutenant of Korean Air Force.

'My desire'

At the end of his autobiography Baekbeomilji, Kim expressed his desire with which he carried all his lifetime:

If god asked me what was my wish, I would reply unhesitatingly,
"Korean independence."
If he asked me what was my second wish, I would again answer,
"My country's independence."
If he asked me what was my third wish, I would reply in an even louder voice,
"My wish is the complete independence of my country Korea."
My fellow brethren. This is my only wish. I have lived seventy years of my life for this wish, am living my life for this wish, and will live my life only to fulfill this wish.
...Recently, some of our brothers have said that they wanted our nation to be a part of a federation of another country. I don't believe this, and if there is really someone who does, I can only say that he is crazy and has lost his mind.
I've studied the ideas of Confucius, Buddha, and Jesus;I respect them as saints, but even if there's a heaven made by them, it's not a nation created by our nation, and I will never take our nation there.
It is because, a nation which shared blood and history is clear, and just like my body can't be another's, the reason that a certain nation can't become another is the same as brothers living in the same house. If two gather and become one, one would be higher and the other lower, so it becomes a basic problem that one orders from above, and the other obeys from below.
And so-called leftists deny the motherland of blood, and say this and that about the so-called motherland of ideology, ignoring brothers of blood-ties, and claims the so-called comrade of ideology and international class of proletariat, and speak as if nationalism is outside the truth.
This is foolish thinking. Philosophies change and theories of politics and economics are only a snap, but a nation's success is everlasting.
...I want our nation to be the most beautiful in the world. By this I do not mean the

most powerful nation. Because I have felt the pain of being invaded by another nation, I do not want my nation to invade others. It is sufficient that our wealth makes our lives abundant;it is sufficient that our strength is able to prevent foreign invasions. The only thing that I desire in infinite quantity is the power of a noble culture. This is because the power of culture both makes ourselves happy and gives happiness to others.

AN CHANG-HO
Undying Beacon for The Korean
Independence Movement
(November 9, 1876 - March 10, 1938)

Ahn Changho, sometimes An Chang-ho (Korean pronunciation: [antɕʰaŋho]; 안창호: 安昌浩, November 9, 1876 - March 10, 1938) was a Korean independence activist and one of the early leaders of the Korean-American immigrant community in the United States. He is also referred to as his pen name Dosan (도산:島山 [tosʰan]). He established the Shinminhoe (New Korea Society) when he returned to Korea from the US in 1907. It was the most important organization to fight the Japanese occupation of Korea. He established the Young Korean Academy (흥사단:興士團) in San Francisco in 1913 and was a key member in the founding of the Provisional Government of the Republic of Korea in Shanghai in 1919. Ahn is one of two men believed to have written the lyrics of the Aegukga, the South Korean national anthem. Besides his work for the Independence Movement, Dosan wanted to reform the Korean people's character and the entire social system of Korea. Educational reform and modernizing schools were two key efforts of Dosan. He was the father of actor Philip Ahn and U.S. Navy officer Susan Ahn Cuddy.

Background and education

Ahn was born Ahn Ch'i-sam, on the 6th day of the 10th lunar month 1878 in Kangso Pyeongan province, in present-day South Pyongan, North Korea. His birth date is equivalent to 10 November 1878 on the Gregorian calendar but he chose to use the date 9 November 1878 on his vita. Ahn is the family name, chi is the generation marker, and sam refers to the fact that he was the third son of Ahn Kyon-jin (father), and Hwang (Mother). Dosan is of the family of the Sunheung Ahn (순흥안씨:順興安氏) lineage.

It is believed that he changed his name to Chang-ho when he began public speaking as a teenager. His father also changed his name from Ahn Kyo Jin (not Ahn Kyon Jin as previously entered - He is another person and in no way related to Ahn Chang Ho. This error has been repeated numerous times due to this incorrect information posted here.) to Ahn Heung-guk, (assumed to be his father's name).

In 1894, Ahn moved to Seoul where he attended Save the World School (Gusae Hakdang) in 1895, a Presbyterian missionary-sponsored school in Seoul run by Horace G. Underwood and Rev. F.S. Miller. Dosan eventually converted to Christianity. While Dosan was a student at Gusae he worked for Dr. Oliver R. Avison at Jejungwon, the first medical institution in Korea which became Severance Hospital and is now part of Yonsei University Medical Center.

On November 8, 2013 Dosan was posthumously given an Honorary Diploma by Yonsei University in recognition of his attendance at Gusae Hakdang as a student and for his work there as a teaching assistant; and, for his work at Jejungwon while at Gusae and at Severance Hospital in the early 1900s.

Immigration to America

In October 1902, Ahn came to San Francisco with his wife Helen (Hye Ryeon Lee/이 혜련) to pursue a better education. They were the first married couple to come from Korea to the Mainland. Their passports from King Kojong were numbers 51 and 52. Ahn Changho started work there picking oranges in the fields. While living in San Francisco, California, he witnessed two Korean Ginseng merchants fighting in the streets over sales

National Association annual convention in 1915

turf. Ahn was apparently upset by this display of incivility among his country-men overseas, so he began to invest time into reforming the earliest local Korean community members, rising to become one of the first leaders of the Korean-American community.[1]

He founded the Friendship Society (Chinmoke Hoe/친목회) in 1903, the first group that was organized exclusively for Koreans in the United States. April 5, 1905, he established the Mutual Assistance Society (MAS)(Kongrip Hyophoe/공립협회), the first Korean political organization in the United States. The MAS would eventually merge with the United Korean Society (Hapsong Hyophoe/합성협회) in Hawaii to become the Korean National Association (Daehan Inguk Hoe) (대한인국민회;大韓人國民會) in 1909, the official agent of Koreans in the United States until the end of World War II.[2]

Return to Korea

In 1926 departing from San Pedro, California by ship, Dosan traveled back to China, never returning to the United States. During Dosan's anti-Japanese activism in Korea, he was arrested and imprisoned by the Japanese Imperialist government at least five times. He was first arrested in 1909 in connection with Ahn Chung Gun's assassination of Itō Hirobumi, the Japanese Resident General of Korea. Dosan was tortured and punished many times during the years of his activism. In 1932 he was arrested in Shanghai, China in connection with Yun Bong-gil's bombing at Hongkew Park (April 29, 1932). He was a naturalized Chinese citizen at this time and illegally extradited back to Korea, where he was convicted of violating Japan's "Preservation of Peace Laws" and sentenced to five years in Taejon prison.

Death

In 1937, Japanese authorities arrested Ahn, but due to complications from imprisonment under harsh conditions, inhumane torture and severe internal illness, he was released on bail and transferred to the Kyungsung University Hospital where he died on March 10, 1938.

Legacy and memorials

Many consider Ahn Chang-ho to be one of the key moral and philosophical leaders of Korea during the 20th century. In the turmoil immediately before and during the Japanese occupation of Korea, he called for the moral and spiritual renewal of the Korean people through education as one of the important components in their struggle for independence and building a democratic society. Dosan also included economic and military compo-

165

nents in his independence movement strategies.

A memorial park called Dosan Park (Korean:도산공원) and hall were built to honor him in Gangnam-gu, Seoul.[3] Another memorial was built in downtown Riverside, California to honor him. Ahn's family home on 36th Place in Los Angeles has been restored by the University of Southern California, on whose campus it sits (albeit in a different location). Dosan never lived in the house on the USC campus since the Ahn family moved there in 1935 many years after Dosan had gone back to Shanghai.

At the request of Congresswoman Diane Watson, the USPS Post Office in Koreatown at Harvard and 6th Street was named Dosan Ahn Chang Ho Station. This was the first USPS naming honoring an Asian.

In 2011, the Ellis Island Foundation installed a plaque honoring Dosan to commemorate the 100th year anniversary of his entrance to the United States through Ellis Island from London on September 3, 1911. He sailed from Glasgow aboard the SS Caledonia.

The City of Los Angeles, in the early 1990s, declared the nearby intersection of Jefferson Boulevard and Van Buren Place - across from the Korean National Association and Korean Presbyterian church - to be named "Dosan Ahn Chang Ho Square" in his honor. A main freeway interchange in downtown Los Angeles where the 10 Freeway and 110 Freeway meet is named after Dosan Ahn Chang Ho. The third pattern of Taekwondo which is made up of 24 movements is called Do-San or Dosan in his honor. This is the pattern is required to advance from 7th Kup Yellow Belt with Green Tag to 6th Kup Green Belt.

In 2012, Ahn was posthumously inducted into the International Civil Rights Walk of Fame at the Martin Luther King Jr. National Historic Site in Atlanta, Georgia. His grandson Philip Cuddy accepted the honor at the ceremony in Atlanta on behalf of Dosan.

November 8, 2013 Dosan was given an Honorary Diploma by his alma mater Yonsei University in recognition of his service as teaching assistant at Gusae Hakdang and for his work at Jejungwon and Severance Hospital. Dosan was also a good influence on many Yonsei and Severance Medical School alumni. Susan Cuddy's son, Philip Cuddy, initiated the awarding of the honorary diploma providing the historical records to Yonsei President accepted the diploma in a ceremony in Seoul on behalf of Dosan.

AN JUNG-GEUN
The Patriot, Assassin, Hero
(September 2, 1879 – March 26, 1910)

An Jung-geun (hangul:안중근 hanja:安重根 Korean pronunciation:[andʑuŋɡɯn];Bapti smal name: Thomas) was a Korean independence activist,[1][2][3] nationalist,[4][5] and pan-Asianist.[6][7]

On October 26, 1909, he assassinated Itō Hirobumi, a four-time Prime Minister of Japan and former Resident-General of Korea, following the signing of the Eulsa Treaty, with Korea on the verge of annexation by Japan.[8] Ahn was posthumously awarded the Order of Merit for National Foundation in 1962 by the South Korean government, the most prestigious civil decoration in the Republic of Korea, for his efforts for Korean independence.[9]

Biography

Early accounts

Ahn was born on September 2, 1879, in Haeju, Hwanghae-do, the first son of Ahn Tae-Hun (안태훈;安泰勳) and Baek Cheon-Jo (백천조;白川趙), of the family of the Sunheung Ahn (순흥안씨;順興安氏) lineage. His childhood name was Ahn Eung-chil (안 응칠;安應七;[anuŋteʰil]). As a boy, he learned Chinese literature and Western sciences, but was more interested in martial arts and marksmanship. Kim Gu (김구;金九), future leader of the Korean independence movement who had taken refuge in Ahn Tae-Hun's house at the time, wrote that young Ahn Jung-Geun was an excellent marksman, liked to read books, and had strong charisma.[10]

At the age of 25, he started a coal business, but devoted himself to education of Korean people after the Eulsa Treaty by establishing private schools in northwestern regions of Korea. In 1907 he exiled himself to Vladivostok to join in with the armed resistance against the Japanese colonial rulers. He was appointed a lieutenant general of an armed Korean resistance group and led several attacks against Japanese forces before his eventual defeat.

Religion
At the age of 16, Ahn entered the Catholic Church with his father, where he received his baptismal name "Thomas" (토마스), and learned French. While fleeing from the Japanese, Ahn took refuge with a French priest of the Catholic Church in Korea named Wilhelm (Korean name, Hong Seok-ku;홍석구;洪錫九) who baptized and hid him in his church for several months. The priest encouraged Ahn to read the Bible and had a series of discussions with him. He maintained his belief in Catholicism until his death, going to the point of even asking his son to become a priest in his last letter to his wife.[11]

Assassination of Ito Hirobumi

In October 1909, Ahn passed the Imperial Japanese guards at the Harbin Railway Station. Ito Hirobumi had come back from negotiating with the Russian representative on the train. Ahn shot Ito three times with an FN M1900 pistol on the railway platform. He also shot Kawagami Toshihiko (川上俊彦), the Japanese Consul General, Morita Jiro (森泰二郎), a Secretary of Imperial Household Agency, and Tanaka Seitaro (田中淸太郎), an executive of South Manchuria Railway, who were seriously injured. After the shooting,

Ahn yelled out for Korean independence in Russian, stating "Корея! Ура!", and waving the Korean flag.

Afterwards, Ahn was arrested by Russian guards who held him for two days before turning him over to Japanese colonial authorities. When he heard the news that Ito had died, he made the sign of the cross in gratitude. Ahn was quoted as saying, "I have ventured to commit a serious crime, offering my life for my country. This is the behavior of a noble-minded patriot."[11] Despite the orders from the Bishop of Korea not to administer the Sacraments to Ahn, Fr. Wilhelm disobeyed and went to Ahn to give the Last Sacraments. Ahn insisted that the captors call him by his baptismal name, Thomas.

In the court, Ahn insisted that he be treated as a prisoner of war, as a lieutenant general of the Korean resistance army, instead of a criminal, and listed 15 crimes Ito had committed which convinced him to kill Ito.[12]

"15 reasons why Ito Hirobumi should be killed.

1. Assassinating the Korean Empress Myeongseong
2. Dethroning the Emperor Gojong
3. Forcing 14 unequal treaties on Korea.[13]
4. Massacring innocent Koreans
5. Usurping the authority of the Korean government by force
6. Plundering Korean railroads, mines, forests, and rivers
7. Forcing the use of Japanese banknotes
8. Disbanding the Korean armed forces
9. Obstructing the education of Koreans
10. Banning Koreans from studying abroad
11. Confiscating and burning Korean textbooks
12. Spreading a rumor around the world that Koreans wanted Japanese protection
13. Deceiving the Japanese Emperor by saying that the relationship between Korea and Japan was peaceful when in truth it was full of hostility and conflicts
14. Breaking the peace of Asia
15. Assassinating the Emperor Komei.[14]

I, as a lieutenant general of the Korean resistance army, killed the criminal Ito Hirobumi because he disturbed the peace of the Orient and estranged the relationship between Korea and Japan. I hoped that if Korea and Japan be friendlier and are ruled peacefully, they would be a model all throughout the five continents. I did not kill Ito misunderstanding his intentions."

Imprisonment and death

Ahn's Japanese captors showed sympathy to him. He recorded in his autobiography that the public prosecutor, Mizobuchi Takao, exclaimed "From what you have told me, it is clear that you are a righteous man of East Asia. I can't believe a sentence of death will be imposed on a righteous man. There's nothing to worry about." He was also given New Year's delicacies and his calligraphy was highly admired and requested.[11] After six trials, Ahn was sentenced to death by the Japanese colonial court in Ryojun (Port Arthur).

Ahn was angered at the sentence, though he expected it.[11] He had hoped to be viewed as a prisoner of war instead of an assassin.[11] On the same day of sentencing at two o'clock in the afternoon, his two brothers Jeong-Geun and Gong-Geun met with him to deliver their mother's message, "Your death is for the sake of your country, and don't ask for your life cowardly. Your brave death for justice is a final filial regards to your mother." [15]

Judge Hirashi, who presided over Ahn's trial, had promised Ahn that a stay of execution for at least a few months would be granted, but Tokyo ordered prompt action. Prior to his execution, Ahn made two final requests;that the wardens help him finish his essay, "On Peace in East Asia", and for a set of white silk Korean clothes to die in. The warden was able to grant the second request and resigned shortly afterwards. Ahn requested to be executed as a prisoner of war, by firing squad. But instead it was ordered that he should be hanged as a common criminal. The execution took place in Ryojun, on March 26, 1910. His grave in Lu Shun has not been found.[16]

Views

Some historians hold that Itō's death resulted in the acceleration of the final stage of the colonization process,[11] but the claim has been disputed by some.[17]

According to Donald Keene, author of Emperor of Japan: Meiji and His World, 1852–1912, Ahn Jung-Geun was an admirer of Emperor Meiji of Imperial Japan.[11] One of the 15 'charges' Ahn leveled against Ito was that he had deceived the Emperor of Japan, whom Ahn felt desired peace in East Asia and Korean independence. Ahn requested that Meiji be informed of his reasons for his assassination of Ito in the hopes that if Meiji understood his reasons, the emperor would realize how mistaken Ito's policies were and would rejoice. Ahn also felt sure that most Japanese felt similar hatred for Ito, an opinion he formed from talking with Japanese prisoners in Korea.[11] While Ahn was staying in the prison and on the trial, many Japanese prison guards, lawyers and even prosecutors were inspired by Ahn's great spirit, righteousness, and humanity.[18]

Taegukgi by Ahn Jung-geun longing for the Independence of Korea

Legacy

The assassination of Ito by Ahn was praised by Koreans and many Chinese as well, who were struggling against Japanese invasion at the time. Well-known Chinese political leaders such as Yuan Shikai, Sun Yat-sen, and Liang Qichao wrote poems acclaiming An.[19]

In the 2010 Ahn Jung-Geun Symposium in Korea, Wada Haruki (和田春樹), an activist who once worked at Tokyo University, evaluated Ahn by quoting Ito Yukio (伊藤之雄), a fellow history scholar in Kyoto University.[20] In his text published in 2009, Ito Yukio claims that the reign by Ito Hirobumi resulted in strong resistance from Koreans as it was considered the first step for annexation of Korea due to the cultural differences, and that Ahn is not to be blamed even if he assassinated Ito without understanding Ito's ideology (2009, Ito).

On March 26, 2010, a nationwide centenary tribute to Ahn was held in South Korea, including a ceremony led by the Prime Minister Chung Un-Chan and tribute concerts.

Ancestry

Ahn's family produced many other Korean independence activists. Ahn's cousin An My-eong-Geun (안명근;安明根) attempted to assassinate Terauchi Masatake, the first Japanese Governor-General of Korea (조선총독;朝鮮總督) who executed the Japan-Korea Annexation Treaty in 1910. He failed, however, and was imprisoned for 15 years;he died in 1926. Ahn's brothers Ahn Jeong-Geun (안정근;安定根) and Ahn Gong-Geun (안공근;安恭根), as well as Ahn's cousin Ahn Gyeong-Geun (안경근;安敬根) and nephew Ahn Woo-Saeng (안우생;安偶生), joined the Provisional Government of the Republic of Korea in Shanghai, China, which led by Kim Gu, and fought against Japan. Ahn Chun-Saeng (안춘생;安春生), another nephew of Ahn's, joined the National Revolutionary Army of China, participated in battles against Japanese forces at Shanghai, and joined the Korean Liberation Army in 1940. Later, he became a lieutenant general of the Republic of Korea Army and a member of the National Assembly of South Korea.

Pan-Asianism

Ahn strongly believed in the union of the three great countries in East Asia, China, Korea, and Japan in order to counter and fight off the "White Peril", namely, the European countries engaged in colonialism, and restore peace to East Asia. He followed the progress of Japan during the Russo-Japanese War and claimed that he and his compatriots were delighted at hearing of the defeat of one of the agents of the White Peril, but were disappointed that the war ended before Russia was totally subjugated.

Ahn felt that with the death of Itō, Japan and Korea could become friends because of the many traditions that they shared. He hoped that this friendship, along with China, would become a model for the world to follow. His thoughts on Pan-Asianism were stated in his essay, "On Peace in East Asia" (東洋平和論;동양평화론) that he worked on and left unfinished before his execution.[11][21] In this work, Ahn recommends the organization of combined armed forces and the issue of joint banknotes among Korea, Japan, and China. Sasagawa Norikatsu (笹川紀勝), a Professor of Law at Meiji University, highly praises Ahn's idea as an equivalent of the European Union and a concept that preceded the concept of United Nations by 10 years.[22]

Calligraphic works

Ahn is highly renowned for calligraphy works. While he was in prison, many prison guards such as Chiba Toshichi (千葉十七) who respected him, made requests to Ahn for calligraphy works.[18] He left many calligraphy works which were written in the jail of Lushun although he hadn't studied calligraphy formally. He would leave on his calligraphy works a signature of "大韓國人" (Great Korean) and a handprint of his left hand

171

"Unless reading
everyday, thorns grow
in the mouth."

that was missing the last joint of the ring finger, which he had cut off with his comrades in 1909 as a pledge to kill Ito. Some of the works were designated as Treasure No. 569 of the Republic of Korea in 1972.[23] One of his famous works is "一日不讀書口中生荊棘" (일일부독서 구중생형극;Unless one reads every day, thorns grow in the mouth), a quote from the Analects of

Confucius.Memorial Halls

Memorial halls for Ahn were erected in Seoul in 1970 by the South Korean government and in Harbin by the Chinese government in 2006.[24] South Korean President Park Geun-Hye raised the idea of erecting a monument for Ahn while meeting with Chinese President Xi Jinping during a visit to China in June 2013. Thus another memorial hall honoring Ahn Jung-Geun was opened on Sunday, 19 January 2014 in Harbin. The hall, a 200-square meter room, features photos and memorabilia.[25]

According to local sources in China dated on 22 March 2017, the Ahn Jung-geun Memorial Hall located at Harbin Railway Station was recently relocated to a Korean art museum in Harbin City amid China's retaliation over South Korea's deployment of the U.S. THAAD antimissile system.[26]

Controversies

Historically, the Japanese government has generally deemed Ahn Jung-geun as a terrorist and criminal, while South Korea has upheld Ahn as a national hero. In January 2014, Yoshihide Suga, a Japanese government spokesman, described the Harbin memorial hall in China as "not conducive to building peace and stability" between East Asian countries.[27] China, on the other hand, "said that Ahn was a 'famous anti-Japanese high-minded person,'" while "South Korea's foreign ministry said Ahn was a 'highly respected figure.'"

In February 2017, South Korean police were criticized for using a picture of Ahn in posters put up in the city of Incheon.[28] The poster warned of terrorism, and many South Korean citizens online criticized the police, asking "if it was meant to imply if Ahn was a terrorist." A police officer in the Korea Times apologized and clarified that there was no intention to associate Ahn with terrorism, and all posters were taken down.

In popular culture

The North Korean film An Jung Gun Shoots Ito Hirobumi is a dramatized story of the event.[29] The South Korean film Thomas An Jung-geun (토마스 안중근) is another dramatized story of the event.[30] Released on September 10, 2004, it is directed by Seo Se-won. Ahn Jung-Geun is played by actor Yu Oh-seong and Ito Hirobumi is played by Yoon Joo-sang.

SHIN CHAE-HO
Founder of Korean Ethnic Nationalist Historiography
(1880–1936)

Shin Chae-ho (신채호;申采浩) was a Korean independence activist, historian, anarchist, nationalist, and a founder of Korean ethnic nationalist historiography (민족사학 minjok sahak;sometimes shortened to minjok).[2]:7[3]:27[4]:52 He is held in high esteem in both North[5]:112–3 and South Korea.[6]:26–7 Two of his works, A New Reading of History (Doksa Sillon), written in 1908, and The Early History of Joseon (Joseon Sanggosa), published in 1931, are considered key works of nationalist historiography in modern Korea.[7]:445 He argued that modern Koreans and the people of Manchuria were of a single race which has an ancestral claim to both Korea and Manchuria,[6]:26[8]:3 Shin also studied Korean mythology.[4]:53 During his exile in China, Shin joined the Eastern Anarchist Association and wrote anti-imperialist and pro-independence articles in various outlets;his anarchist activities lead to his arrest and subsequent death in prison, February 21, 1936.[7]:447[9]:128

Biography

Early years

Shin was born on November 7, 1880. His grandfather was an official in the royal advisory department. His pen name was "Dansaeng", which he later changed to "Danjae". Shin was taught various Neo-Confucian books and concepts by his grandfather, and later enrolled in the Confucian academy Seonggyungwan,[7]:441–2 receiving a doctoral degree in 1905.[10] Shin, to a limited capacity, read Italian literature and history and published some Italian-related works;There is some speculation that Dante might be an influence on Shin Chae-ho's work, in particular Dream Sky (1916).[11]:313

Shin went on to work for the editorial boards for two newspapers, the Hwangseong Shin-mun and the Daehan Maeil Shinbo, and became the leader of the underground "patriotic enlightenment" group, the Sinminhoe.[7]:443 His group would later migrate to Manchuria in 1910[8]:3 and attract such radicals as Yi Tong-hwi, a Korean Bolshevik who participated in "The Conspiracy case of 1911,"[12]:6–7 which was an effort to assassinate Japanese Governor-General Terauchi, leading to the arrests of several Sinminhoe members and eventually the dissolution of the Sinminhoe.[13]:46

Abroad

Shin went into voluntary exile in 1910 when Japan declared its annexation of Korea;he then traveled to Vladisvostok, then throughout China.[7]:444–5 Shin never returned to Korea,[6]:27 and since he refused to file for citizenship with the Empire of Japan he became stateless.[1] Shin avoided politicized organizations until the March First Independence Movement, in 1919, which spurred him to join the Korean Provisional Government in Shanghai.[7]:445 Shin quickly became frustrated with the Provisional Government,[9]:123–4 culminating in a clash with interim leader Syngman Rhee (I Seung-man) and Shin leaving to embrace anarchism[14]:34 and draft the "Declaration of Korean Revolution" for the Righteous Brotherhood (Uiyeoldan) in 1923.[7]:445 Shin went on to join the Eastern Anarchist Association (동방무정부주의연맹;東方無政府主義聯盟) in 1926.[7]:446

174

Arrest and death

Shin was arrested by the Japanese Military Police in Taiwan in May 1928 for the attempted smuggling of 12,000 yuan in forged banknotes out of Taiwan under the pseudonym "Yu Byeong-taek" (유병택;柳炳澤) in an effort to help fund the Eastern Anarchist Association's general activities and bomb factory.[7]:446 He was sentenced to a 10-year prison term by the Dalian District Court to be served in Lüshun Prison.[15] Shin died while in solitary confinement at Lüshun Prison of a brain hemorrhage on the 21st of February, 1936.[15][16]:156[7]:447 The Republic of Korea posthumously awarded Shin with the "Presidential Order of Merit for National Foundation" in 1962 and citizenship on April 13, 2013.[1]

Thought

The Minjok and Korean Ethnic Nationalism

Shin Chae-ho wrote extensively on a theory of ethnic history which sought to challenge tShin Chae-ho wrote extensively on a theory of ethnic history which sought to challenge traditional border concepts in Korea and encourage Korean nationalism. This theory is broadly referred to as the Korean minjok (민족;民族);[17]:188 An early form of the minjok is found in his article "New History Reader."[18]:6–7 Shin's minjok works contested the traditional conception of Korea as a geographically defined "peninsular nation" (반도국;pandoguk), which was born out of politics associated with the Mandate of Heaven in classical Chinese political philosophy.[6]:29 This Chinese hegemony was interpreted as Sinocentric by Shin, and others, as it placed border control in the hands of the Chinese Court.[3]:27[6]:29–30

Shin's minjok historiographical work traced a nation's history by its racial genealogy and lineage, relying on heritable race and culture.[19]:16 The minjok was defined by the terms of its history, and history was shaped by the minjok, hence these two concepts were reciprocal and inseparable. For Shin, "if one dismisses the minjok, there is no history";to ignore or to down-play the minjok was to devitalize history itself.[6]:32

Within the greater minjok history of a nation there was a host race, the chujok (주족);the identification of the chujok was necessary for tracing the authentic history of a nation, and solidified an ethnocentric national history. For Korea, the chujok was the ancient Korean-Manchurian Kingdom of the Buyeo (부여;夫餘),[6]:32 which, by Shin's estimate, began 5,000 years ago with the birth of Dangun, the legendary son of a bear who was transformed into a human by the god Whanin.[19]:16 By combining mythology and genealogy, a common ancestry of Koreans and Manchurians was traced, effectively making them family.[6]:33 Shin thereby attempted to erase the geographical border between Korea and Manchuria in favour of ethnic re-unification.[17]:231

Distinct from the minjok was the state, the gukga (국가;國家;or kukka). The minjok as a more basal concept than the gukga and did not substantially change between generations, whereas the gukga could change between kingdoms, government, and rules.[6]:40

By defining the minjok as a rich and powerful ethnic history, Shin constructed an anti-

175

imperialism and anti-colonialism social defence. Largely, the goal was rejection of both Chinese and Japanese governmental oversight and influence.[6]:42 Contemporaneous Japanese historians also argued that Koreans and Manchurians were the same group, but their efforts were to prove Korea was historically indistinct from other nations and thus mitigate Korea's importance.[6]:30

Social Darwinism

Shin is sometimes called a social Darwinist, a popular concept in the early 20th century. Within Shin's work, the Manchurian-Korean Buyeo minjok is interpreted as the standard of measure for historical progress in Korea.[6]:34 Shin described a racial history of conflict between the various races of East Asia, as well as a political history. Towards this progress, Shin's minjok project was laid out in terms of racial victories: specifically for the Buyeo, victory would be complete reunification of the race and then-on defending against cultural assimilation and imperialism.[6]:35

This "Darwinian-Spencerian" framework, which prized ethnic nationalism and purity, allowed Shin to write a race-centred history of Korea that attempted to shut down the Japanese colonial justifications by conjoining ethnic history and progress, necessarily making harmful the adulteration of Korean society with Japanese culture, not a progressive one. [17]:34–5 This is somewhat analogous to Nordicism, or progressivist ethnography, but from a Korean-centric perspective.

Shin did not describe Korea as the "victor" of these racial battles. Shin described a slow fall of the minjok, primarily attributing a high point to King Muyeol of Silla, and then descent through the fall of Barhae and slow fracturing of Korean social unity through politics and war. Shin praised the Koryeo and Choseon dynasties, but insisted that the successes that they brought were only partial, lamenting that if scholars "are searching for a full unification, it cannot be found after Tangun."[6]:35–6

Juche

Shin Chae-ho is often credited as the primary source in the Juche (주체;主體: meaning Self-reliance or Autonomy;sometimes spelt Chuch'e) political ideology. Juche aspires towards a country's complete autonomy, both in a national sense and in an historical sense.[19]:5 However, it is not clear whether the North Korean Juche is modelled upon or is merely similar to Shin's Juche.[17]:270–2 Scholars such as Sheila Miyoshi Jager have written that strong references about the history of North Korean ideology are uncommon, but similarities in language, symbolism, and the concepts make Shin Chae-ho a good candidate as an influence on Kim Il Sung and his own Juche state ideology.[19]:5 Shin's Juche concept is also specifically Korean;however it bears a likeness to Japanese Kokutai (Kukche).[20]:135

Anarchism

Shin Chae-ho's anarchist philosophy is largely ignored by contemporary Korean scholars. [17]:272 One of his later works, The Dream Sky, is considered one of these anarchist-themed works, and explores themes of "clear understanding," an individual's "own way",

176

and praises "human struggle" as a righteous path. The book also challenged literary standards by ending on an ellipsis and breaking historical continuity by borrowing characters from Korean history.[11]:324–5

Legacy

In South Korea, after the emancipation from Japan, Shin was not considered an important author. The term minjok was decried as politically unacceptable by Shin's old acquaintance from the Provisional Government, and now the first president of South Korea, Syngman Rhee. The new South Korean government favoured the term kukka, which implied loyalty to the Republic of Korea, over Shin's minjok. In the 1960s, Rhee's political reKime ended and anti-imperialism sentiments redoubled, followed by scholars pursuing a new autonomous history of Korea, and revived the term minjok. By 1908, Shin Chae-ho had become a powerful figure in Korean historiography, but concepts like minjok, among others, are interpreted in ways that favour the South Korean Government over the North's.[6]:40–1

The Park military reKime in South Korea pushed for capitalist economic development, noting that dismantling the North Korean communist state would do the minjok saengjon good. Following nationalist trends, some South Korean Minjung movements made appeals to national self-reliance (민족정체성 minjok juchesung).[21]:442–3

North Korea also sponsored re-reading Shin, among other Korean authors. In the Democratic People's Republic of Korea, Kim Il Sung is said to be the leader of the minjok, and follows similar genealogical tracings of Koreans into ancient Korean-Manchuria. [6]:39–40[17]:271

Shin Chae-ho is held in high esteem by North Korea[5]:112–3 and made a lasting impact on the Korean perception of Japan and imperialism generally.[3]:27 Two of his works, Doksa Sillon ("A New Reading of History"), written in 1908, and Joseon Sanggosa ("The Early History of Joseon"), published in 1931, are particularly important in the nationalist historiography of modern Korea.[7]:446[8]:3

A consequence of Shin's nationalistic thought might be the discouragement of the Korean diaspora – the closer a Korean was to Korean soil the closer they were to their cultural "space." For Shin, space, culture, and patriotism became inseparable.[17]:239 A worry of some Koreans is their ethno-cultural continuation, and the loss of "Korean-ness" as Koreans either travel abroad or adopt foreign customs.[22]

Criticism

Standards of education

Shin Chae-ho's high standards of education and early enrollment of children in school (at age 4) were criticized as excessive. He responded that some four-year-olds already knew the first one thousand characters in Chinese and that some had already begun the Children's First Learning Programme (Dongmong seonseup). He also argued that historical standards of education were steeper than the contemporary standards.[7]:453 All the while, Shin believed all Korean citizens should learn both Hangeul and Hanja to aid in preserving Korean identity, rather than subject themselves to the Chinese language system, and to study Korean patriotic literature.[7]:458–9

Concerns with Minjok thought

As part of the minjok historiography, Shin rebuked some scholars for focusing too much on geography and borders rather than minjok ethnic boundaries;he called these scholars "territorial historians". However, his own works consistently employed territorial terms, boundaries, borders that only differ by how Shin justified them by a very ancient Korea, while the "territorial historians'" terms are usually traced to younger Chinese courts. This is aggravated by the fact that Shin had few, if any, compelling references for his historical claims, making his boundaries largely arbitrary or folk-history based.[6]:31
Dream Sky borrowed from Dante's Divine Comedy
Shin Chae-ho's Dream Sky at times resembles Dante's Divine Comedy. If Shin had knowingly presented a Korean-ized Divine Comedy as an authentic work of Korean fiction, it would be an adulteration of the minjok historiography project by Shin's own standards of ethno-cultural autonomy. Whether or not Shin even read Dante's Divine Comedy is purely speculative.[11]:313

YU GWAN-SUN
The Martyr of The Korean
Independence Movement
(December 16, 1902 – September 28, 1920)

Yoo Gwansun, also known as Yoo Kwan-soon (hangul:유관순 hanja:柳寬順), was an organizer in what would come to be known as the March 1st Movement against Imperial Japanese colonial rule of Korea in South Chungcheong.[1] The March 1st Movement was considered a peaceful demonstration by the Korean people against Japanese rule. Yoo Gwansun became one of the most well-known participants in this movement, and eventually, a symbol of Korea's fight for independence.

Early life and education

Yoo Gwansun was born in Cheonan, in the South Chungcheong Province of Korea on November 17, 1902. From early childhood, Gwansun's father encouraged her to develop a strong devotion to God and Korean national pride. She was considered an intelligent child and would memorize Bible passages upon hearing them only once. One of her teachers, named Alice Sharp, referred her to the Ewha Womans University in Seoul, known today as Ewha University. She was able to attend the school through a scholarship program that required recipients to work as a teacher after graduation. In 1919, while she was a student at the University's high school, she witnessed the beginnings of the March First Movement. Gwansun, along with a five-person group, took part in the movement and participated in demonstrations in Seoul. On March 10, 1919,all of the schools, including [2] the Ewha Women's School, were temporarily closed by the governor-general of Korea, and Gwansun returned home to Cheonan.[3]

Political Activism

Independence Demonstration

On March 1, 1919, Seoul was overflowing with marches by people from around the country protesting Japanese involvement in Korea. Gwansun left Seoul after the Japanese government ordered all Korean schools to close response to the ongoing independence protests. She returned to her home in Jiryeong-ri (now Yongdu-ri) and, while there, took a more active role in the protest movement.[4][5][6]

Aunae Market Demonstration and Arrest

Along with her family, Gwansun began to encourage public resentment against the Japanese occupation. She visited churches to tell others of the demonstrations in Seoul, and she planned an independence demonstration with Cho In-won and Kim Goo-Eung. This included people from neighboring towns, including Yeongi, Chungju, Cheonan and Jincheon. The demonstration took place on April 1, 1919, in Aunae Marketplace at 9:00 a.m.. About 3,000 demonstrators participated,[2] shouting, *"Long Live Korean Independence!"* ("대한독립만세"). By 1:00 p.m, the Japanese police responded by arresting Yoo and several other demonstrators. Chaos ensued and shots were fired killing both of Gwansun's parents and injuring Jo In-Won. As a result of the Aunae Marketplace demonstration, there were nineteen casualties and thirty others were injured by the Japanese Military.[2]

The Japanese police offered Gwansun a lighter sentence in exchange her admission of guilt and cooperation in finding the other protest collaborators. However, she refused to reveal the identity or whereabouts of any of her collaborators even after being tortured.[7]

Imprisonment and Utterance

After Gwansun's arrest, she was initially detained at the Cheonan Japanese Military Police Station then transferred to the Gongju Police Station prison. At her trial, Gwansun argued the proceedings were controlled by the Japanese colonial administration, the law of the governor-general of Korea, and was overseen by an assigned Japanese judge. Despite her attempts to obtain what she believed was a fair trial, Gwansun received a guilty verdict on counts of sedition and security law violations and was sentenced to five years imprisonment at Seodaemun Prison. During her imprisonment, Gwansun continued to support the Korean independence movement which caused her to be punished a number of times by Japanese prison officers.

On March 1, 1920, Gwansun prepared a massive demonstration with her fellow inmates in honor of the first anniversary of the March 1st Independence Movement.[2] Because of her continuing protest activities, Gwansun was then taken to a different, underground prison [2] and died three months before her release on September 28, 1920, the result of complications due to the torture and beatings she received.[8] According to records discovered in November 2011, of the 45,000 who were arrested in relation to the protests during that period, 7,500 died at the hands of the Japanese authorities.[9][10]

After Death

Japanese prison officials initially refused to release Gwansun's body in an attempt to hide the evidence of torture. Authorities eventually released her body in a Saucony Vacuum Company oil crate due to threats made by Lulu Frey and Jeannette Walter, the principals of Gwansun's former school, who voiced their suspicions of torture to the public. Walter, who dressed Gwansun for her funeral proceedings, later assured the public in 1959 that her body had not been cut into pieces as had been alleged.[11] On October 14, 1920, Yoo Gwansun's funeral was held at the Jung-dong Church by Minister Kim Jong-wu and her body was buried in the public Itaewon cemetery, which was eventually destroyed. After Korea gained independence, a shrine was built in honor of Yoo Gwansun with the cooperation of South Chungcheong and Cheonan.[12]

Legacy

Gwansun became known as Korea's "Joan of Arc" and was posthumously awarded the Order of Independence Merit in 1962.[13] While the March 1st Movement did not immediately gain freedom for Korea, the Japanese colonial government soon implemented more lenient political controls. Because she did not abandon her convictions, even after her arrest, Gwansun became a symbol of the Korean fight for independence through her unrelenting protests and resistance.[14]

SOHN KEE-CHUNG
Korea's First Olympic Gold Medalist
(August 29, 1912 – November 15, 2002)

Sohn Kee-chung(손기정;孫基禎) was a Korean athlete and long-distance runner. He became the first Korean to medal at the Olympic Games, winning gold in the marathon at the 1936 Berlin Olympics as a member of the Japanese delegation.[1]

Sohn competed under the Japanese name Son Kitei, as Korea was part of the Japanese Empire during his career.[1]

Early life

Sohn Kee-chung at the 1936 Olympics

Sohn Kee-chung was born in what is now Sinuiju, North P'yŏngan Province, North Korea, which occupied by Japan at the time. He studied at Yangjeong High School in Seoul and Meiji University in Tokyo, where he graduated in 1940.

Athletics career

Sohn first competed in the 1,500 and 5,000 m, but turned to longer distances after winning an eight-mile race in October 1933. Between 1933 and 1936, he ran 12 marathons;he finished in the top three on all occasions and won nine.[1] On November 3, 1935 in Tokyo, Japan, Sohn set a world record in the marathon with a time of 2:26:42. [2][3] According to the International Association of Athletics Federations, this record remained unbroken until Sohn's own trainee, Suh Yun-Bok, won the 1947 Boston Marathon.[2][4]

1936 Berlin Olympics

Sohn, competing for the Empire of Japan, won the gold medal at the 1936 Summer Olympics in the marathon. He ran the 42.195 kilometres (26.219 mi) course in 2:29:19.2, breaking the Olympic record. His Korean teammate Nam Sung-yong took the bronze medal. As Korea was under Japanese occupation at the time, the International Olympic Committee (IOC) officially credited Japan with Sohn's gold and Nam's bronze in the 1936 Summer Olympics medal count.

On December 9, 2011, the IOC recognized Sohn's Korean nationality in his official profile. It cited his efforts to sign his Korean name and stressing Korea's status as a separate nation during interviews. The move was part of the Korean Olympic Committee's repeated requests to acknowledge Sohn's background. However, the IOC ruled out changing the nationality and registered name per official records to prevent historical distortions.[5]

Political significance

Under orders from Tokyo, Sohn Kee-chung had to compete using the Latin alphabet name of Son Kitei. It is the romanization of Japanese pronunciation of 孫基禎, his Ko-

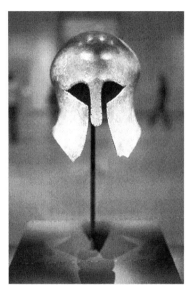

The Corinthian helmet that was awarded to Sohn Kee-chung, on display at the National Museum of Korea.

rean name in hanja.[6]

Sohn refused to acknowledge the Japanese anthem while it was played at his award ceremony and later told reporters that he was ashamed to run for Japan. [3] When the Dong-a Ilbo published a photograph of Sohn at the medal ceremony, it altered the image to remove the Japanese flag from his running tunic. The act enraged the Japanese Governor-General of Korea Minami Jiro in Seoul. The Kempetai military police imprisoned eight people connected with the newspaper and suspended its publication for nine months. [7][8]

Hellenic prize

For winning the marathon, Sohn was to have received an ancient Corinthian helmet (circa BCE 800–700), which was discovered at Olympia, Greece, and later purchased by a newspaper in Athens to give as an Olympic award. However, the IOC believed that presenting such a valuable gift to a runner would violate its amateur rules. The helmet was placed in a Berlin museum where it remained for fifty years. It was finally presented to Sohn in 1986.[9][10] On March 7, 1987, the helmet was categorised as the 904th treasure of South Korea. There was initially a plan to award replicas of this helmet to the winners of the 2006 Sohn Kee-chung marathon,[11] but winners got only chance to wear that replica.[12]

Later life

Sohn spent the remainder of his career in South Korea coaching other notable runners such as Suh Yun-Bok, the winner of the Boston Marathon in 1947;[1] Ham Kee-Yong, winner of the Boston Marathon in 1950;and Hwang Young-Cho, who was the gold medalist of the 1992 Summer Olympics marathon, and whom Sohn Kee-chung especially went to Barcelona to see. Sohn also became the Chairman of the Korean Sporting Association. At the 1988 Summer Olympics in Seoul, he was given the honor of carrying the Olympic torch into the stadium at the opening ceremony.[1][13]

Sohn authored an autobiography entitled My Motherland and Marathon (나의조국과 마라톤).

He was honoured with the Korean Order of Civil Merit (국민훈장).

Death and legacy

Sohn died at midnight on November 15, 2002, at age 90 from pneumonia. He was buried at the Daejeon National Cemetery. The Sohn Kee-chung Memorial Park in Seoul was

184

established in his honor.[13] He was also posthumously made a Grand Cordon (Blue Dragon) of the Order of Sport Merit.

In popular culture

The historical Korean drama Bridal Mask referenced Sohn Kee-chung's Olympic win and the subsequent arrest of Korean journalists in its twenty-first episode.[14] In a parade scene, spectators waved Japanese flags to a Korean boxer parading through on a jeep. Despite the joyous occasion, the boxer's face remained staid, never smiling, with the Japanese flag put onto his shirt. The boxer recently won an international sports title, a first for a Korean. However, due to the Japanese occupation, the boxer represented Japan, rather than Korea, and the Empire of Japan claimed that victory.

As the parade continued, suddenly, spectators unveiled their Korean flags, which they got the night before, waved them, and shouted for Korea. In solidarity with the crowd, the boxer then ripped the Japanese flag from his shirt. With tearful eyes and a determined face, he raised his fists and repeatedly cheered with the crowd, "Manseh!", a pro-Korean independence slogan.

Reporter Song took a picture of this emotional scene. The picture appeared in the newspaper's front page the next day, and government officials learned about this incident. The picture also angered Kimura, a high-ranking police officer. At the police station, he ordered officers to arrest the boxer and punish him harshly for disrespecting Japan. Consequently, the police arrested him and the journalists, and the government closed the newspaper.

LEE JUNG-SEOB
The Master of Korean Modern Painting
(April 10, 1916 - September 6, 1956)

Lee Jung Seob (Seop) (이중섭:李仲燮)was born in 1956 to a rich family in the now North Korea region of Pyeongwon, South Pyeongan Province. He studied in Pyeong-yang, Jeongju (situated in North Pyeongan Province in North Korea) and Tokyo. During the Japanese colonial period, he started his career as an artist. He went back to Wonsan, South Hamgyeong Province (North Korea) and remained here until Korea got back its independence in the year 1945. During the Korean War of 1950 to 1953 he sought refuge from the war in Busan and Jeju Island. He still kept on moving from one place to another even after the end of the war; he moved around Tongyeong, Seoul, and Daegu. Lee died in 1956 at 41 years of age. Despite where he was located or the terrible conditions of life, Lee insistently carried on with his strong interest in artistry.

Despite living during the most unstable times in the Korean history characterized by colonial administration, warfare and disunity, Lee maintained his way of living and continued using his artistic skills to convey his thoughts and feelings. Even through the colonial administration when the Japanese suppressed any symbols of Korean culture and customs, Lee fearlessly created bull paintings; a long-established representation of the people of Korea. In spite of the prevailing conditions at the time such as poverty, imper-manence and war he still created paintings that made people happy despite the hardships, demonstrating the cheer and happiness of his childhood days.

In the aftermath of the warfare he focused on bull painting inculcated with energy that proclaimed his determination and belief. Most importantly Lee strived to truly and hon-estly convey his emotions in his works of art. Additionally he desired to represent the Ko-rean people by actualizing the traditional principles of art of Korea as a country. However Lee's life was without a doubt full of misfortune; he got detached from his family, lived his final days in desolate isolation while agonizing from anorexia and mental illness, was swindled of his money and got into debt. As it happens to very many artists, Lee died in isolation and left behind a trail of desolate, sad works of art.

Pyeongwon, Pyeongyang, Jeongju, Tokyo, and Wonsan 1916-50

Lee was born in September 1916 in Pyeongwon, South Pyeongan Province. He went to Jongno Primary School in Pyeongyang; his maternal relatives resided in Pyeongyang . In 1930, he started studying art at Osan High School situated in Jeongju. This school was exclusively funded by the people of Korea it was under the instruction of Im Yongryeon (b. 1901) who was a Yale University graduate. Lee headed to Tokyo in 1936 to further his studies in art at the Imperial Art Institute first and then between 1931 and 1941 he studied at Bunka Gakuin. During the time Lee studied in Tokyo Japan was predominantly conservative; Bunka Gakuin was a private institution and was well known for its liberal mood. During the time that Lee studied at Bunka Gakuin, he joined other senior students who took part in an exposition arranged by the Association of Free Artists (Jiyu bijutsuka kyokai).

Lee's work was applauded by various influential critics; as a result Lee was welcomed to the Association of Free Artists. Later in the year 1941, Lee in conjuction with other Korean artists based in Tokyo such as Lee Qoedee, Jin Hwan, Choi Jaedeok, and Kim Jongchan created the Association of New Artists (Shin bijutsuka kyokai). They organized an exposition in Tokyo and it was honored by those in the field of art.

In 1943, the Pacific War had extended to its apex and Lee went back to Wonsan, Korea to his family. Lee married a Japanese woman he met while studying at Bunka Gakuin, Yamamoto Masako in May 1945 precedent to Korea getting its independence.

Seogwipo and Busan 1950-53

The Korean War broke out in June 1950 and Wonsan was under attack, in December 1950 Lee was forced retreat to Busan. He fled with his wife and their two sons but was unable to bring along his mother and his works of art. As a result none of Lee's work done before the year 1950 was lost. Busan was overcrowded forcing Lee and his family in 1951 to shift to Jeju Island where they lived a poor but contented life. They stayed in Jeju Island for almost a year before going back to Busan in December the same year. In Busan they lived a life of destitution moving from one refugee camp to another until Lee's wife became tired of their condition of living. In July 1952 she left their two sons to Japan and Lee was left behind. Despite all this Lee kept on striving in his work, creating paintings, book covers, magazines and illustrations; he even continued taking part in expositions. Sadly majority of his creations in Busan are not in existent; it is purported that they were damaged by a fire.

Postcard Paintings

Lee and his wife to be Yamamoto Masako met as students at Bunka Gakuin University in Tokyo. Lee remained in Tokyo up till 1953 even after completing his studies; throughout this period his sent his wife to be postcards. Intriguingly these postcards the messages in these postcards were not written; Lee instead created a small scale painting on one of the sides of the postcards and added an address on the other side. Of these postcards Lee sent to Yamamoto, approximately ninety of them are known about a number of them were displayed in the National Museum of Modern and Contemporary Art. The postcard paintings in the beginning are lightly colored and are more dreamlike and astounding. Additionally they are meticulously done with the lines made using carbon paper. With time Lee became more confident in his art and his subsequent paintings displayed more audacity and vigor. We are able to figure out the progression in the relationship between Lee and Yamamoto by observing the transitions in the postcard paintings.

Tinfoil Paintings

Lee in addition came up with new painting methods for instance creating paintings on the tinfoil of cigarette packages. To achieve this he first made small marks on the tinfoil, applied some paint on the tinfoil and finally cleared off the paint; the result is that only

188

the marked lines are painted. Even though the lines are horizontal the images produced appear to have a number of layers credited to the well-marked lines. The shiny surface of the tinfoil further improves the beauty of the painting. This approach remarkably brings back the tradition of decorated Goryeo celadon or metal ware decorated with silver. Evidently Lee held Korean tradition in high regard and for this reason knowingly adopted this style in the tinfoil paintings.

It is alleged that over time Lee created approximately 300 paintings from tinfoil. He used a sharp tool to n the tinfoil; he produced images of his joyous life with his family in Seogwipo, in Jeju Islands as well as images portraying poverty, hardships and misfortunes in the society. Lee stated that the tinfoil paintings were meant to be used as basic sketches for the paintings he intended to produce. In fact he always wanted to produce large paintings in public places so that they could be seen and understood by a lot of people.

Tongyeong 1953-1954

After the Korean War came to an end Lee lectured at the School of Lacquerware inset with Mother-of-pearl in Tongyeong between July 1953 and June 1954. Yu Kangyul (1920-76) a skilled artist who had relocated to North Korea assisted Lee get this lecturing job. Lee used the favourable conditions at Tongyeonga and the general stability in the country to create a significant number of fresh art work. This included his well-known Bull series and the multiple oil paintings of the alluring Tongyeong sceneries. Additionally he developed his career; he held his first ever single exposition and also took part in the Four Young Artists Exhibition.

Letter Paintings

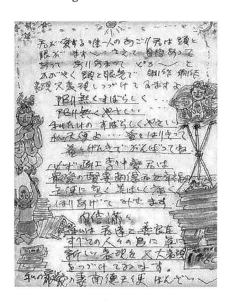 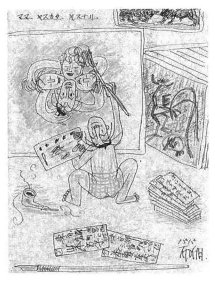

In the thick of havoc during the Korean War, in July 1952 Lee's wife and their two sons escaped to Japan. Lee was left alone and it is during this time that he moved from place to place; in spite of this he always communicated with his family abroad. In the beginning his letters were happy and loving full of anticipation that they would meet and be together again soon. Very many of these letters contained pleasant artworks for his sons and clearly demonstrated his fatherly care and affection. Things changed mid-1955, Lee was driven into desperation and nearly completely stopped communicating with his family and it is also alleged that he also stopped reading letters from his wife. About seventy of these letters making up around 150 pages are still in existence; a number of these letters are exhibited in the national museum. These letters serve as documented records showing the relation between Lee's life and art. Moreover these letters should be regarded as works of art separately since they are depicted by the delightful harmony from the unconstrained handwritten words and the captivating spontaneous artworks.

Seoul 1954-1955

Lee relocated to Seoul while his sons and wife still lived in Japan. He temporarily lived with his friends and allies in Nusang-dong and Sangsu-dong. It is during this period that Lee engaged in a business endeavor; he sold Japanese books at a profit in Korea. He was however defrauded by an intermediary and fell into debt. In January 1955 in an attempt to pay off his debts so that he could get back together with his family, Lee tried to sell his artwork by holding a single exposition at the Gallery of Midopa Department Store which is today Lotte Department Store. He sold about twenty of his artwork during this exposition but never got the money for the sales made; he therefore continued being hugely in debt.

Daegu 1955

After the January 1955 exposition in Seoul, with assistance from Ku Sang (1919-2004) an immediate companion and poet, Lee put up another single exposition in April of the same year. This exhibition was held at the Gallery of the US Information Service in Daegu. The Daegu exhibition was more devastating than that held in Seoul. This highly affected Lee and he went into depression. He harshly berated himself for being unable to provide for his family and for begging for free food, he stopped believing he was a good artist and felt like he was lying to the world about his skills. Lee experienced mental illness and anorexia; he recuperated at Ku Sang's house in the vicinity of Daegu and kept working on his art work.

Jeongneung, Seoul 1956

Beginning in December 1955, Lee frequented a number of hospitals. He later shifted to Jeongneung in Seoul; he temporarily lived with Han Mook (painter, b. 1914), Park Yeonhee (novelist, 1918-2008), and Jo Yeongam (poet, 1920-?). Meanwhile he did some artworks for scholarly magazines and produced his final works of art the River of No Return set being one of them. Unfortunately he got hospitalized again as a result of hepatitis and malnutrition (arising from anorexia). He passed away on September 6, 1956 at Seoul Red Cross Hospital still not united with his family. His associates ordered a tomb and tombstone for him and he was buried at Manguri Public Cemetery in Seoul.

KIM IL-SUNG
The First President of North Korea
(April 15, 1912 – July 8, 1994)

Official portrait, issued after his death in 1994

Kim Il-sung (English: /ˈkɪmˈɪlˈsʌŋ,ˈsʊŋ/;[1] Korean: 김일성, Hanja:金日成 Korean pronunciation: [ki.mil.ʂʌŋ] or [kim.il.ʂʌŋ]; born Kim Sŏng-ju (김성주:金成柱) was the leader of North Korea from its establishment in 1948 until his death in 1994.[2] He held the posts of Premier from 1948 to 1972 and President from 1972 to 1994. He was also the leader of the Workers' Party of Korea (WPK) from 1949 to 1994 (titled as chairman from 1949 to 1966 and as general secretary after 1966). Coming to power after the overthrow of Japanese rule in 1945, he authorized the invasion of South Korea in 1950 triggering a defense of South Korea by the United Nations led by the United States. A cease-fire in the Korean War was signed on 27 July 1953. He was one of the longest-serving non-royal heads of state in the 20th century, in office for more than 45 years.

Under his leadership, North Korea became a workers' state with a publicly owned planned economy. It had close political and economic relations with the Soviet Union. By the 1960s and 1970s, North Korea enjoyed a relatively high standard of living, outper-forming the South, which was riddled with political instability and economic crises.[3][4][5] The situation reversed in the 1980s, as a stable South Korea became an economic powerhouse fueled by Japanese and American investment and military aid, and internal economic development while North Korea stagnated.[6] Differences between North Ko-rea and the Soviet Union made the countries less aligned in world politics, central among these differences being Kim Il-sung's philosophy of Juche, which focused on Korean pa-triotism and self-reliance. Despite this, the country still received funds, subsidies, and aid from the USSR (and the Eastern Bloc) until the latter's dissolution in 1991. The resulting loss of economic aid adversely affected the North's economy. During this period, North Korea also remained critical of United States imperialism, once even seizing the Ameri-can ship USS Pueblo (AGER-2) in 1968.

Kim Il Sung's mass popularity came to dominate domestic politics. At the 6th WPK Con-gress in 1980, his son Kim Jong-il, was elected as Politburo Standing Committee member and his heir to supreme leadership.

Kim Il-sung's birthday is a public holiday in North Korea and is called the "Day of the Sun".

Early life

Controversy about origins

Controversy surrounds Kim's life before the founding of North Korea, with some sources labeling him an impostor. Several sources indicate that the name "Kim Il-sung" had previously been used by a prominent early leader of the Korean resistance, Kim Kyung-cheon.[7]:44 The Soviet officer Grigory Mekler, who worked with Kim during the Soviet occupation, said that Kim assumed this name from a former commander who had died.[8] However, historian Andrei Lankov has argued that this is unlikely to be true. Several witnesses knew Kim before and after his time in the Soviet Union, including his superior, Zhou Baozhong, who dismissed the claim of a "second" Kim in his diaries.[9]:55 His-torian Bruce Cumings pointed out that Japanese officers from the Kwantung Army have attested to his fame as a resistance figure.[10]:160–161 Historians generally accept that, while Kim's exploits were exaggerated by the personality cult that was built around him, he was a significant guerrilla leader.[11][12][13]

Family background

Many North Koreans believe Kim-il-Sung is an "almighty god" who "created the world" in seven days as a divine spirit millions of years ago, and came to Earth as a human in 1912 as a messianic figure.[15][16]:12 He was born to Kim Hyŏng-jik and Kang Pan-sŏk, who gave him the name Kim Sŏng-ju; Kim also had two younger brothers, Ch'ŏl-chu (or Kim Chul Joo) and Kim Yŏng-ju.[16]:15

Kim's family is said to have originated from Jeonju, North Jeolla Province. His great-grandfather, Kim Ung-u, settled in Mangyong-dae in 1860. Kim is reported to have been born in the small village of Mangyungbong (then called Namni) near Pyongyang on 15 April 1912.[15][16]:12

According to Kim, his family was not very poor, but was always a step away from poverty. Kim said that he was raised in a Presbyterian family, that his maternal grandfather was a Protestant minister, that his father had gone to a missionary school and was an elder in the Presbyterian Church, and that his parents were very active in the religious community.[17][18][19] According to the official version, Kim's family participated in anti-Japanese activities and in 1920 they fled to Manchuria. Like most Korean families, they resented the Japanese occupation of the Korean peninsula, which began on 29 August 1910.[16]:12 Another view seems to be that his family settled in Manchuria, as many Koreans had at the time to escape famine. Nonetheless, Kim's parents, especially Kim's mother Kang Ban Suk, played a role in the anti-Japanese struggle that was sweeping the peninsula.[16]:16 Their exact involvement—whether their cause was missionary, nationalist, or both—is unclear nevertheless.[9]:53 Still, Japanese repression of opposition was brutal, resulting in the arrest and detention of more than 52,000 Korean citizens in 1912 alone.[16]:13 This repression forced many Korean families to flee Korea and settle in Manchuria.

Communist and guerrilla activities

In October 1926 Kim founded the Down-With-Imperialism Union.[20] Kim attended Whasung Military Academy in 1926, but finding the academy's training methods outdated, he quit in 1927. From that time, he attended Yuwen Middle School in Jilin up to 1930,[21] where he rejected the feudal traditions of older-generation Koreans and became interested in Communist ideologies; his formal education ended when the police arrested and jailed him for his subversive activities. At seventeen Kim had become the youngest member of an underground Marxist organization with fewer than twenty members, led by Hŏ So, who belonged to the South Manchurian Communist Youth Association. The police discovered the group three weeks after it formed in 1929, and jailed Kim for several months.[9]:52[22]

In 1931 Kim joined the Communist Party of China—the Communist Party of Korea had been founded in 1925, but had been thrown out of the Comintern in the early 1930s for being too nationalist. He joined various anti-Japanese guerrilla groups in northern China. Feelings against the Japanese ran high in Manchuria, but as of May 1930 the Japanese had not yet occupied Manchuria. On 30 May 1930 a spontaneous violent uprising in eastern Manchuria arose in which peasants attacked some local villages in the name of resisting "Japanese aggression."[23] The authorities easily suppressed this unplanned, reckless and unfocused uprising. Because of the attack, the Japanese began to plan an occupation of Manchuria.[24] In a speech before a meeting of Young Communist League delegates on 20 May 1931 in Yenchi County in Manchuria, Kim warned the delegates against such unplanned uprisings as the 30 May 1930 uprising in eastern Manchuria.[25]

Four months later, on 18 September 1931, the "Mukden Incident" occurred, in which a relatively weak dynamite explosive charge went off near a Japanese railroad in the town of Mukden in Manchuria. Although no damage occurred, the Japanese used the incident as an excuse to send armed forces into Manchuria and to appoint a new puppet government.[26] In 1935, Kim became a member of the Northeast Anti-Japanese United Army, a guerrilla group led by the Communist Party of China. Kim was appointed[by whom?] the same year to serve as political commissar for the 3rd detachment of the second division, consisting of around 160 soldiers.[9]:53 Here Kim met the man who would become his mentor as a Communist, Wei Zhengmin, Kim's immediate superior officer, who served at the time as chairman of the Political Committee of the Northeast Anti-Japanese United Army. Wei reported directly to Kang Sheng, a high-ranking party member close to Mao Zedong in Yan'an, until Wei's death on 8 March 1941.[27]

In 1935 Kim took the name Kim Il-sung, meaning "Kim become the sun".[28] Kim was appointed commander of the 6th division in 1937, at the age of 24, controlling a few hundred men in a group that came to be known as "Kim Il-sung's division". While commanding this division he executed a raid on Poch'onbo, on 4 June 1937. Although Kim's division only captured the small Japanese-held town just within the Korean border for a few hours, it was nonetheless considered[by whom?] a military success at this time, when the guerrilla units had experienced difficulty in capturing any enemy territory. This accomplishment would grant Kim some measure of fame among Chinese guerrillas, and North Korean biographies would later exploit it as a great victory for Korea. For their part the Japanese regarded Kim as one of the most effective and popular Korean guerrilla leaders.[10]:160–161[29] He appeared on Japanese wanted lists as the "Tiger".[30] The Japanese "Maeda Unit" was sent to hunt him in February 1940, but he was able to destroy it.[31] Kim was appointed commander of the 2nd operational region for the 1st Army, but by the end of 1940 he was the only 1st Army leader still alive. Pursued by Japanese troops, Kim and what remained of his army escaped by crossing the Amur River into the Soviet Union.[9]:53–54 Kim was sent to a camp at Vyatskoye near Khabarovsk, where the Soviets retrained the Korean Communist guerrillas. Kim became a Major in the Soviet Red Army and served in it until the end of World War II in 1945.

Return to Korea

The Soviet Union declared war on Japan on 8 August 1945, and the Red Army entered Pyongyang on 24 August 1945. Stalin had instructed Lavrentiy Beria to recommend a Communist leader for the Soviet-occupied territories and Beria met Kim several times before recommending him to Stalin.[15][32][33]

Kim arrived in the Korean port of Wonsan on 19 September 1945 after 26 years in exile.

194

[33][34] According to Leonid Vassin, an officer with the Soviet MVD, Kim was essentially "created from zero". For one, his Korean was marginal at best; he had only had eight years of formal education, all of it in Chinese. He needed considerable coaching to read a speech (which the MVD prepared for him) at a Communist Party congress three days after he arrived.[7]:50

In December 1945, the Soviets installed Kim as chairman of the North Korean branch of the Korean Communist Party.[35] Originally, the Soviets preferred Cho Man-sik to lead a popular front government, but Cho refused to support a UN-backed trusteeship and clashed with Kim.[36] General Terentii Shtykov who led the Soviet occupation of northern Korea, supported Kim over Pak Hon-yong to lead the Provisional People's Committee for North Korea on 8 February 1946.[37] As chairman of the committee, Kim was "the top Korean administrative leader in the North," though he was still de facto subordinate to General Shtykov until the Chinese intervention in the Korean War.[33][35][37]

To solidify his control, Kim established the Korean People's Army (KPA), aligned with the Communist Party, and he recruited a cadre of guerrillas and former soldiers who had gained combat experience in battles against the Japanese and later against Nationalist Chinese troops.[38] Using Soviet advisers and equipment, Kim constructed a large army skilled in infiltration tactics and guerrilla warfare. Prior to Kim's invasion of the South in 1950, which triggered the Korean War, Joseph Stalin equipped the KPA with modern, Soviet-built heavy tanks, trucks, artillery, and small arms. Kim also formed an air force, equipped at first with Soviet-built propeller-driven fighters and attack aircraft. Later, North Korean pilot candidates were sent to the Soviet Union and China to train in MiG-15 jet aircraft at secret bases.[39]

Leader of North Korea

Rise of cult of personality

Despite United Nations plans to conduct all-Korean elections, the Democratic People's Republic of Korea was proclaimed on 9 September 1948, with Kim as the Soviet-designated premier. In May 1948, the south had declared statehood as the Republic of Korea.

On 12 October, the Soviet Union recognized Kim's government as sovereign of the entire peninsula, including the south.[40] The Communist Party merged with the New People's Party to form the Workers Party of North Korea (of which Kim was vice-chairman). In 1949, the Workers Party of North Korea merged with its southern counterpart to become the Workers' Party of Korea (WPK) with Kim as party chairman.[41]

By 1949, Kim and the communists had consolidated rule in North Korea.[7]:53 Around this time, the cult of personality was promoted by the people, the first statues of Kim appeared, and the people began calling him the "Great Leader".[7]:53

Korean War

Archival material suggests[42][43][44] that North Korea's decision to invade South Korea was Kim's initiative, not a Soviet one. Evidence suggests that Soviet intelligence, through its espionage sources in the US government and British SIS, had obtained information on the limitations of US atomic bomb stockpiles as well as defense program cuts, leading Stalin to conclude that the Truman administration would not intervene in Korea. [45]

The People's Republic of China acquiesced only reluctantly to the idea of Korean re-unification after being told by Kim that Stalin had approved the action.[42][43][44] The Chinese did not provide North Korea with direct military support (other than logistics channels) until United Nations troops, largely US forces, had nearly reached the Yalu River late in 1950. At the outset of the war in June and July, North Korean forces captured Seoul and occupied most of the South, save for a small section of territory in the southeast region of the South that was called the Pusan Perimeter. But in September, the North Koreans were driven back by the US-led counterattack that started with the UN landing in Incheon, followed by a combined South Korean-US-UN offensive from the Pusan Perimeter. North Korean history emphasizes that the United States had previously invaded and occupied the South, allegedly with the intention to push further north and into the Asian continent. Based on these assumptions, it portrays the KPA invasion of the South as a counter-attack.[46] By October, UN forces had retaken Seoul and invaded the North to reunify the country under the South. On 19 October, US and South Korean troops captured P'yŏngyang, forcing Kim and his government to flee north, first to Sinuiju and eventually into Kanggye.[47][48]

On 25 October 1950, after sending various warnings of their intent to intervene if UN forces did not halt their advance,[49] Chinese troops in the thousands crossed the Yalu River and entered the war as allies of the KPA. There were nevertheless tensions between Kim and the Chinese government. Kim had been warned of the likelihood of an amphibious landing at Incheon, which was ignored. There was also a sense that the North Koreans had paid little in war compared to the Chinese who had fought for their country for decades against foes with better technology.[50] The UN troops were forced to withdraw and Chinese troops retook P'yŏngyang in December and Seoul in January 1951. In March, UN forces began a new offensive, retaking Seoul and advanced north once again halting at a point just north of the 38th Parallel. After a series of offensives and counter-offensives by both sides, followed by a grueling period of largely static trench warfare that lasted from the summer of 1951 to July 1953, the front was stabilized along what eventually became the permanent "Armistice Line" of 27 July 1953. Over 2.5 million people died during the Korean war.[51]

Chinese and Russian documents from that time reveal that Kim became increasingly desperate to establish a truce, since the likelihood that further fighting would successfully unify Korea under his rule became more remote with the UN and US presence. Kim also resented the Chinese taking over the majority of the fighting in his country, with Chinese forces stationed at the center of the front line, and the Korean People's Army being mostly restricted to the coastal flanks of the front.[52]

Consolidating power

Kim Il-sung (centre) and Kim Tu-bong (second from right) at the joint meeting of the New People's Party and the Workers' Party of Korea in Pyongyang, 1946.

With the end of the Korean War, despite the failure to unify Korea under his rule, Kim il-sung proclaimed the war a victory in the sense that he had remained in power in the North. However, the three-year war left North Korea devastated, and Kim immediately embarked on a large reconstruction effort. He launched a five-year national economic plan to establish a command economy, with all industry owned by the state and all agriculture collectivized. The economy was focused on heavy industry and arms production. Both South and North Korea retained huge armed forces to defend the 1953 Demilitarized Zone, and US forces remained in the South.

In the ensuing years, Kim established himself as an independent leader of international communism. In 1956, he joined Mao in the "anti-revisionist" camp, which did not accept Nikita Khrushchev's program of de-Stalinization, yet he did not become a Maoist himself. At the same time, he consolidated his power over the Korean communist movement. Rival leaders were eliminated. Pak Hon-yong, leader of the Korean Communist Party, was purged and executed in 1955. Choe Chang-ik appears to have been purged as well. [53][54] The 1955 Juche speech, which stressed Korean independence, debuted in the context of Kim's power struggle against leaders such as Pak, who had Soviet backing. This was little noticed at the time until state media started talking about it in 1963.[55] [56]

During the 1956 August Faction Incident, Kim Il-sung successfully resisted efforts by the Soviet Union and China to depose him in favor of Soviet Koreans or the pro-Chinese Yanan faction.[57][58] The last Chinese troops withdrew from the country in October 1958, which is the consensus as the latest date when North Korea became effectively independent, though some scholars believe that the 1956 August incident demonstrated independence.[57][58]

Later rule

Despite his opposition to de-Stalinization, Kim never officially severed relations with the Soviet Union. He did not take part in the Sino-Soviet Split. After Khrushchev was replaced by Leonid Brezhnev, Kim's relations with the Soviet Union became closer. At the same time, Kim was increasingly alienated by Mao's unstable style of leadership, especially during the Cultural Revolution in the late 1960s. Kim in turn was denounced by Mao's Red Guards.[59]

At the same time, Kim reinstated relations with most of Eastern Europe's communist countries, primarily Erich Honecker's East Germany and Nicolae Ceaușescu's Roma-

Kim greets visiting Romanian President
Nicolae Ceauşescu in Pyongyang, 1971.
(The Romanian National Archives)

nia. Ceauşescu, in particular, was heavily influenced by Kim's ideology, and the personality cult that grew around him in Romania was very similar to that of Kim. Kim and Albania's Enver Hoxha (another independent-minded Stalinist) would remain fierce enemies[60] and relations between North Korea and Albania would remain cold and tense right up until Hoxha's death in 1985. Although a resolute anti-communist, Zaire's Mobutu Sese Seko was also heavily influenced by Kim's style of rule.[61] At the same time, Kim was establishing an extensive personality cult. North Koreans were taught that Kim was the "Sun of the Nation" and could do no wrong. Kim developed the policy and ideology of Juche in opposition to the idea of North Korea as either a Soviet or a Chinese satellite state.

In the mid-1960s, Kim became impressed with the efforts of North Vietnam's Ho Chi Minh to reunify Vietnam through guerilla warfare and thought something similar might be possible in Korea. Infiltration and subversion efforts were thus greatly stepped up against US forces and the leadership in South Korea. These efforts culminated in an attempt to storm the Blue House and assassinate President Park Chung-hee. North Korean troops thus took a much more aggressive stance toward US forces in and around South Korea, engaging US Army troops in fire-fights along the Demilitarized Zone. The 1968 capture of the crew of the spy ship USS Pueblo was a part of this campaign.

A new constitution was proclaimed in December 1972, under which Kim surrendered the premiership and became President of North Korea. On 14 April 1975, North Korea discontinued most formal use of its traditional units and adopted the metric system.[62] In 1980, he decided that his son Kim Jong-il would succeed him, and increasingly delegated the running of the government to him. The Kim family was supported by the army, due to Kim Il-sung's revolutionary record and the support of the veteran defense minister, O Chin-u. At the Sixth Party Congress in October 1980, Kim publicly designated his son as his successor. In 1986, a rumor spread that Kim had been assassinated, making the concern for Jong-il's ability to succeed his father actual. Kim dispelled the rumors, however, by making a series of public appearances. It has been argued, however, that the incident helped establish the order of succession—the first patrifilial in a Communist state—which eventually would occur upon Kim Il-Sung's death in 1994.[63]

From about this time, North Korea encountered increasing economic difficulties. The practical effect of Juche was to cut the country off from virtually all foreign trade in order to make it entirely self-reliant. The economic reforms of Deng Xiaoping in China from 1979 onward meant that trade with the moribund economy of North Korea held decreasing interest for China. The collapse of communism in Eastern Europe and the Soviet Union, from 1989–1991, completed North Korea's virtual isolation. These events led to mounting economic difficulties because Kim refused to issue any economic or democratic reforms.[64]

As he aged, starting in the late 1970s, Kim developed a calcium deposit growth on the right side of the back of his neck. Its close proximity to his brain and spinal cord made it inoperable. Because of its unappealing nature, North Korean reporters and photographers, from then on, always filmed Kim while standing from his same slight-left angle to hide the growth from official photographs and newsreels, which became an increasingly difficult task as the growth reached the size of a baseball by the late 1980s.[65]

To ensure a full succession of leadership to his son and designated successor Kim Jong-il, Kim turned over his chairmanship of North Korea's National Defense Commission—the body mainly responsible for control of the armed forces as well as the supreme commandership of the country's now million-man strong military force, the Korean People's Army—to his son in 1991 and 1993. So far, the elder Kim—even though he is dead—has remained the country's president, the general-secretary of its ruling Worker's Party of Korea, and the chairman of the Party's Central Military Commission, the party's organization that has supreme supervision and authority over military matters.

In early 1994, Kim began investing in nuclear power to offset energy shortages brought on by economic problems. This was the first of many "nuclear crises". On 19 May 1994, Kim ordered spent fuel to be unloaded from the already disputed nuclear research facility in Yongbyon. Despite repeated chiding from Western nations, Kim continued to conduct nuclear research and carry on with the uranium enrichment program. In June 1994, former U.S. President Jimmy Carter travelled to Pyongyang for talks with Kim. To the astonishment of the United States and the International Atomic Energy Agency, Kim agreed to halt his nuclear research program and seemed to be embarking upon a new opening to the West.[66]

Personal life

Kim Il-sung married twice. His first wife, Kim Jong-suk (1919–1949), gave birth to two sons before her death in childbirth during the delivery of a stillborn girl. Kim Jong-il was his oldest son. The other son (Kim Man-il, or Shura Kim) of this marriage died in 1947 in a swimming accident. Kim married Kim Sung-ae in 1952, and it is believed that he had three children with her: Kim Yŏng-il (not to be confused with the former Premier of North Korea of the same name), Kim Kyŏng-il and Kim Pyong-il. Kim Pyong-il was prominent in Korean politics until he became ambassador to Hungary. Since 2015 Kim Pyong-il has been ambassador to the Czech Republic.

Kim was reported to have other illegitimate children.[67] They included Kim Hyŏn-nam (born 1972, head of the Propaganda and Agitation Department of the Workers' Party since 2002).[68]

In sum, Kim Il-sung had six legitimate children and eight legitimate grandchildren. On his death in 1994, his eldest son Kim Jong-il succeeded him as supreme leader of North Korea.

Death

On 8 July 1994, Kim Il-sung collapsed from a sudden heart attack at the age of 82. After the heart attack, Kim Jong-il ordered the team of doctors who were constantly at his father's side to leave, and arranged for the country's best doctors to be flown in from Pyongyang. After several hours, the doctors from Pyongyang arrived, but despite their efforts to save him, Kim Il-sung died. After the traditional Confucian Mourning period, his death was declared thirty hours later.[69]

Kim Il-sung's death resulted in nationwide mourning and a ten-day mourning period was declared by Kim Jong-il. His funeral in Pyongyang was attended by hundreds of thousands of people who were flown into the city from all over North Korea. Kim Il-sung's body was placed in a public mausoleum at the Kumsusan Palace of the Sun, where his preserved and embalmed body lies under a glass coffin for viewing purposes. His head rests on a traditional Korean pillow and he is covered by the flag of the Workers' Party of Korea. Newsreel video of the funeral at Pyongyang was broadcast on several networks, and can now be found on various websites.[70]

Legacy

The Mansudae Grand Monuments, depicting large bronze statues of Kim Il-sung and his son Kim Jong-il.
By Nicor (Own work) [CC BY-SA 3.0 (http://creativecommons.org/licenses/by-sa/3.0)], via Wikimedia Commons

There are over 500 statues of Kim Il-sung in North Korea, similar to the many statues and monuments put up by East Bloc leaders to themselves.[71] The most prominent are at Kim Il-sung University, Kim Il-sung Stadium, Mansudae Hill, Kim Il-sung Bridge and the Immortal Statue of Kim Il-sung. Some statues have reportedly been destroyed by explosions or damaged with graffiti by North Korean dissidents.[7]:201[72] Yŏng Saeng ("eternal life") monuments have been erected throughout the country, each dedicated to the departed "Eternal Leader".[73] It is claimed that it is traditional for North Korean newlyweds, immediately after their wedding, to go to the nearest statue of Kim Il-sung and lay flowers at his feet.[74]

Kim Il-sung's image is prominent in places associated with public transportation, hanging at every North Korean train station and airport.[71] It is also placed prominently at the border crossings between China and North Korea. Thousands of gifts to Kim Il-sung from foreign leaders are housed in the International Friendship Exhibition.

Kim Il-sung's birthday, "Day of the Sun", is celebrated every year as a public holiday in North Korea.[75] The associated April Spring Friendship Art Festival gathers hundreds of artists from all over the world.[76]

Works

Kim Il-sung was the author of many works. According to North Korean sources these amount to approximately 10,800 speeches, reports, books, treatises and others.[77] Some, such as the 100-volume Complete Collection of Kim Il Sung's Works (김일성전집), are published by the Workers' Party of Korea Publishing House.[78] Shortly before his death, he published an eight volume autobiography With the Century.[36]:26

According to official North Korean sources, Kim Il-sung was the original writer of The Flower Girl, a revolutionary theatrical opera, which was adapted into a locally produced feature film in 1972.[79][80][14]:178

RHEE SYNGMAN
The First President of South Korea

(April 18, 1875 – July 19, 1965)

Syngman Rhee (Korean: 리승만: 李承晚, pronounced [i.sɯŋ.man]) was a South Korean statesman, the first and the last Head of State of the Provisional Government of the
Republic of Korea, and President of South Korea from 1948 to 1960. His three-term
presidency of South Korea (August 1948 to April 1960) was strongly affected by Cold
War tensions on the Korean Peninsula.

Rhee was regarded as an anti-Communist and a capitalist strongman, and he led South
Korea through the Korean War. His presidency ended in resignation following popular
protests against a disputed election. He died in exile in Honolulu, Hawaii.

Early life (1875–95)

Syngman Rhee was born on April 18, 1875;[2] his birthday is also stated as March 26,[3]
the lunar date,[2] and April 26.[4][5] Rhee was born in Hwanghae Province[3] into a
rural family of modest means as the third son out of three brothers and two sisters. His
two older brothers both died in infancy.[2] Rhee's family traced its lineage back to King
Taejong of Joseon.[6] He is a 16th-generation descendant of Grand Prince Yangnyeong.
In 1877, at the age of two, Rhee and his family moved to Seoul.[7]

In Seoul, he had traditional Confucianism education in various seodang in Nakdong (낙
동; 駱洞) and Dodong (도동; 桃洞).[7] He was portrayed as a potential candidate for
gwageo, the Korean civil service examination. When Rhee was nine years old, he was
rendered virtually blind through smallpox and was cured by Horace Newton Allen, an
American medical missionary.[6]

In 1894, when reforms abolished the gwageo system, Rhee enrolled in the Pai Chai
School (배재학당; 培材學堂),[2] an American Methodist school,[4][5] in April. He studied English and sinhakmun (신학문; 新學問; "new subjects"). Near the end of 1895, he
joined a Hyeopseong Club (협성회; 協成會) created by Seo Jae-pil, who returned from
the United States. He worked as the head and the main writer of the newspapers Hye-
opseong-hoe Hoebo (협성회회보; 協成會會報; literally Hyeopseong Club Newsletter)
and Maeil Sinmun (매일신문; 每日新聞; "The Daily Newspaper"),[7] the latter being
the first daily newspaper in Korea.[8] During this period, he earned money by teaching
Americans Korean. He converted to Christianity in school.[8] In 1895, he graduated from
Pai Chai School.[2]

Independence activities (1896–1904)

Rhee was implicated in a plot to take revenge for the assassination of Empress Myeongseong; however, a female American physician helped him avoid the charges. At this
point, he converted to Christianity.[2] Rhee acted as one of the forerunners of Korea's
grassroots movement through organizations such as the Hyeopseong Club and the Independence Club (독립협회; 獨立協會). He organized several protests against corruption
and the influences of the Empire of Japan and the Russian Empire.[8] As a result, in
November 1898, he attained the rank of Uigwan (의관; 議官) in the Imperial Legislature,
the Jungchuwon (중추원; 中樞院).[7]

After entering civil service, he was implicated in a plot to remove King Gojong from power through the recruitment of Park Yeong-hyo. As a result, he was imprisoned in the Gyeongmucheong Prison (경무청 ; 警務廳) in January 1899.[7] Other sources place the year arrested as 1897[4][5][8] and 1898.[2]

Rhee attempted to escape on the 20th day of imprisonment but was caught and was sentenced to life imprisonment through the Pyeongniwon (평리원 ; 平理院). He was imprisoned in the Hanseong Prison (한성감옥서 ; 漢城監獄署). In prison, Rhee translated and compiled The Sino–Japanese War Record (청일전기 ; 淸日戰紀), wrote The Spirit of Independence (독립정신), compiled the New English–Korean Dictionary (신영한사전) and wrote in the Daeguk Newspaper (뎨국신문).[7] He was also tortured.[8]

Political activities in the U.S. (1904–10, 1912–45), China and Korea (1910–12)

Syngman Rhee in 1905 dressed to meet Theodore Roosevelt.
In 1904, Rhee was released from prison at the outbreak of the Russo-Japanese War with the help of Min Yeong-hwan (민영환 ; 閔泳煥).[2] In November 1904, with the help of Min Yeong-hwan and Han Gyu-seol (한규설 ; 韓圭卨), Rhee moved to the United States. In August 1905, Rhee and Yun Byeong-gu (윤병구 ; 尹炳求)[7] met with the Secretary of State John Hay and U.S. President Theodore Roosevelt at peace talks in Portsmouth, New Hampshire and attempted to convince the US to help preserve independence for Korea,[9] but the attempt was unsuccessful.[7]

Rhee continued to stay in the United States; this move has been described as an "exile."[8] He obtained a Bachelor of Arts from George Washington University in 1907, and a Master of Arts from Harvard University in 1908.[2][6] In 1910,[2] he obtained a Ph.D. from Princeton University[4][5] with the thesis "Neutrality as influenced by the United States" (미국의 영향하에 발달된 국제법상 중립).[7]

In August 1910, he returned to Japanese occupied Korea.[7][note 1] He served as a YMCA coordinator and missionary.[10][11] In 1912, he was implicated in the 105-Man Incident,[7] and was shortly arrested.[2] However, he fled to the United States in 1912[4] with M. C. Harris's rationale that Rhee was going to participate in the general meeting of Methodists in Minneapolis as the Korean representative.[7][note 2]

In the United States, Rhee attempted to convince Woodrow Wilson to help the people involved in the 105-Man Incident, but failed to bring any change. Soon afterwards, he met Park Yong-man, who was in Nebraska at the time. In February 1913, as a consequence of the meeting, he moved to Honolulu and took over the Han-in Jung-ang Academy (한인중앙학원 ; 韓人中央學園).[7] In Hawaii, he began to publish the Pacific Ocean Magazine (태평양잡지 ; 太平洋雜誌).[2] In 1918, he established the Han-in Christian Church (한인기독교회 ; 韓人基督敎會). During this period, he opposed Park Yong-man's stance on foreign relations of Korea and brought about a split in the community.[7] In December 1918, he was chosen as one of the Korean representatives to the Paris Peace Conference, 1919 by the Korean National Association (대한인국민회 ; 大韓人國民會), but failed to obtain permission to travel to Paris. After giving up traveling to Paris, Rhee held the First Korean Congress (한인대표자대회) in Philadelphia with Seo Jae-pil to make plans for the declaration and action of independence of Korea.[7]

204

Following the March 1st Movement in 1919, Rhee discovered that he was appointed to the positions of Foreign Minister in the Noryeong Provisional Government (노령임시정부;露領臨時政府), Prime Minister for the Provisional Government of the Republic of Korea in Shanghai, and a position equivalent to President for the Hansung Provisional Government (한성임시정부;漢城臨時政府). In June, in the acting capacity of the President of the Republic of Korea, he notified the prime ministers and the chairmen of peace conferences of Korea's independence. On August 25, Rhee established the Korean Commission to America and Europe (구미위원부;歐美委員部) in Washington, D.C. On September 6, Rhee discovered that he had been appointed acting president for the Provisional Government in Shanghai.[4][5] From December 1920 to May 1921, he moved to Shanghai and was the acting president for the Provisional Government.[7]

However, Rhee failed to efficiently act in the capacity of Acting President due to conflicts inside the provisional government in Shanghai. In October 1920, he returned to the US to participate in the Washington Naval Conference. During the conference, he attempted to set the problem of Korean independence as part of the agenda and campaigned for independence, but was unsuccessful.[2][7] In September 1922, he returned to Hawaii to focus on publication, education, and religion. In November 1924, Rhee was appointed the position of President-for-Life in the Korean Comrade Society (대한인동지회;大韓人同志會).[7]

In March 1925, Rhee was impeached as the president of the Provisional Government in Shanghai over allegations of misuse of power[12] and was removed from office. Nevertheless, he continued to claim the position of President by referring to the Hansung Provisional Government and continued independence activities through the Korean Commission to America and Europe. In the beginning of 1933, he participated in the League of Nations conference in Geneva to bring up the question of Korean independence.[7]

In November 1939, Rhee and his wife left Hawaii for Washington. He focused on writing the book Japan Inside Out and published it during the summer of 1941. With the attack on Pearl Harbor and the consequent Pacific War which began on December 1941, Rhee used his position as the chairman of the foreign relations department of the provisional government in Chongqing to convince President Franklin D. Roosevelt and the United States Department of State to approve the existence of the Korean provisional government. As part of this plan, he cooperated with anti-Japan strategies conducted by the Office of Strategic Services. In 1945, he participated in the United Nations Conference on International Organization as the leader of the Korean representatives to request the participation of the Korean provisional government.[7]

Presidency

After the surrender of Japan on September 2, 1945,[13] Rhee was flown to Tokyo aboard a U.S. military aircraft.[14] Over the objections of the State Department, the American military government allowed Rhee to return to Korea by providing him with a passport in October 1945, despite the refusal of the State Department to issue Rhee with a passport. [15] The British historian Max Hastings wrote that there was "at least a measure of corruption in the transaction" as the American OSS agent Preston Goodfellow who provided

Syngman Rhee in 1905 dressed to meet Theodore Roosevelt.

Rhee with the passport that allowed him to return to Korea was apparently promised by Rhee that if he came to power, he would reward Goodfellow with commercial concessions."[15] Following the independence of Korea and a secret meeting with Douglas MacArthur, Rhee was flown in mid-October 1945 to Seoul aboard MacArthur's personal airplane, The Bataan.[14]

After the return to Korea, he assumed the posts of president of the Independence Promotion Central Committee (독립촉성중앙위원회 ; 獨立促成中央協議會), chairman of the Korean People's Representative Democratic Legislature (대한국민대표민주의원 ; 大韓國民代表民主議院), and president of the Headquarters for Unification (민족통일총본부 ; 民族統一總本部). At this point, he was strongly anti-communist and opposed foreign intervention; he opposed Soviet Union and United States' proposal in the Moscow Conference (1945) to establish a trusteeship for Korea and the cooperation between the left-wing (communist) and the right-wing (nationalist) parties. He also refused to join the U.S.–Soviet Cooperation Committee (미소공동위원회 ; 美蘇共同委員會) as well as the negotiations with the north.[7] The Korean nationalist movement had for decades been torn by factionalism and in-fighting, and most of the leaders of the independence movement hated each other as much as they hated the Japanese. Rhee, who had lived for decades in the United States, was a figure known only from afar in Korea, and therefore regarded as a more or less acceptable compromise candidate for the conservative factions. More importantly, Rhee spoke fluent English whereas none of his rivals did, and therefore he was the Korean politician most trusted and favored by the American occupation government. The British diplomat Roger Makins later recalled, "the American propensity to go for a man rather than a movement — Giraud among the French in 1942, Chiang Kai-shek in China. Americans have always liked the idea of dealing with a foreign leader who can be identified as 'their man'. They are much less comfortable with movements." Makins further added the same was the case with Rhee, as very few Americans were fluent in Korean in the 1940s or knew much about Korea, and it was simply far easier for the American occupation government to deal with Rhee than to try to understand Korea. Rhee was "acerbic, prickly, unpromising" and was regarded by the U.S. State Department, which long had dealings with him as "a dangerous mischief-maker", but the American General John R. Hodge decided that Rhee was the best man for the Americans to back because of his fluent English and his ability to talk with authority to American officers about American subjects. Once it become clear from October 1945 onward that Rhee was the Korean politician most favored by the Americans, other conservative leaders fell in behind him. Hastings wrote, "In an Asian society, where politics are often dominated by an instinctive desire to fall in behind the strongest force, Rhee's backing from the military government was the decisive factor in his rise to power."[15]

When the first U.S.–Soviet Cooperation Committee meeting was concluded without a result, he began to argue on June 1946 that the government of Korea must be established as an independent entity.[7] In the same month, he created a plan based on this idea[2] and moved to Washington, D.C. from December 1946 to April 1947 to lobby support for the plan. During the visit, Harry S. Truman's policies of Containment and the Truman Doctrine, which was announced on March 1947, enforced Rhee's anti-communist ideas. [7]

Syngman Rhee and Douglas MacArthur at the Ceremony inaugurating the government of the Republic of Korea.

On November 1947, the United Nations General Assembly recognized Korea's independence and established the United Nations Temporary Commission on Korea (UNTCOK) through Resolution 112.[16] [17] In May 1948, the South Korean Constitutional Assembly election was held under the oversight of the UNTCOK.[7] He was elected without competition to serve in the South Korean Constitutional Assembly (대한민국제헌국회 ; 大韓民國制憲國會) and was consequently selected to be Speaker of the Assembly. Rhee was highly influential in creating the policy stating that the president of South Korea had to be elected by the National Assembly.[2] The 1948 Constitution of the Republic of Korea was adopted on July 17, 1948.[18]

On July 20, 1948, Rhee was elected president of the Republic of Korea[4][5][18] in the South Korean presidential election, 1948 with 92.3% of the vote; the second candidate, Kim Gu, received 6.7% of the vote.[19] On August 15, the Republic of Korea was formally established in South Korea[18] and Rhee was inaugurated as the first President of the Republic of Korea.[2][7] Rhee himself had been an independence activist, and his relations with the chinilpa Korean elites who had collaborated with the Japanese were, in the words of the South Korean historian Kyung Moon Hwang, often "contentious," but in the end an understanding was reached in which, in exchange for their support, Rhee would not purge the elites.[20] In particular, the Koreans who had served in the colonial-era National Police, whom the Americans had retained after August 1945, were promised by Rhee that their jobs would not be threatened by him. Upon independence in 1948, 53% of South Korean police officers were men who had served in the National Police during the Japanese occupation.[21]

Political repression

Soon after taking office, Rhee enacted laws that severely curtailed political dissent. There was much controversy between Rhee and his leftist opponents. Allegedly, many of the leftist opponents were arrested and in some cases killed. The most controversial issue has been Kim Gu's assassination. On 26 June 1949, Kim Gu was assassinated by Ahn Doo-hee, who confessed that he assassinated Kim Gu by the order of Kim Chang-ryong. The assassin was described by the British historian Max Hastings as one of Rhee's "creatures".[22] It soon became apparent that Rhee's governing style was going to be authoritarian.[23] He allowed the internal security force (headed by his right-hand man, Kim Chang-ryong) to detain and torture suspected communists and North Korean agents.

His government also oversaw several massacres, including the suppression of the Jeju Uprising on Jeju island, where South Korea's Truth Commission reported 14,373 victims, 86% at the hands of the security forces and 13.9% at the hands of communist rebels,[24] Mungyeong massacre.

Korean War

Both Rhee and Kim Il-sung wanted to unite the Korean peninsula under their respective governments, but the United States refused to give South Korea any heavy weapons in order to ensure that its military could only be used for preserving internal order and self-defense. By contrast, Pyongyang was well equipped with Soviet aircraft and tanks. According to John Merrill, "the war was preceded by a major insurgency in the South and serious clashes along the thirty-eighth parallel," and 100,000 people died in "political disturbances, guerrilla warfare, and border clashes".[25]

At the outbreak of hostilities on June 25, 1950, all South Korean resistance at the 38th parallel was overwhelmed by the North Korean offensive within a few hours. By June 26, it was apparent that the Korean People's Army (KPA) would occupy Seoul. Rhee stated, "Every Cabinet member, including myself, will protect the government, and parliament has decided to remain in Seoul. Citizens should not worry and remain in their workplaces."[26] However, Rhee had already left the city with most of his government on June 27. At midnight on June 28, the South Korean military destroyed the Han Bridge, thereby preventing thousands of citizens from fleeing. On June 28, North Korean soldiers occupied Seoul.

Syngman Rhee awarding a medal to U.S. Navy Rear Admiral Ralph A. Ofstie during the Korean War in 1952.

During the North Korean occupation of Seoul, Rhee established a temporary government in Busan and created a defensive perimeter along the Naktong Bulge. A series of battles ensued, which would later be known collectively as the Battle of Naktong Bulge. After the Battle of Inchon in September 1950, the North Korean military was routed, and the United Nations (UN)— of whom the largest contingents were the Americans and South Koreans—not only liberated all of South Korea, but overran much of North Korea. In the areas of North Korea taken by the UN forces, elections were supposed to be administered by the United Nations, but instead were taken over and administered by the South Koreans. After the Chinese entered the war in November 1950, the UN forces were thrown into retreat. During this period of crisis, Rhee ordered the December Massacres of 1950.

Hastings notes that, during the war, Rhee's official salary was equal to $37.50 (U.S. dollars) per month. Both at the time and since, there has been much speculation about precisely how Rhee managed to live on a salary equivalent to $37.50 per month. The entire Rhee regime was notorious for its corruption, with everyone in the government from the President downwards stealing as much they possibly could from both the public purse and aid from the United States, making the Rhee regime one of the most dishonest and corrupt governments in South Korean history. The Rhee regime engaged in the "worst excesses of corruption," with the soldiers in the Army of the Republic of Korea (ROK) going unpaid for months as their officers embezzled their pay, equipment provided by the United States being sold on the black market, and the size of the ROK Army being bloated by hundreds of thousands of "ghost soldiers" who only existed on paper, allowing their officers to steal pay that would have been due had these soldiers actually existed. The problems with low morale experienced by the ROK Army were largely due to the corruption of the Rhee regime. The worst scandal during the war—indeed of the entire Rhee government—was the National Defense Corps Incident. Rhee created the National Defense Corps in December 1950, intended to be a paramilitary militia, comprising men not in the military or police who be drafted into the corps for internal security duties. In the months that followed, thousands of National Defense Corps men either starved or froze to death in their unheated barracks, as the men lacked winter uniforms. Even Rhee could not ignore the deaths of so many of the National Defense Corps and ordered an investigation. It was revealed that commander of the National Defense Corps, General Kim Yun Gun, had stolen millions of American dollars that were intended to heat the barracks and feed and clothe the men. General Kim and five other officers were publicly shot at Daegu on August 12, 1951, following their convictions for corruption.[27]

In the spring of 1951, Rhee—who was upset about MacArthur's dismissal by President Truman—lashed out in a press interview against Britain, whom he blamed for MacArthur's sacking.[28] Rhee was absolutely committed to reunifying Korea under his leadership and strongly supported MacArthur's call for going all-out against China, even at the risk of provoking a nuclear war with the Soviet Union. Rhee declared, "The British troops have outlived their welcome in my country." Shortly thereafter, Rhee told an Australian diplomat about the Australian troops fighting for his country, "They are not wanted here any longer. Tell that to your government. The Australian, Canadian, New Zealand and British troops all represent a government which is now sabotaging the brave American effort to liberate fully and unify my unhappy nation."[28]

Rhee was strongly against the armistice negotiations the U.S. entered into in 1953. Accordingly, in April of the same year, he demanded of President Eisenhower a total withdrawal of his troops from the peninsula if an armistice were to be signed, declaring that the ROK would rather fight on its own than negotiate a cease-fire. He also deliberately carried out some actions that would deter the armistice and reignite conflicts in the region, the most provocative one being his unilateral release of 25,000 prisoners of war in June 1953.[29] Such actions upset China and the North, which hindered the progress of armistice talks. Moreover, for such unpredictability in his authoritarian leadership, the Truman and Eisenhower administrations considered him one of the "rogue allies" in East Asia and engaged in "powerplay", or the construction of asymmetric alliances, which helped the U.S. maximize economic and political influence over the ROK and increase ROK's dependency on the United States.[30]

On July 27, 1953, at last, "one of the 20th century's most vicious and frustrating wars"[31] came to an end with no apparent victor. Ultimately, the armistice agreement was signed by military commanders from China and the North, with the United Nations Command, led by the U.S., signing "on the behalf of the international community."[32] Its signatories did not include the ROK, however, as Rhee refused to agree to the armistice, and neither was it supposed to be a permanent cease-fire, as a peace treaty was never signed. Nevertheless, to this very day, the armistice remains the only means for security and peace on the Korean peninsula.[32]

Re-election

Because of widespread discontent with Rhee's corruption and political repression, it was considered unlikely that Rhee would be re-elected by the National Assembly. To circumvent this, Rhee attempted to amend the constitution to allow him to hold elections for the presidency by direct popular vote. When the Assembly rejected this amendment, Rhee ordered a mass arrest of opposition politicians and then passed the desired amendment in July 1952. During the following presidential election, he received 74% of the vote.[33]

Resignation and exile

After the war ended in July 1953, South Korea struggled to rebuild following nationwide devastation. The country remained at a Third-World level of development and was heavily reliant on U.S. aid. Rhee was easily re-elected for what should have been the final time in 1956 since the 1948 constitution limited the president to two consecutive terms. However, soon after being sworn in, he had the legislature amend the constitution to allow the incumbent president—himself—to run for an unlimited number of terms.

In 1960, the 84-year-old Rhee won his fourth term in office as President with 90% of the vote. His victory was assured after the main opposition candidate, Cho Byeong-ok, died shortly before the March 15 elections.

Rhee wanted his protégé, Lee Ki-poong, elected as Vice President—a separate office under Korean law at that time. When Lee, who was running against Chang Myon (the ambassador to the United States during the Korean War, a member from the opposition Democratic Party) won the vote with a wide margin, the opposition Democratic Party claimed the election was rigged. This triggered anger among segments of the Korean populace on April 19. When police shot demonstrators in Masan, the student-led April Revolution forced Rhee to resign on April 26.

On April 28, a DC-4 belonging to the United States Central Intelligence Agency (CIA), piloted by Capt. Harry B. Cockrell, Jr. and operated by Civil Air Transport, covertly flew Rhee out of South Korea as protesters converged on the Blue House.[34] During the journey, Rhee and Franziska Donner, his Austrian wife, came up to the cockpit to thank the pilot and crew. Rhee's wife offered the pilot a substantial diamond ring in thanks, which was courteously declined. The former president, his wife, and their adopted son subsequently lived in exile in Honolulu, Hawaii.

Personal life

In February 1933, Rhee met Austrian Franziska Donner in Geneva.[35] At the time, Rhee was participating in a League of Nations meeting[35] and Donner was working as an interpreter.[12] In October 1934, they were married[35] in New York City.[12] She also acted as his secretary.[35]

Death

Rhee died of a stroke on July 19, 1965. A week later, his body was returned to Seoul and buried in the Seoul National Cemetery.[36]

REFERENCES

DANGUN WANGGEOM The Founding Father

This article uses material from the Wikipedia article en.wikipedia.org/wiki/Dangun, which is released under the Creative Commons Attribution-Share-Alike License 3.0, which can be viewed at creativecommons.org/licenses/by-sa/3.0/

[1] Encyclopædia Britannica online Korea 'Dangun' http://premium.britannica.co.kr/bol/topic.asp?article_id=b04d1969b
[2] The Story of Dan-gun http://www.academicmartialarts.co.uk/pages/information/korea/mythology/samguk_yusa/the_story_of_dan_gun/
[3] Needham, J;Lu GD (2002). Celestial lancets: a history and rationale of acupuncture and moxa. Routledge. pp. 262. ISBN 0-7007-1458-8.
[4] http://www.san-shin.org/Dan-gun_Myth.html
[5] Tudor, Daniel (2013). Korea: The Impossible Country: The Impossible Country. Tuttle Publishing. pp. [1]. ISBN 146291022X.
[6] Tudor, Daniel (2013). Korea: The Impossible Country: The Impossible Country. Tuttle Publishing. pp. [2]. ISBN 146291022X.
[7] Richmond, Simon;Yu-Mei Balasingamchow (2010). Lonely Planet Korea. Lonely Planet. p. 25. ISBN 1742203566.
[8] Hong, Sung-wook (2008). Naming God in Korea: The Case of Protestant Christianity. OCMS. p. 56. ISBN 1870345665.
[9] Lim, SK (2011). Asia Civilizations: Ancient to 1800 AD. Asiapac Books Pte Ltd. p. 76. ISBN 9812295941.
[10] KCNA
[11] Hong, Sung-wook (2008). Naming God in Korea: The Case of Protestant Christianity. OCMS. pp. [3]. ISBN 1870345665.
[12] Mason, David A. (1999). Spirit of the Mountains: Korea's San-Shin and Traditions of Mountain-worship. Hallim Publishing. pp. [4]. ISBN 1565911075.
[13] Kemerly, Tony;Steve Snyder (2013). Taekwondo Grappling Techniques: Hone Your Competitive Edge for Mixed Martial Arts. Tuttle Publishing. pp. [5]. ISBN 1462909914.
[14] Tertitskiy, Fyodor (6 June 2016). "The good things in North Korea". NK News. Retrieved 20 July 2016.
[15] G. John, Ikenberry;Chung-in Moon (2008). The United States and Northeast Asia: debates, issues, and new order Asia in world

KING SEJONG THE GREAT

This article uses material from the Wikipedia article en.wikipedia.org/wiki/Sejong_the_Great, which is released under the Creative Commons Attribution-Share-Alike License 3.0, which can be viewed at creativecommons.org/licenses/by-sa/3.0/

[1] Encyclopedia of World History, Vol II, P362 Sejong, Edited by Marsha E. Ackermann, Michael J. Schroeder, Janice J. Terry, Jiu-Hwa Lo Upshur, Mark F. Whitters, ISBN 978-0-8160-6386-4
[2] Yŏng-gyu, Pak (2004). Han'gwŏn ŭro ingnŭn Chosŏn Wangjo sillok (Ch'op'an. ed.). Seoul: Tŭllyŏk. p. 55. ISBN 89-7527 029-7
[3] Yŏng-gyu, Pak (2004). Han'gwŏn ŭro ingnŭn Chosŏn Wangjo sillok (Ch'op'an. ed.). Seoul: Tŭllyŏk. p. 55. ISBN 89-7527-029-7
[4] Pratt, Keith (2006). Everlasting Flower: A History of Korea.
[5] http://web.archive.org/web/20080516063253/http://www.asiaquarterly.com/content/view/167/43/
[6] <<Learning Sejong Silok in one book>> ISBN 890107754X
[7] https://web.archive.org/web/20090114065908/http://preview.britannica.co.kr/bol/topic.asp?article_id=b01g3496a. Archived from the original on January 14, 2009. Retrieved October 25, 2008
[8] Sejong.prkorea.com. Retrieved 2016-02-22.
[9] People.aks.ac.kr. 2005-11-30. Retrieved 2016-02-22.
[10] <<Learning Sejong Silok in one book>> ISBN 890107754X
[11] Haralambous, Yannis;Horne, P. Scott. Fonts & Encodings. "O'Reilly Media, Inc.". p. 155. ISBN 9780596102425. Retrieved 8 October 2016.
[12] Selin, Helaine. Encyclopaedia of the History of Science, Technology, and Medicine in Non-Westen Cultures. Springer Science & Business Media. pp. 505–506. ISBN 9789401714167. Retrieved 27 July 2016.
[13] Kim (1998), 57
[14] Bueb125.com.ne.kr. Retrieved 2016-02-22.
[15] Kim (1998), 51
[16] https://web.archive.org/web/20110722135645/http://www.reportnet.co.kr/knowledge/pop_preview.html?dn=2075262. Archived from the original on July 22, 2011. Retrieved October 25, 2008.
[17] Urimal.cs.pusan.ac.kr. Retrieved 2016-02-22.
[18] Kim Jeong Su(1990), <<(History and Future of Hangul>> ISBN 8930107230
[19] Hannas, Wm C. Asia's Orthographic Dilemma. University of Hawaii Press. p. 57. ISBN 9780824818920. Retrieved 20 September 2016.
[20] Chen, Jiangping. Multilingual Access and Services for Digital Collections. ABC-CLIO. p. 66. ISBN 9781440839559. Retrieved 20 September 2016.
[21] "Invest Korea Journal". 23. Korea Trade-Investment Promotion Agency. 1 January 2005. Retrieved 20 September 2016. They later devised three different systems for writing Korean with Chinese characters: Hyangchal, Gukyeol and Idu. These systems were similar to those developed later in Japan and were probably used as models by the Japanese.
[22] "Korea Now". 29. Korea Herald. 1 July 2000. Retrieved 20 September 2016.
[23] Hunmin Jeongeum Haerye, postface of Jeong Inji, p. 27a, translation from Gari K. Ledyard, The Korean Language Reform of 1446, p. 258
[24] Koerner, E. F. K.;Asher, R. E. Concise History of the Language Sciences: From the Sumerians to the Cognitivists. Elsevier. p. 54. ISBN 9781483297545. Retrieved 13 October 2016.
[25] Korean Spirit and Culture Promotion Project. Fifty Wonders of Korea Volume I: Culture and Art. 2nd ed. Seoul: Samjung Munhwasa, 2009. 28-35.
[26] "Tour Guide". Tourguide.vo.kr. Retrieved 2016-02-22.

YI SUN-SIN, The Admiral Who Saved The Nation

This article uses material from the Wikipedia article en.wikipedia.org/wiki/Yi_Sun-sin, which is released under the Creative Commons Attribution-Share-Alike License 3.0, which can be viewed at creativecommons.org/licenses/by-sa/3.0/

[1] Hawley, Samuel (2005). The Imjin War, Japan's Sixteenth-Century Invasion of Korea and Attempt to Conquer China. Seoul: The Royal Asiatic Society, Korea Branch. p. 490. ISBN 89-954424-2-5.
[2] The Influence of the Sea on The Political History of Japan (1921), Admiral George Alexander Ballard, ISBN 0-8371-5435-9
[3] Cummins, Joseph (2008). The War Chronicles: From Chariots to Flintlocks. Fair Winds. p. 275. ISBN 1616734035.
[4] Sawyer, M.F. (2007). Married to Islam. iUniverse. ISBN 0595423272.
[5] Yi Sun-sin, Nanjung Ilgi, p. 314
[6] "Admiral Yi Sun-sin A brief overview of his life and achievements" Korean Spirit and Culture, Series I, Diamond Sutra Recitation Group.
[7] Admiral Yi Sun-sin at Koreanhero.net
[8] Was Yi Baek-rok a victim of Kimyeo literati purge?(in Korean)
[9] Turnbull, Stephen. 2002. p. 90-1.
[10] Strauss, Barry. pp. 11
[11] Turnbull, Stephen. 2002. p. 90-2.
[12] Strauss, Barry. pp. 12
[13] Turnbull, Stephen. 2002. p. 93.
[14] Turnbull, Stephen. 2002. p. 98-107.
[15] Strauss, Barry. pp. 13
[16] Strauss, Barry. pp. 14
[17] Hawley, Samuel: The Imjin War. Japan's Sixteenth-Century Invasion of Korea and Attempt to Conquer China, The Royal Asiatic Society, Korea Branch, Seoul 2005, ISBN 89-954424-2-5, p.195f.
[18] War Diary, the autobiographical diary of Admiral Yi Sun-Sin
[19] Yi Sun-sin, Nanjung Ilgi, p. 315
[20] Hawley (2005), p. 552
[21] Hawley (2005), p. 553
[22] Choi (2002), p. 213
[23] Ha (1979), p. 237
[24] Hawley (2005), pp. 549–550
[25] Choi (2002), p. 222
[26] Hawley (2005), p. 555
[27] Hawley (2005), p. 557
[28] http://www.seoprise.com/board/view_nw.php?uid=6970&table=global_2

[1] Yi, Ki-baek. A New History of Korea. Harvard University Press. pp. 38–40. ISBN 9780674615762. Retrieved 11 October 2016.
[2] "Hangugui segyemunhwayusan yeohaeng: Segyega injeonghan hangugui areumdaum"(in Korean). Sang Sang Press. p. 209. ISBN 9791186163146. Retrieved 19 November 2016.
[3] Kim, Djun Kil. The History of Korea, 2nd Edition. ABC-CLIO. p. 32. ISBN 9781610695824. Retrieved 11 October 2016.
[4] Kim, Jinwung. A History of Korea: From "Land of the Morning Calm" to States in Conflict. Indiana University Press. p. 35. ISBN 0253000785. Retrieved 11 October 2016.
[5] Hall, John Whitney. The Cambridge History of Japan. Cambridge University Press. p. 362. ISBN 9780521223522. Retrieved 29 July 2016.
[6] Yi, Hyŏn-hŭi;Pak, Sŏng-su;Yun, Nae-hyŏn. New history of Korea. Jimoondang. p. 201. ISBN 9788988095850. Retrieved 29 July 2016. He launched a military expedition to expand his territory, opening the golden age of Goguryeo.
[7] Embree, Ainslie Thomas. Encyclopedia of Asian history. Scribner. p. 324. ISBN 9780684188997. Retrieved 29 July 2016. Nevertheless, the reigns of Kwanggaet'o and his successor Changsu (413-491) constituted the golden age of Koguryo.
[8] Roberts, John Morris;Westad, Odd Arne. The History of the World. Oxford University Press. p. 443. ISBN 9780199936762. Retrieved 15 July 2016.
[9] Gardner, Hall. Averting Global War: Regional Challenges, Overextension, and Options for American Strategy. Palgrave Macmillan. pp. 158–159. ISBN 9780230608733. Retrieved 15 July 2016.
[10] Laet, Sigfried J. de. History of Humanity: From the seventh to the sixteenth century. UNESCO. p. 1133. ISBN 9789231028137. Retrieved 10 October 2016.
[11] Walker, Hugh Dyson. East Asia: A New History. AuthorHouse. pp. 6–7. ISBN 9781477265178. Retrieved 19 November 2016.
[12] Tudor, Daniel. Korea: The Impossible Country: The Impossible Country. Tuttle Publishing. ISBN 9781462910229. Retrieved 15 July 2016.
[13] Kotkin, Stephen;Wolff, David. Rediscovering Russia in Asia: Siberia and the Russian Far East: Siberia and the Russian Far East. Routledge. ISBN 9781317461296. Retrieved 15 July 2016.
[14] "Gwanggaetodaewanggwa Jangsuwang" (in Korean). ebookspub. ISBN 9791155191323. Retrieved 11 October 2016.
[15] Park, Yeon Hwan;Gerrard, Jon. Black Belt Tae Kwon Do: The Ultimate Reference Guide to the World's Most Popular Black Belt Martial Art. Skyhorse Publishing Inc. p. 1. ISBN 9781620875742. Retrieved 11 October 2016.
[16] Ebrey, Patricia Buckley;Walthall, Anne. Pre-Modern East Asia: A Cultural, Social, and Political History, Volume I: To 1800. Cengage Learning. p. 103. ISBN 1133606512. Retrieved 11 October 2016.
[17] Lee, Hyun-hee;Park, Sung-soo;Yoon, Nae-hyun (2005). New History of Korea. Jimoondang. pp. 199–202. ISBN 9788988095850.
[18] "King Gwanggaeto the Great (1)". KBS World Radio. Korea Communications Commission. Retrieved 7 October 2016.
[19] Kimsanghun. tong segyesa 1: illyu tansaengeseo jungse sidaekkaji: oeuji anko tongeuro ihaehaneun (in Korean). Dasan Books. ISBN 9788963702117. Retrieved 11 October 2016.
[20] Injae, Lee;Miller, Owen;Jinhoon, Park;Hyun-Hae, Yi. Korean History in Maps. Cambridge University Press. p. 49. ISBN 9781107098466. Retrieved 11 October 2016.
[21] Ichangu, geurim : ihuigeun, geul : choeseungpil,gamsu : sesangi kkamjjang nollan uri yeoksa jingirok (in Korean). Tteuindol Press. ISBN 9788958074731. Retrieved 11 October 2016.
[22] "Ilbon Gulle Beoseonan Choechoui Gwanggaetodaewangbimun Haeseokbon Nawa". Ohmynews. 9 February 2014. Retrieved 11 October 2016.
[23] Yi, Ki-baek. A New History of Korea. Harvard University Press. p. 37. ISBN 9780674615762. Retrieved 11 October 2016.
[24] Injae, Lee;Miller, Owen;Jinhoon, Park;Hyun-Hae, Yi. Korean History in Maps. Cambridge University Press. p. 30. ISBN 9781107098466.
[25] Sin Hyeongsik. A Brief History of Korea. Ewha Womans University Press. ISBN 9788973006199. Retrieved 11 October 2016.
[26] Middleton, John. World Monarchies and Dynasties. Routledge. p. 505. ISBN 9781317451587. Retrieved 11 October 2016.
[27] Buswell, Robert E. (2004). Encyclopedia of Buddhism: A - L. New York: Macmillan Reference USA, Thomson Gale. p. 430. ISBN 9780028657196.
[28] Kim, Jinwung. A History of Korea: From "Land of the Morning Calm" to States in Conflict. Indiana University Press. p. 34. ISBN 0253000785. Retrieved 11 October 2016.
[29] Kang, Jae-eun. The Land of Scholars: Two Thousand Years of Korean Confucianism. Homa & Sekey Books. pp. 37–38. ISBN 9781931907309. Retrieved 11 October 2016.
[30] "Guk Yangwang". KOCCA. Korea Creative Content Agency. Retrieved 11 October 2016.
[31] "King Gogukyang". KBS World Radio. Retrieved 11 October 2016.
[32] "Goguryeo's Worldview and Three Kingdoms". Korea Now. Korea Herald. 33: 32. 1 January 2004. Retrieved 31 December 2016. They called their king "taewang" ("the greatest king"). Taewang was a title equivalent to "emperor" and referred to the ruler of the entire world of Goguryeo. In short, the practice of calling their king "taewang" was based on Goguryeo's independent worldview.
[33] Iyunseop. Gwanggaetodaewanggwa Jangsuwang" (in Korean). ebookspub. pp. 89–91. ISBN 9791155191323. Retrieved 11 October 2016.
[34] Hall, John Whitney. The Cambridge History of Japan. Cambridge University Press. p. 362. ISBN 9780521223522. Retrieved 29 July 2016.
[35] Kim, Bu-sik. Samguk Sagi: Volume 18. Retrieved 7 July 2016.
[36] Yi, Hyun-hui;Pak, Song-su;Yun, Nae-hyon (2005). New History of Korea. Seoul: Jimoondang. p. 170. ISBN 8988095855.
[37] Jeon ho-tae, "Koguryo, the origin of Korean power & pride", Dongbuka History Foundation, 2007. ISBN 8991448836 p.137
[38] Institute of Korean Studies;Seoul National University (2004). "Korean studies". Korean Studies (17): 15–16.
[39] Bourgoin, Suzanne Michele, ed. (1998). "Kwanggaet'o". Encyclopedia of World Biography: Kilpatrick-Louis. Gale Research. p. 94.
[40] Holcombe, Charles (2001). The Genesis of East Asia : 221 B.C. - A.D. 907. Honolulu: Associate for Asian Studies [u.a.] p. 174. ISBN 9780824824655. Retrieved 17 June 2016.
[41] Walker, Hugh Dyson. East Asia: A New History. AuthorHouse. p. 137. ISBN 9781477265161. Retrieved 29 July 2016. He also conquered Sushen tribes in the northeast, Tungusic ancestors of the Jurcid and Manchus who later ruled Chinese "barbarian conquest dynasties" during the twelfth and seventeenth centuries.
[42] Iyunseop. Gwanggaetodaewanggwa Jangsuwang (in Korean). ebookspub. pp. 93–95. ISBN 9791155191323. Retrieved 11 October 2016.
[43] "King Gwanggaeto the Great (2)". KBS World Radio. Korea Communications Commission. Retrieved 11 October 2016.
[44] Johanseong. Yeoksauiteoningpointeu14_Samguguijeonseonggi (in Korean). Book21 Publishing Group. ISBN 9788950944087. Retrieved 11 October 2016.
[45] Lee, Peter H.;Ch'oe, Yongho;Kang, Hugh H. W. Sources of Korean Tradition: Volume One: From Early Times Through the Sixteenth Century. Columbia University Press. p. 26. ISBN 9780231515313. Retrieved 21 October 2016.
[46] "Koguryo". Journal of Northeast Asian History. 4 (1-2): 57. 2007.
[47] Kamstra, Jacques H. Encounter Or Syncretism: The Initial Growth of Japanese Buddhism. p. 38.
[48] Batten, Bruce Loyd. Gateway to Japan: Hakata in War And Peace, 500-1300. p. 16.
[49] Walker, Hugh Dyson. East Asia: A New History. AuthorHouse. p. 137. ISBN 9781477265161. Retrieved 29 July 2016.
[50] Kimunhoe. Tehangukgwa Monggol, Geu Cheonnyeonui Bimireul Chajaseo". Pressian. Korea Press Foundation. Retrieved 11 October 2016.
[51] "Gogohakja Sonbogi Gyosu". Sisa Journal. Retrieved 11 October 2016.
[52] "[Chowon silkeurodeureul gada](14)chowolloga hanbandokkajite." Gyeonghyangsinmun. The Kyunghyang Shinmun. Retrieved 11 October 2016.
[53] Koerner, E. F. K.;Asher, R. E. Concise History of the Language Sciences: From the Sumerians to the Cognitivists. Elsevier. p. 54. ISBN 9781483297545. Retrieved 13 October 2016.
[54] Haralambous, Yannis;Horne, P. Scott. Fonts & Encodings. "O'Reilly Media, Inc.". p. 155. ISBN 9780596102425. Retrieved 8 October 2016.
[55] Selin, Helaine. Encyclopaedia of the History of Science, Technology, and Medicine in Non-Westen Cultures. Springer Science & Business Media. pp. 505–506. ISBN 9789401714167. Retrieved 27 July 2016.
[56] "Daehanmingung guseokguseok". Visit Korea. Korea Tourism Organization. Retrieved 7 July 2016.
[57] "Gwanggaetotaewangbi/dongsang". Guri City. Retrieved 7 July 2016.

QUEEN SEONDEOK - The First Queen of Korea

[1] Il-yeon: Samguk Yusa: Legends and History of the Three Kingdoms of Ancient Korea, translated by Tae-Hung Ha and Grafton K. Mintz. Book One, page 57. Silk Pagoda (2006). ISBN 1-59654-348-5
[2] Silla Korea and the Silk Road by Koreasociety
[3] Lee 2008, p. 137
[4] Lee 2008, p. 139
[5] Wollock 2011, p. 254
[6] Lee 2008, p. 140
[7] (7. Silla and Wa) - Bidam Archived October 5, 2011, at the Wayback Machine.

KIM HONG-DO - The Master of Korean Painting

[1] Turner 2003, p. (18)53
[2] KBS. http://rki.kbs.co.kr/english/program/program_koreanstory_detail.htm??lang=e&current_page=11&No=23530
[3] Pratt 1999, p. 211
[4] Naver. http://terms.naver.com/entry.nhn?cid=200000000&docId=1073375&categoryId=200001108 (in Korean)
[5] Britannica. http://preview.britannica.co.kr/bol/topic.asp?article_id=b03g2103b (in Korean)
[6] Chansol 2015
[7] TWA 2013

JANG YOUNG-SIL - The Genius Engineer

[1] "The genealogy of A-san Jang-si", book 1, pp.4, 1872,
[2] Jonghwa Ahn, Kook-Jo-In-Mool-Ji, 1909, v.1, A biographical dictionary of Korea
[3] The article of 16 SEP 1433, Chosun Wangjo Sillok, King Sejong
[4] Dae-Dong-Woon-Boo-Goon-Ok, 1587
[5] Teun Koetsier;Marco Ceccarelli (5 April 2012). Explorations in the History of Machines and Mechanisms: Proceedings of HMM2012. Springer. p. 87. ISBN 978-94-007-4132-4.
[6] Moon-Ik-Gong Sillok, 1738
[7] p. 17 Baek Seokgi. (1987). Woongjin Wi-in Jeon-gi #11 Jang Yeong-sil. Woongjin Publishing.
[8] p. 46-49 Baek Seokgi. (1987). Woongjin Wi-in Jeon-gi #11 Jang Yeong-sil. Woongjin Publishing.
[9] a b Korean History Project
[10] p. 55 Baek Seokgi. (1987). Woongjin Wi-in Jeon-gi #11 Jang Yeong-sil. Woongjin Publishing.
[11] p. 56 Baek Seokgi. (1987). Woongjin Wi-in Jeon-gi #11 Jang Yeong-sil. Woongjin Publishing.
[12] p. 77 Baek Seokgi. (1987). Woongjin Wi-in Jeon-gi #11 Jang Yeong-sil. Woongjin Publishing.
[13] Indiana University Resources
[14] Introduction to the Folk Museum
[15] The Invention of Movable Type
[16] Glossary of Korean Studies
[17] p. 63 Baek Seokgi. (1987). Woongjin Wi-in Jeon-gi #11 Jang Yeong-sil. Woongjin Publishing.
[18] Federation of Busan and Technology
[19] p. 68 Baek Seokgi. (1987). Woongjin Wi-in Jeon-gi #11 Jang Yeong-sil. Woongjin Publishing.
[20] p. 71 Baek Seokgi. (1987). Woongjin Wi-in Jeon-gi #11 Jang Yeong-sil. Woongjin Publishing.
[21] p. 72-73 Baek Seokgi. (1987). Woongjin Wi-in Jeon-gi #11 Jang Yeong-sil. Woongjin Publishing.
[22] p. 75 Baek Seokgi. (1987). Woongjin Wi-in Jeon-gi #11 Jang Yeong-sil Woongjin Publishing.
[23] "Silent clock tick - jagyeokru adoptive father and one". Kaeri Web Magazine (Korean Atomic Energy Research Institute). March–April 2002. Archived from the original on May 2, 2005. Retrieved May 30, 2015.
[24] p. 87-91 Baek Seokgi. (1987). Woongjin Wi-in Jeon-gi #11 Jang Yeong-sil. Woongjin Publishing.
[25] The Culture and Civilization of Ancient India in Historical Outline;Kosambi, 1982
[26] p. 97 Baek Seokgi. (1987). Woongjin Wi-in Jeon-gi #11 Jang Yeong-sil. Woongjin Publishing.
[27] Visit Busan Museum Guide
[28] American Meteorological Society press
[39] Education About Asia, Vol. 6, #2, Fall, 2001.
[30] Friendly Korea brief on Korean history
[31] p. 101 Baek Seokgi. (1987). Woongjin Wi-in Jeon-gi #11 Jang Yeong-sil. Woongjin Publishing.
[32] p. 108-111 Baek Seokgi. (1987). Woongjin Wi-in Jeon-gi #11 Jang Yeong-sil. Woongjin Publishing.

JANG BO-GO - The Emperor of The Sea

[1] Tagliacozzo, Eric. Asia Inside Out. Harvard University Press. ISBN 9780674286344. Retrieved 17 March 2017.
[2] Shin, Gi-Wook;Choi, Joon. Global Talent: Skilled Labor as Social Capital in Korea. Stanford University Press. p. 68. ISBN 9780804794381. Retrieved 17 March 2017.
[3] Chong Sun Kim, "Slavery in Silla and its Sociological and Economic Implications", in Andrew C. Nahm, ed. Traditional Korea, Theory and Practice (Kalamazoo, MI: Center for Korean Studies, 1974), p. 33.
[4] Quoted in Edwin O. Reischauer, Ennin's Diary;the Record of a Pilgrimage to China in Search of the Law (New York: Ronald Press, 1955), p. 288.
[5] Il-yeon: Samguk Yusa: Legends and History of the Three Kingdoms of Ancient Korea, translated by Tae-Hung Ha and Grafton K. Mintz. Book Two, page 103. Silk Pagoda (2006). ISBN 1-59654-348-5
[6] KBS Global Marketing
[7] www.shenyanglvxing.com. Retrieved 17 March 2017.

JEONG YAK-YONG - The Joseon Dynasty's Social Reformer

[1] Setton, Mark. Chong Yakyong. page 54
[2] Setton, Mark. Chong Yakyong. page 55
[3] Setton, Mark. Chong Yakyong. page 59
[4] Setton, Mark. Chong Yakyong. page 62
[5] Setton, Mark. Chong Yakyong. page 63
[6] Setton, Mark. Chong Yakyong. page 66
[7] Jeong Min:Joseonui Chamunhwa p. 144
[8] Jeong Min:Joseonui Chamunhwa p. 209
[9] Jeong Min:Joseonui Chamunhwa p. 278
[10] Brother Anthony etc:Korean Tea Classics page 9
[11] http://eng.cfe.org/mboard/bbsDetail.asp?cid=mn2007713123749&pn=3&idx=971
[12] https://docs.google.com/viewer?a=v&q=cache:QBlEV3IADmcJ:www.ekoreajournal.net/upload/pdf/PDF4948+Jeong+Yakyong+idea&hl=en&gl=us&pid=bl&srcid=ADGEEShJFLe6lO7AHd3Kt6-jTjJ30D3F49-bS5op5VvY0DNk7A6_LfgGmdxjtAX25SJ-rchyxVNGnRvzSuqbrAAC5aR3FvDIgMxcYT1oW_FPXGiaXefGsUoyX7GJANwMzwtSMuE_Mkn4&sig=AHIEtbSOPybiHQgT7Pl-orGGvncRRQoQ-A
[13] (Jong Chun Park) (2006). "Tasan's theory of sacrificial rites -in the case of Mokminsimseo". Tasanhak. 9: 81–122. Abstract, Introduction
[14] Kihl, Young Whan (2004). Transforming Korean Politics: Democracy, Reform, and Culture. Armonk, New York: M.E. Sharpe. p. 48. ISBN 978-0-7656-1427-8.
[15] Palais, James B. (1996). Confucian Statecraft and Korean Institutions: Yu Hyŏngwŏn and the Late Chosŏn Dynasty. Seattle, Washington: University of Washington Press. pp. https://books.google.com/books?id=kwpSxkUYCSAC&pg=PA372 372–379. ISBN 978-0-295-97455-2.
Print

YU GWANSUN - The Patriotic Martyr

[1] Bright Figures in Korean History, Kim, Han-ryong Compiler, Daeil Publishing
[2] "Yu Gwan-sun, the Indefatigable Independence Fighter". KBS World Radio. Korea Communications Commission. 2013. Retrieved 30 November 2016.
[3] http://www.cheonan.go.kr/yugwansun/sub01_03.do, Yu Gwan-sun Historic Site
[4] Books, L. L. C. (1 May 2010). "Korean People Who Died in Prison Custody: Yoo Gwan-Sun, Yun Dong-Ju, Pak Paengnyeon, Kim Jeong-Ho,". General Books LLC – via Google Books.
[5] Famous Koreans: Six Portraits -Yoo, Kwan-Sun (1904–20) - By Mary Connor at aasianst.org
[6] http://www.cheonan.go.kr/yugwansun/sub01_04.do, Yu Gwan-sun Historic Site
[7] http://www.cheonan.go.kr/yugwansun/sub01_05.do, Yu Gwan-sun Historic Site
[8] Lonely Planet;Simon Richmond (1 November 2012). Lonely Planet Seoul. Lonely Planet. pp. 294–. ISBN 978-1-74321-363-6.
[9] Connor, Mary. "Famous Koreans Six Portratis". Retrieved 5 May 2015.
[10] http://www.cheonan.go.kr/yugwansun/sub01_06.do, Yu Gwan-sun Historic Site
[11] Interview with Jeanette Walter quoted in Living Dangerously in Korea: The Western Experience 1900-1950, Clark, Donald N. (Norwalk, CT: Eastbridge, 2003). "... when I was in Korea in 1959, I was interviewed by a group from Kwansoon's school, and I assured them on tape that her body was not mutilated. I had dressed her for burial."
[12] http://www.cheonan.go.kr/yugwansun/sub01_07.do, Yu Gwan-sun Historic Site
[13] "Korea's Joan of Arc latest figure in East Asia's colonial propaganda war | The National". Retrieved 2016-11-30.
[14] McMurray, Nathan. "Society: The March 1st Independence Movement and its big sister". 10 Magazine. Retrieved 2015-05-05.

WONHYO - The Great Master-Monk

[1] Muller, Charles A. (1995). "The Key Operative Concepts in Korean Buddhist Syncretic Philosophy: Interpenetration and Essence-Function in Wŏnhyo, Chinul and Kihwa" cited in Bulletin of Toyo Gakuen University No. 3, March 1995, pp 33-48.Source: [1] (accessed: September 18, 2008) Archived August 28, 2008, at the Wayback Machine.
[2] "wonhyo - Buddhistdoor - Buddhist Glossary". Glossary.buddhistdoor.com. Retrieved 2012-08-13.
[3] Sources Of East Asian Tradition: Premodern Asia - Google Books. Books.google.com. Retrieved 2012-08-13.
[4] Keel, Hee-Sung (2004). "Korea";cited in Buswell, Robert E. (2004). Encyclopedia of Buddhism. Volume 1. New York, USA: Macmillan Reference USA. ISBN 0-02-865719-5 (Volume 1): pp.432
[5] (in Korean) Establishment and History of Bunhangsa Korea Temple
[6] Keel, Hee-Sung (2004). "Korea";cited in Buswell, Robert E. (2004). Encyclopedia of Buddhism. Volume 1. New York, USA: Macmillan Reference USA. ISBN 0-02-865719-5, pp.431-432
[7] Byeong-Jo Jeong;Wŏnhyo (2010). Master Wonhyo: an overview of his life and teachings, Korean spirit and culture series, vol. 6, Seoul : Diamond Sutra Recitation Group, page 50
[8] Chun Ock-bae, 2010, "Why WonhyoNow?," The Korea Times, April 16, p. 14.
[9] "Wonhyo Publication Project". Stony Brook University, Center for Korean Studies. Retrieved 2 May 2013.
[10] WTF Poomsae

AN JUNG-GEUN - The Patriot, Assassin, Hero

WONHYO - The Great Master-Monk

[1] Ahn was the chief of staff of the Korean Righteous army
[2] "What Defines a Hero?". Japan Society. Archived from the original on 2007-10-04. Retrieved 2008-01-29.
[3] "Ito, Hirobumi". Portrait of Modern japanese Historical Figures. Archived from the original on 29 January 2008. Retrieved 2008-01-29.
[4] "Ito Hirobumi". Encyclopædia Britannica. Retrieved 2008-01-29.
[5] Dudden, Alexis (2005). Japan's Colonization of Korea: Discourse and Power. University of Hawaii Press. ISBN 0-8248-2829-1.
[6] "Peace of East Asia" Thesis written by An Jung-geun in 1910
[7] Shin, Gi-Wook (2006). Ethnic Nationalism in Korea. Stanford University Press. ISBN 0-8047-5408-X.
[8] Ito, Hirobumi | Portraits of Modern Japanese Historical Figures at www.ndl.go.jp
[9] [1] Doosan Encyclopedia
[10] Kim, G. (1928/1997, p.48)
[11] Keene, Donald (2002). Emperor of Japan: Meiji and His World, 1852–1912. Columbia University Press. pp. 662–667. ISBN 0-231-12340-X.
[12] Kang.(2007, p.131)
[13] For example, see the article Eulsa Treaty
[14] Komei, who was strongly opposed to radical political changes, died at the age of 35. The official cause of death was smallpox. But there has been a theory widely believed at the time that the emperor was actually poisoned by the anti-Bakufu clique. See for example Chung (1910/2004, p.61), Jansen (1961, p.282), Nam (1999, p.111), and Ravina (2004, p.135).
[15] Ahn Jung-Geun, The Great Patriot Martyr of Korea, Patriot Ahn Memorial Hall, November 1995, p. 5
[16] http://naver007.exblog.jp/i8/ (3)
[17] [2] 2010 Nocut News article
[18] "Research notes of Ippei Wakabayashi" "Archived copy" (PDF). Archived from the original (PDF) on 2011-06-13. Retrieved 2011-03-31.
[19] [3] 2009 Joongang Ilbo Article
[20] [4] 2010 Kyunghyang News Article
[21] "On Peace in East Asia" (in Korean) Archived April 18, 2014, at the Wayback Machine.
[22] [5] 2010 Segye Ilbo article
[23] An Jung Geun calligraphy, Treasure No. 569
[24] [6] 2009 Asian Business Article
[25] [7]
[26] "China Relocates Ahn Jung-geun Memorial Hall". KBS World Radio. March 22, 2017.
[27] "Japan protest over Korean assassin Ahn Jung-geun memorial in China". BBC News. 2014-01-20. Retrieved 2017-03-09.
[28] "South Korean police in terrorism poster gaffe". BBC News. 2017-02-13. Retrieved 2017-03-09.
[29] DVD in North Korea Books
[30] "Thomas Ahn Jung-geun". Retrieved 10 December 2013.

KIM KOO - Leader of Korean Independence Movement

http://www.newsis.com/ar_detail/view.html/?ar_id=NISX20140817_0013113564&cID=10201&pID=10200
Japan Center for Asian Historical Records Reference code: A04010024500
New Encyclopedia of Korean History Seoul:Gyohaksa, 1983, ISBN 89-09-00506-8
[1] Doosan Encyclopedia
a b c http://legacy.www.hani.co.kr/section-021109000/2007/04/021109000200704120655080.html
Bruce Cumings, Korea's Place in the Sun: A Modern History, W W Norton and Co, New York, 1997, p 197.

a b c Bruce Cumings, "Hangukjeonjaengui giwon" translated by Kim Ja Dong. Ilwolseogak p. 286

Richard Robinson, "Migukeui baeban: migunjeonggwa namjoseon" translated by Jeong Mi-ok. Gwahakgwa sasang, 1988 p 78

Richard Robinson, "Migukeui baeban: migunjeonggwa namjoseon" translated by Jeong Mi-ok. Gwahakgwa sasang, 1988 p 77

Lee Cheol-seung, Park Gap-dong, "Geonguk 50nyeon daehanminguk ireotgae sewotda". Gyemyeongsa, 1998 p. 238

Kang Joon-man, "Hanguk hyeondaesasanchaek - 1940nyeondaepyeon 2gwon". Inmulgwasasangsa. 2004 p 66

Jang Taek-sang, "Daehanminguk geongukgwa na". Changrangjangtaesang ginyeomsaeophoe. 1993) p. 73

Lankov, Andrei (September 4, 2008). "What Happened to Kim Ku?". Korea Times. Archived from the original on December 22, 2015.

Jager, Sheila Miyoshi (2013). Brothers at War – The Unending Conflict in Korea. London: Profile Books. pp. 48, 496. ISBN 978-1-84668-067-0.

Cumings, Bruce. The origins of the Korean War: liberation and the emergence of separate reKimes 1945-1947. (Princeton;Guildford: Princeton University Press, 1981.), 219. ISBN 978-0691101132

Jager, Sheila Miyoshi (2013). Brothers at War – The Unending Conflict in Korea. London: Profile Books. p. 496. ISBN 978-1-84668-067-0.

[2] 2010 Pressian article

"National Reunification Prize Winners", Korean Central News Agency, 1998-05-07, archived from the original on 2013-06-02, retrieved 2012-09-13

a b [3] Korean Cultural Heritage Information Center

[4] 2004 online poll

[5] 2005 survey by Dongailbo

[6] 2007 survey by CBS

[7] 2007 survey by Maeil Business

[8] Yonhap News Article

Kim Koo (in Korean). Wikisource link to baekbeomilji. Wikisource.[7] Jeong Min:Joseonui Chamunhwa p. 144

[8] Jeong Min:Joseonui Chamunhwa p. 209

[9] Jeong Min:Joseonui Chamunhwa p. 278

[10] Brother Anthony etc:Korean Tea Classics page 9

[11] http://eng.cfe.org/mboard/bbsDetail.asp?cid=mn2007713123749&pn=3&idx=971

[12] https://docs.google.com/viewer?a=v&q=cache:QBlEV3lADmcJ:www.ekoreajournal.net/upload/pdf/PDF4948+Jeong+Yakyong+idea&hl=en&gl=us&pid=bl&srcid=ADGEE ShJFLe6lO7AHd3Kt6-jTjJ30D3F49-bS5op5VvY0DNk7A6_LfgGmdxjtAX25SJ rchyxVNGnRvzSuqbrAAC5aR3FvDIgMxcYT1oW_FPXGiaXefGsUoyX7GJANwMzwtSMuE_ Mkn4&sig=AIIIEtbSOPybIHQg17Pl-orGGvncRRQoQ-A

[13] (Jong Chun Park) (2006). "Tasan's theory of sacrificial rites -in the case of Mokminsimseo". Tasanhak. 9: 81–122. Abstract, Introduction

[14] Kihl, Young Whan (2004). Transforming Korean Politics: Democracy, Reform, and Culture. Armonk, New York: M.E. Sharpe. p. 48. ISBN 978-0-7656-1427-8.

[15] Palais, James B. (1996). Confucian Statecraft and Korean Institutions: Yu Hyŏngwŏn and the Late Chosŏn Dynasty. Seattle, Washington: University of Washington Press. pp. https://books.google.com/books?id=kwpSxkUYCSAC&pg=PA372 372–379. ISBN 978-0-295 97455-2. Print

KIM YU-SHIN - General Who Led The Unification of Kingdoms

This article uses material from the Wikipedia article en.wikipedia.org/wiki/Kim_Yu-sin, which is released under the Creative Commons Attribution-Share-Alike License 3.0, which can be viewed at creativecommons.org/licenses/by-sa/3.0/

McBride, Richard D., II. "Hidden Agendas in the Life Writings of Kim Yusin." Acta Koreana 1 (August 1998): 101-142.

McBride, Richard D., II. "The Structure and Sources of the Biography of Kim Yusin." Acta Koreana 16, no. 2 (December 2013): 497–535.

SOHN KEE-CHUNG, Korea's First Olympic Gold Medalist

This article uses material from the Wikipedia article en.wikipedia.org/wiki/Sohn_Kee-chung, which is released under the Creative Commons Attribution-Share-Alike License 3.0, which can be viewed at creativecommons.org/licenses/by-sa/3.0/

[1] Son Gi-Jeong. www.sports-reference.com

[2] "12th IAAF World Championships In Athletics: IAAF Statistics Handbook. Berlin 2009." (PDF). Monte Carlo: IAAF Media & Public Relations Department. 2009. p. 565. Archived from the original on August 6, 2009. Retrieved July 29, 2009.

[3] Men's World Record Times – 1932 to 1938. Marathonguide.com. Retrieved on June 9, 2015.

[4] However, Shu's performance was set on a course considered to be short by some[who?] road racing authorities, which means Sohn's world best would have lasted until the early 1950's. (See the Association of Road Racing Statistician's web pages regarding the Boston Marathon and World Best Progressions.)

[5] The Chosun Ilbo (English Edition): Daily News from Korea – Late Recognition for Korean Olympic Athlete Sohn Kee-chung. English.chosun.com (December 16, 2011). Retrieved on 2015-06-09

[6] Sohn Kee-chung. beijing2008.cn

[7] Bull, Andy (August 27, 2011). "The forgotten story of Sohn Kee-chung, Korea's Olympic hero". The Guardian.

[8] Athletics at the 1936 Berlin Summer Games: Men's Marathon. sports-reference.com

[9] James Markham (August 18, 1986). "GERMANS LOOK BACK, GINGERLY, TO THE '36 GAMES". New York Times.

[10] Marathon Winner in '36 Berlin Games Will Be Given Prize—50 Years Late. Reuters. August 10, 1986

[11] http://www.hani.co.kr/arti/sports/baseball/158635.html (Korean). The Hankyoreh. September 20, 2006.

[12] http://media.daum.net/society/nation/others/view.html?cateid=100011&newsid=20061111144710635&p=yonhap (Korean)". Media Daum/Yonhap News Agency. November 11, 2006.

[13] "Sohn Kee-chung". Korea Times. Retrieved November 4, 2010.

[14] "Bridal Mask" boxer recalls Son Gi-jeong". HanCinema. HanCinema. August 15, 2012. Retrieved February 17, 2015.

SHIN CHAE-HO - Founder of Korean Ethnic Nationalist Historiography

This article uses material from the Wikipedia article en.wikipedia.org/wiki/Shin_Chaeho, which is released under the Creative Commons Attribution-Share-Alike License 3.0, which can be viewed at creativecommons.org/licenses/by-sa/3.0/

[1] Bae, Ji-sook. "Independence Fighter to Get Family Register". www.koreatimes.co.kr. Korea Times. Archived from the original on 25 June 2014. Retrieved 25 June 2014.

[2] Ch'oe, Yŏng-ho (1980). "An outline history of Korean historiography". Korean Studies. 4: 1–27. doi:10.1353/ks.1980.0003.

[3] Park, So-yang (Jan 2012). "Speaking with the Colonial Ghosts and Pungsu Rumour in Contemporary South Korea (1990-2006): The Pungsu (Feng Shui) Invasion Story Surrounding the Demolition of the Former Japanese Colonial-General Builsing and Iron Spikes". Journal for Cultural Research. 16 (1): 21–42. doi:10.1080/14797585.2011.633834.

[4] Robinson, Michael (1986). "Nationalism and the Korean Tradition, 1896-1920: Iconoclasm, Reform, and National Identity". Korean Studies. 10: 35–53. doi:10.1353/ks.1986.0001.

[5] David-West, Alzo (2011). "Between Confucianism and Marxism-Leninism: Juche and the Case of Chŏng Tasan". Korean Studies. 35: 93–121. doi:10.1353/ks.2011.0007.

[6] Schmid, Andre (Feb 1997). "Rediscovering Manchuria: Sin Ch'aeho and the Politics of Territorial History in Korea". The Journal of Asian Studies. 56 (1): 26–46. JSTOR 2646342. doi:10.2307/2646342.

[7] Shin, Yong-ha (2004). "The philosophical world of Sin Chae-ho". In Lee, Seung-Hwan;Korean National Commission for UNESCO. Korean Philosophy: Its Tradition and Modern Transformation. Seoul, South Korea: Elizabeth, NJ - Hollym. pp. 441–461. ISBN 1565911784.

[8] Armstrong, Charles (1995). "Centering the Periphery: Manchurian Exile(s) and the North Korean State". Korean Studies. 19: 1–16. doi:10.1353/ks.1995.0017.

[9] Robinson, Michael (1984). "National Identity and the Thought of Sin Ch'aeho: Sadaejuŭi and Chuch'e in History and Politics". Journal of Korean Studies. 5: 121–142. doi:10.1353/jks.1984.0003.

[10] Kuiwon. "Shin Chaeho - On the road to mount Baekdu". Koreabridge.

[11] Park, Sang-jin (Dec 2012). "The literary value of Sin Ch'ae-ho's Dream Sky: A marginal alteration of Dante's Comedy". Acta Koreana. 15 (2): 311–340. doi:10.18399/acta.2012.15.2.003.

[12] Suh, Dae-sook (1967). The Korean Communist Movement 1918-1948. Princeton, New Jersey: Princeton University Press.

[13] Tikhonov, Vladimir (2012). "The Race and Racism Discourses in Modern Korea 1890s-1910s". Korean Studies. 36: 31–57. doi:10.1353/ks.2012.0008.

[14] Tikhonov, Vladimir (2007). "Masculinizing the nation: Gender ideologies in traditional Korea and in the 1890s-1900s Korean enlightenment discourse". The Journal of Asian Studies. 66 (4): 1029–1065. doi:10.1017/s0021911807001283.

[15] "Historical Figures". Daejeon Jung-gu. Archived from the original on 20 April 2015. Retrieved 20 April 2015.

[16] Korea Times, Dec. 3, 1994. Cited by Bruce Cumings (2005), Korea's Place in the Sun (updated edition), New York and London: W. W. Norton.

[17] Schmid, Andre (2002). Korea Between Empires, 1895-1919. New York: Columbia University Press.

[18] Lee, Ki-Balk (September 1979). "Nationalism in Tanjae's Historical Study". Korea Journal. 19 (9): 4–10.

[19] Jager, Sheila Miyoshi (Feb 1996). "Women, resistance, and the divided nation: The romantic rhetoric of Korean reunification". The Joural of Asian Studies. 55 (1): 3–21.

JSTOR 2943634. doi:10.2307/2943634.
[20] Robinson, Michael (1984). "National identity and thought of Sin Ch'aeho: Sadaejuŭi and Chuch'e in history and politics". Journal of Korean Studies. 5: 121–142. doi:10.1353/jks.1984.0003.
[21] Sung, Min-kyu (2009). "The 'truth politics' of anti-North Koreanism: the post-ideological cultural representation of North Korea and the cultural criticisms of Korean nationalism". Inter-Asia Cultural Studies. 10 (3): 439–459. doi:10.1080/14649370902949457.
[22] Burgess, Chris (2007). "'Loss' and 'Recovery' of Voice amongst Korean International Marriage Migrants: Discourses of Korean-ness in Contemporary Japan". Electronic Journal of Contemporary Japanese Studies. 7. Archived from the original on April 25, 2009. Retrieved 24 July 2015.

SOH JAIPIL - Founder of The First Korean Newspaper in Hangul

[1] http://www.segye.com/Articles/NEWS/SOCIETY/Article.asp?aid=20110407005238 The Segyenews 2011.04.07 (in Korean)
[2] http://terms.naver.com/entry.nhn?cid=1593&docId=574510 Soh Jaipil (in Korean)
[3] Seo Jae-pil: pioneering reformer, independence fighter koreatimes 2011.12.28 (in English)
[4] http://www.imaeil.com/sub_news/sub_news_view.php?news_id=50661&yy=2007 imail 2007.11.20 (in Korean)
[5] http://news.hankooki.com/lpage/culture/201005/h2010051721354086330.htm The Hanguk (in Korean)

SIN SAIMDANG - Korea's Own Renaissance Woman

[1] (in Korean) http://100.naver.com/100.nhn?docid=101834 Sin Saimdang at Doosan Encyclopedia
[2] (in Korean) http://people.aks.ac.kr/front/tabCon/ppl/pplView.aks?pplId=PPL_6JOa_A1504_2_0006348 Sin Saimdang at The Academy of Korean Studies
[3] "'Best mom' chosen as face of currency". Reuters. Nov 6, 2007.

Yi I - Joseon's Most Prominent Scholar and Philosopher

[1] Daehwan, Noh. "The Eclectic Development of Neo-Confucianism and Statecraft from the 18th to the 19th Century," Archived June 14, 2011, at the Wayback Machine. Korea Journal. Winter 2003.
[2] (in Korean) Yi I at Doosan Encyclopedia
[3] (in Korean) Yi I at The Academy of Korean Studies
[4] (in Korean) [1] at Encyclopedia of Korean Culture
[5] Lee Eunjik translated by Jeong Hongjun, Great Joseon Masters Vol.2 p35, Ilbit Publishing, Seoul, 2005. ISBN 89-5645-087-0
[6] (in Korean) Dongho Mundap at Doosan Encyclopedia
[7] Choi Beomseo, Unofficial History of Joseon Vol. 2 p52, Garam Publishing, Seoul, 2003. ISBN 89-8435-143-1
[8] Lee Hyun-hee, Park Sung-soo, Yoon Nae-hyun, translated by The Academy of Korean Studies, New History of Korea p393, Jimoondang, Paju, 2005. ISBN 89-88095-85-5
[9] WorldCat Identities: Yi, I 1536-1584
[10] (in Korean) Maneon Bongsa at Doosan Encyclopedia
[11] (in Korean) Seonhak Jibyo at Doosan Encyclopedia
[12] (in Korean) Gyeokmong Yogyel at Doosan Encyclopedia
[13] (in Korean) Gyeongyeon Ilgi at Doosan Encyclopedia
[14] (in Korean) Yulgok Jeonseo at Doosan Encyclopedia
[15] (in Korean) Yulgongno at Doosan Encyclopedia
[16] (in Korean) Money bill designs at Naver dictionary
[17] Yulgok Taekwondo pattern
[18] Cha Yeonggu, Theory and Actuality of National Defense Policies p86, Oruem, Seoul, 20

Yi Hwang - Joseon's Most Prominent Scholar and Philosopher

[1] Daehwan, Noh. "The Eclectic Development of Neo-Confucianism and Statecraft from the 18th to the 19th Century," Archived June 14, 2011, at the Wayback Machine. Korea Journal. Winter 2003.
[2] http://100.naver.com/100.nhn?docid=128831 (in Korean) Yi Hwang at Doosan Encyclopedia
[3] http://100.nate.com/dicsearch/pentry.html?s=K&i=266750&v=43 (in Korean) Yi Hwang at Encyclopedia of Korean Culture
[4] http://people.aks.ac.kr/front/tabCon/ppl/pplView.aks?pplId=PPL_6JOa_A1501_1_0011100 (in Korean) Yi Hwang at The Academy of Korean Studies
[5] http://news.naver.com/main/read.nhn?mode=LSD&mid=sec&sid1=103&oid=0000043131 (in Korean) Seoul Sinmun, 2005-05-18. Retrieved 2010-07-07.
[6] http://100.nate.com/dicsearch/pentry.html?s=B&i=180790&v=43 (in Korean) Yi Hwang at Britannica Korea
[7] Lee Hyun-hee, Park Sung-soo, Yoon Nae-hyun, translated by The Academy of Korean Studies, New History of Korea pp 392–393, Jimoondang, Paju, 2005. ISBN 89-88095-85-5
[8] WorldCat Identities: http://www.worldcat.org/identities/lccn-n81-79070 1501–1570;Yi, Hwang 1501–1570: May 23, 2015
[9] Michael C. Kalton et al., The Four-Seven Debate. An Annotated Translationnof the Most Famous Controversy in Korean Neo-Confucian Thought, SUNY Press, Albany, 1994
[10] http://100.naver.com/100.nhn?docid=92451 (in Korean) Seonghaksipdo at Doosan Encyclopedia
[11] Ten Diagrams, Michael C. Kalton, Columbia University Press, 1988
[12] http://100.naver.com/100.nhn?docid=156033 (in Korean) Toegyero at Doosan Encyclopedia
[13] http://news.naver.com/main/read.nhn?mode=LSD&mid=sec&sid1=101&oid=019&aid=0000127499 (in Korean) The new 1,000 won bill, Maeil Business News, 2006-01-17. Retrieved 2010-07-08.
[14] http://news.naver.com/main/read.nhn?mode=LSD&mid=sec&sid1=104&oid=001&aid=0001046333 (in Korean) Historical names in Taekwondo, Yonhap News, 2005-07-10. Retrieved 2010-07-08.

JUMONG - The Holy King of The East

[1] Korea Herald. (2004) Korea now, p. 31;excerpt; "The Chinese also insist that even though Goguryeo was part of Chinese domain, Silla and Baekje were states subjected to China's tributary system."
[2] Pratt, Keith L. (1999). Korea: a historical and cultural dictionary. p. 482.
[3] Kwak, p. 99., p. 99, at Google Books;excerpt, "Korea's tributary relations with China began as early as the fifth century, were regularized during the Goryeo dynasty (918-1392), and became fully institutionalized during the Yi dynasty (1392-1910)."
[4] Seth, Michael J. (2006). A concise history of Korea, p. 64, p. 64, at Google Books;excerpt, "China found instead that its policy of using trade and cultural exchanges and offering legitimacy and prestige to the Silla monarchy was effective in keeping Silla safely in the tributary system. Indeed, the relationship that was worked out in the late seventh and early eighth centuries can be considered the beginning of the mature tributary relationship that would characterize Sino-Korean interchange most of the time until the late nineteenth century;"
[5] Digital Korean Studies https://web.archive.org/web/20050213202825/http://www.koreandb.net:80/KPeople/KPShow.asp?ID=0003672&Type=L. Archived from the original on 2005-02-13. Retrieved 2008-03-06.
[6] http://terms.naver.com/entry.nhn?docId=1185444&mobile&cid=40942&categoryId=33375. Doosan Encyclopedia.
[7] http://terms.naver.com/entry.nhn?docId=1160526&cid=40942&categoryId=31541&mobile. Doosan Encyclopedia.
[8] http://terms.naver.com/entry.nhn?docId=531903&cid=46620&categoryId=46620&mobile. Encyclopedia of Korean Culture.

[9] China, Japan, Korea: Culture and Customs By Ju Brown, John Brown
[10] Retrieved on March 6th of 2008. https://web.archive.org/web/20050213202825/http://www.koreandb.net:80/KPeople/KPShow.asp?ID=0003672&Type=L. Archived from the original on 2005-02-13. Retrieved 2008-03-06.
[11] http://www.seelotus.com/gojeon/gojeon/seol-hwa/dong-myeong-wang.htm (Kor)
[12] History of Korea (Korean) https://web.archive.org/web/20080312044422/http://www.koreandb.net:80/KoreanKing/html/person/p121_03672.htm. Archived from the original on 2008-03-12. Retrieved 2008-03-06.
[13] <<Samguksagi>>
[14] <<Samguksagi>> Goguryeo, volume 13.

YI SEONG-GYE - The First King of The Joseon Dynasty

This article uses material from the Wikipedia article en.wikipedia.org/wiki/Taejo_of_Joseon, which is released under the Creative Commons Attribution-Share-Alike License 3.0, which can be viewed at creativecommons.org/licenses/by-sa/3.0/

[1] http://terms.naver.com/entry.nhn?docId=541111&cid=46622&categoryId=46622&mobile. Encyclopedia of Korean Culture. Retrieved 2017-02-08.
[2] http://terms.naver.com/entry.nhn?docId=1134059&cid=40942&categoryId=33383&mobile. Doosan Encyclopedia. Retrieved 2017-02-09.
[3] Hussain, Tariq. (2006). Diamond Dilemma: Shaping Korea for the 21st Century, p. 45;Hodge, Carl Cavanagh. (2008). Encyclopedia of the Age of Imperialism, 1800-1914: A-K, p. 401.
[4] Goodrich, L. Carrington et al. (1976). Dictionary of Ming biography, 1368-1644, Vol. II, p. 1601.
[5] Titsingh, Isaac. (1834). Annales des empereurs du japon, p. 320;Northeast Asian History Foundation: Korea-Japan relations> Early Modern Period> Foreign Relations in Early Joseon.
[6] Seoul municipality website: About Seoul> History> General Information> Center of Korean Culture.
[7] Seoul municipality: News> Features> Royal Tombs of the Joseon Dynasty> Ggureung Tomb Complex at Guri-si, Gyeonggi-do.
[8] Taejong of Joseon Sillok vol.16, 07 August 1408, entry 3.
[9] Preface to Taejo Sillok, entry 1. The posthumous title "Kangheon" was bestowed from Ming, and was added to Taejo's posthumous name [Taejong Sillok vol.16, 13 October 1408, entry 1].
[10] Gojong Sillok vol.39, 23 December 1899, entry 1. Gojong notably omitted the posthumous title China bestowed on Taejo as a sign of the Empire's "independence" from Qing
[11] http://newfocusintl.com/chosun-north-korea-history/
[12] Kang, Jae-eun et al. (2006). The Land of Scholars, p. 172;Northeast Asian History Foundation > Korea-China relations> Early Modern Period> Korea-China relations during the Joseon.

SAINT ANDREW KIM TAEGON - Korea's First Catholic Priest and a Martyr

This article uses material from the New World Encyclopedia article http://www.newworldencyclopedia.org/entry/Andrew_Kim_Taegon, which is released under the Creative Commons Attribution-Share-Alike License 3.0, which can be viewed at creativecommons.org/licenses/by-sa/3.0/

[1] Robinson, Martin, Andrew Bender, and Rob Whyte. 2004. Korea. Footscray, Vic: Lonely Planet. ISBN 9781740594493
[2] NajuMary Retrieved December 22, 2007.
[3] Joly, Léon. 1907. Le Christianisme et l'extrême Orient: Missions Catholiques de l'Inde, de L'Indo-Chine, de la Chine, de la Corée. Paris: P. Lethielleux. OCLC: 38445976
[4] Saint of the Day Retrieved December 22, 2007.

JEONG MONG-JU - The Symbol of Unwavering Loyalty

This article uses material from the New World Encyclopedia article http://www.newworldencyclopedia.org/entry/Jeong_Mong-ju, which is released under the Creative Commons Attribution-Share-Alike License 3.0, which can be viewed at creativecommons.org/licenses/by-sa/3.0/

[1] Kang, Jae-eun and Suzanne Lee. (2006). The Land of Scholars : Two Thousand Years of Korean Confucianism. p. 191. Paramus, New Jersey: Homa & Sekey Books. ISBN 978-1-931-90737-8;OCLC 60931394.
[2] http://100.nate.com/dicsearch/pentry.html?s=K&i=242963&v=44 (in Korean) Nate / Encyclopedia of Korean Culture
[3] Titsingh, Isaac. (1834). Annales des empereurs du Japon (Nihon Ôdai Ichiran). p. 313. Paris: Oriental Translation Fund of Great Britain and Ireland. OCLC 84067437 (1834).
[4] Kang, Jae-eun and Suzanne Lee. (2006). The Land of Scholars : Two Thousand Years of Korean Confucianism. p. 159. Paramus, New Jersey: Homa & Sekey Books. ISBN 978-1-931-90737-8;OCLC 60931394.

Yeon Gaesomun - Gogyreon's Super Hero Who Saved The Kingdom

This article uses material from the New World Encyclopedia article http://www.newworldencyclopedia.org/entry/Yeon_Gaesomun, which is released under the Creative Commons Attribution-Share-Alike License 3.0, which can be viewed at creativecommons.org/licenses/by-sa/3.0/

[1] Korean Net, Downfall and Succession of Koguryo. Retrieved October 20, 2007.
[2] Samguk Sagi, vol. 21三國志. Retrieved October 20, 2007.
[3] Book of Tang, vols. 3, 199舊唐書. Retrieved October 20, 2007.
[4] New Book of Tang, vols. 2, 220唐書. Retrieved October 20, 2007.
[5] Zizhi Tongjian, vols. 資治通鑑/卷197, 資治通鑑/卷198.
[6] Bo Yang Edition of the Zizhi Tongjian, vol. 47.

EULJI MUNDEOK - Hero of The Great Battle of Salsu

This article uses material from the Wikipedia article en.wikipedia.org/wiki/Eulji_Mundeok, which is released under the Creative Commons Attribution-Share-Alike License 3.0, which can be viewed at creativecommons.org/licenses/by-sa/3.0/

[1] http://www.globalsecurity.org/military/ops/ulchi-focus-lens.htm

KIM BUSIK - Great Scholar Who Led The Compilation of The Samguk Sagi

This article uses material from the Wikipedia article en.wikipedia.org/wiki/Gim_Busik, which is released under the Creative Commons Attribution-Share-Alike License 3.0, which can be viewed at creativecommons.org/licenses/by-sa/3.0/

[1] E. J. Shultz, Military Revolt in Koryŏ: The 1170 Coup d'État, Korean Studies 3, 19 (1979); available at http://www.jstor.org/stable/23717825.
[2] M. J. Seth, A history of Korea : from antiquity to the present, (Rowman and Littlefield, Lanham MA, 2011), p. 80. ISBN 978-0-7425-6715-3
[3] E.J. Shultz, An Introduction to the Samsuk Sagi, Korean Studies 28, 1 (2004).
[4] Seth, p. 78
[5] J. B. Duncan, The Formation of the Central Aristocracy in Early Koryŏ, Korean Studies 12, 39 (1988); available at http://www.jstor.org/stable/23717729.
[6] R. E. Breuker, Establishing a Pluralist Society in Medieval Korea, 918–1170: History, Ideology and Identity in the Koryŏ Dynasty, (Brill, Leiden, 2010), p. 234. ISBN 978-90-04-18325-4
[7] Breuker, p. 261
[8] Y. H. Choe-Wall (ed.), Encyclopaedia of Korean Culture, (Australian National University, 1999), pp. 688-689; available at https://digitalcollections.anu.edu.au/handle/1885/10445.
[9] "Kim Pusik." Encyclopedia of World Biography, available at http://www.encyclopedia.com/doc/1G2-3404703553.html
[10] Y. Kwŏn, Royal Lecture and Confucian Politics in Early Yi Korea, Korean Studies 6, 41 (1982); available at http://www.jstor.org/stable/23717630
[11] E. J. Shultz, Twelfth-Century Koryŏ Politics: The Rise of Han Anin and His Partisans, The Journal of Korean Studies 6, 3 (1988-89); available from http://www.jstor.org/stable/41490196
[12] D. Twitchet and K.-P. Tietze, The Liao, in D. Twitchet and J. K. Fairbank (eds.), The Cambridge History of China, vol. 6, Alien Regimes and Border States, 907—1368 (Cambridge University Press, Cambridge, 1994), Ch. 1. ISBN 978-0-521-24331-5
[13] Breuker, p. 220-224
[14] Seth, p. 99-101
[15] Breuker, Ch. 8

[16] R. E. Breuker, Koryo as an Independent Realm: The Emperor's Clothes? Korean Studies 27, 48 (2003) DOI: 10.1353/ks.2005.0001
[17] Breuker, p. 202
[18] Breuker, p. 228
[19] J.-W. Park, Consultative Politics and Royal Authority in the Goryeo Period, Seoul Journal of Korean Studies 24, (2) 203 (2011).
[20] Breuker, p. 207
[21] K. Pratt, Everlasting flower: a history of Korea, (Reaktion Books, London, 2006), p. 96. ISBN 978-1-86189-273-7
[22] H.-w. Kang, The development of the Korean ruling class from late Silla to early Koryo, (PhD Thesis, University of Washington, 1964), pp. 280-289; available at http://hdl.handle.net/1773/11100
[23] D. McCann, Early Korean Literature: Selections and Introductions (Columbia University Press, 2013), p. 79 ISBN 978-0-231505741
[24] Breuker, p. 377
[25] Breuker, p. 192

HEUNGSEON DAEWONGUN - Regent Who Vigorously Enforced Closed-Door Policy

This article uses material from the Wikipedia article en.wikipedia.org/wiki/Heungseon_Daewongun, which is released under the Creative Commons Attribution-Share-Alike License 3.0, which can be viewed at creativecommons.org/licenses/by-sa/3.0/

[1] Conroy, Hilary. The Japanese Seizure of Korea, 1868-1910: A Study of Realism and Idealism in International Relations. Philadelphia: University of Pennsylvania Press, 1960.
[2] Choe Ching Young. The Rule of the Taewŏn'gun, 1864-1873: Restoration in Yi Korea. Cambridge, Mass.: East Asian Research Center, Harvard University, 1972.
[3] Cumings, Bruce. Korea's Place in the Sun: A Modern History. New York: W.W. Norton & Company, 2005.
[4] Kim, C.I. Eugene and Han-Kyo Kim. Korea and the Politics of Imperialism: 1876-1910. Berkeley and Los Angeles: University of California Press, 1967.
[5] Neff, Robert (21 July 2010). "German merchant's body-snatching expedition in 1868". The Korea Times. Archived from the original on 23 June 2015. Retrieved 22 June 2015.
[6] Su-il, J. (2007). The World Inside Korea How Have We Communicated with the World?. THE REVIEW OF KOREAN STUDIES, 10(2), 189-200. ISO 690

EMPRESS MYEONGSEONG - The Queen Who Fought To Save The Korean Empire

This article uses material from the New World Encyclopedia article http://www.newworldencyclopedia.org/entry/Empress_Myeongseong, which is released under the Creative Commons Attribution-Share-Alike License 3.0, which can be viewed at creativecommons.org/licenses/by-sa/3.0/

[1] The history of the Kyujanggak Royal Library, Seoul National Univ. Ref. code GK17289_00I0079. Retrieved January 18, 2013.
[2] Some sources say that Min was born on September 25, 1851. This is due to the difference in the calendar system.
[3] 3.0 3.1 3.2 3.3 3.4 3.5 3.6 3.7 3.8 Queen Min ("Myongsong hwanghu").Global Korean Network of Los Angeles. Retrieved July 1, 2008.
[4] March 20, 1866 was based on the existing (lunar) calendar of the time.

EMPEROR GOJONG - The First Emperor of The Korean Empire

This article uses material from the New World Encyclopedia article http://www.newworldencyclopedia.org/entry/Emperor_Gojong_of_Korea, which is released under the Creative Commons Attribution-Share-Alike License 3.0, which can be viewed at creativecommons.org/licenses/by-sa/3.0/

[1] M. Volkov, May 2004, Русские в Корее- имена и судьбы (Russians in Korea - Names and Fates). Korusforum Journal, Center for Contemporary Korean Studies, Russian Academy of Sciences (23). Retrieved April 6, 2008.

YI WANYONG - Traitor Who Put Korea Under Japanese Rule

This article uses material from the Wikipedia article https://en.wikipedia.org/wiki/Ye_Wanyong, which is released under the Creative Commons Attribution-Share-Alike License 3.0, which can be viewed at creativecommons.org/licenses/by-sa/3.0/

[0] http://www.chosun.com/national/news/200508/200508040042.html
[1] English JoongAng Ilbo August 30, 2001
[2] "Cho (who spoke fluent Japanese) called that night on Terauchi an told him that he and Ye agreed that unless the name Han-guk and the title of king were retained, no compromise could be reached. They were apparently under the impression that annexation would be a union of two countries, each retaining sovereign status, rather in the manner of Austria-Hungary or Sweden-Norway. Terauchi was surprised by this lack of understanding of Japanese aims, but he finally agreed to allow the country to be known by the old name of Chosen." Keene, Donald. Emperor of Japan: Meiji and his world, 1852-1912 (2002) pg. 674
[3] Committee OKs Seizure of Collaborators' Property The Chosun Ilbo,December 7, 2005
[4] South Korea: Crackdown On Collaborators The New York Times, December 24, 2007

HEO NANSEOLHEON - A Short-Lived Literary Genius

This article uses material from the Wikipedia article https://en.wikipedia.org/wiki/Heo_Nanseolheon, which is released under the Creative Commons Attribution-Share-Alike License 3.0, which can be viewed at creativecommons.org/licenses/by-sa/3.0/

[1] Choe-Wall, Yang-hi. Vision of a Phoenix: the Poems of Hŏ Nansŏrhŏn. Ithaca, NY: East Asia Program, Cornell University, 2003. Print.
[2] Kim-Renaud, Young-Key. Creative Women of Korea: the Fifteenth through the Twentieth Centuries. Armonk, NY: M.E. Sharpe, 2004. Print.
[3] "Heo Gyun and Heo Nanseolheon". PR Korea Times. September 29, 2005. Archived from the original on June 10, 2011. Retrieved October 6, 2008.
[4] kuiwon.wordpress.com
[5] McCann, David R. Early Korean Literature: Selections and Introductions. New York: Columbia UP, 2000. Print.

YEONSANGUN - The Dethroned Tyrant King of The Joseon Dynasty

This article uses material from the Wikipedia article https://en.wikipedia.org/wiki/Yeonsangun_of_Joseon, which is released under the Creative Commons Attribution-Share-Alike License 3.0, which can be viewed at creativecommons.org/licenses/by-sa/3.0/

[1] (in Polish) Joanna Rurarz (2009). Historia Korei. Dialog. ISBN 978-83-89899-28-6. P.234
[2] In traditional East Asian culture the corpse has to be complete in order for the soul to survive in the afterlife and be reincarnated, to mutilate the corpse was seen as not only a punishment in this life but as in the next too
[3] (in Polish) Joanna Rurarz (2009). Historia Korei. Dialog. ISBN 978-83-89899-28-6. P.234-235
[4] (in Polish) Joanna Rurarz (2009). Historia Korei. Dialog. ISBN 978-83-89899-28-6. P.234-235
[5] (in Polish) Joanna Rurarz (2009). Historia Korei. Dialog. ISBN 978-83-89899-28-6. P.234-235
[6] Rurarz, Joanna (2009). Historia Korei [History of Korea] (in Polish). Dialog. pp. 234–35. ISBN 978-83-89899-28-6.
[7] Rurarz 2009, p. 234–35.

DAEJOYOUNG - The Founder of The Balhae Kingdom

This article uses material from the Wikipedia article https://en.wikipedia.org/wiki/Go_of_Balhae, which is released under the Creative Commons Attribution-Share-Alike License 3.0, which can be viewed at creativecommons.org/licenses/by-sa/3.0/

[1] Korean culture and Information Service, "Things Newcomers Need to Know to Live in Korea", 2012. p.16
[2] UNESCO Korean Committee, "Korean History:Discovery of its Characteristics and Developments", VOl.5, Hollym, 2004. ISBN 1565911776 p.134
[3] Lee Injae, Owen Miller, Park Jinhoon, Yi Hyun-hae, Korean History in Maps》, Cambridge University Press, 2014. ISBN 1107098467 p.54
[4] Kichan Bae, "Korea at the crossroads:the history and future of East Asia", Happyreading, 2007. ISBN 8989571464 p.83
[5] South Korean Culture&Education Ministry, "나의조국:재외국민용", 1981. p.102
[6] Patricia Ebrey, Anne Walthall, "Pre-Modern East Asia: A Cultural, Social, and Political History", Vol.I:to 1800, Cengage Learning, 2013. ISBN 1133606512 p.111
[7] Hahoe Hongbowon, "Korea Policy Review", Korean Overseas Information Service, 2006.
[8] UNESCO Korean Committee, "Korean History:Discovery of its Characteristics and Developments", VOl.5, Hollym, 2004. ISBN 1565911776 p.158
[9] "Korea celebrates ties with Oman" Times of Oman, 2014-10-29

[1] "Kim Il Sung". American Heritage Dictionary of the English Language (Fifth ed.). n.d. Retrieved 6 March 2017.
[2] 김일성, 루바의 혁명영웅' 체게바라를 만난 날. DailyNK (in Korean). 15 April 2008. Archived from the original on 29 April 2011.
[3] Buzo, Adrian (2002). The Making of Modern Korea. London: Routledge. p. 140. ISBN 0-415-23749-1.
[4] Cumings, Bruce (2005). Korea's Place in the Sun: A Modern History. New York: W. W. Norton & Company. p. 434. ISBN 0-393-32702-7.
[5]Robinson, Michael E (2007). Korea's Twentieth-Century Odyssey. Honolulu: University of Hawaii Press. p. 153. ISBN 978-0-8248-3174-5.
[6] Bluth, Christoph (2008). Korea. Cambridge: Polity Press. p. 34. ISBN 978-07456-3357-2.
[7] Jasper Becker (1 May 2005). Rogue Regime : Kim Jong Il and the Looming Threat of North Korea. Oxford University Press. ISBN 978-0-19-803810-8. Archived from the original on 18 May 2016.
[8] "Soviets groomed Kim Il Sung for leadership". Vladivostok News. 10 January 2003. Archived from the original on 10 June 2009.
[9] Lankov, Andrei (2002). From Stalin to Kim Il Sung: The Formation of North Korea 1945–1960. Rutgers University Press. ISBN 0813531179.
[10] Cumings, Bruce (1 September 2005). Korea's Place in the Sun: A Modern History (Updated). New York: W W Norton & Co. ISBN 978-0-393-32702-1. Archived from the original on 18 May 2016.
[11] Buzo, Adrian (2002). The Making of Modern Korea. London: Routledge. p. 56. ISBN 0-415-23749-1.
[12] Robinson, Michael E (2007). Korea's Twentieth-Century Odyssey. Honolulu: University of Hawaii Press. p. 87. ISBN 978-0-8248-3174-5.
[13] Oberdorfer, Don; Carlin, Robert (2014). The Two Koreas: A Contemporary History. Basic Books. pp. 13–14. ISBN 9780465031238.
[14] Kim Il-sung (1994). With the Century (PDF). 2. Pyongyang: Foreign Languages Publishing House. OCLC 28377167. Retrieved 17 October 2014.
[15] "Soviet Officer Reveals Secrets of Mangyongdae". Daily NK. Archived from the original on 11 February 2014. Retrieved 2014-04-15.
[16] Baik Bong (1973). Kim il Sung: Volume I: From Birth to Triumphant Return to Homeland. Beirut, Lebanon: Dar Al-talia.
[17] Kimjongilia – The Movie – Learn More Archived 18 September 2010 at the Wayback Machine.
[18] "PETER HITCHENS: North Korea, the last great Marxist bastion, is a real-life Truman show". Daily Mail. London. 8 October 2007. Archived from the original on 21 February 2010.
[19] Byrnes, Sholto (7 May 2010). "The Rage Against God, By Peter Hitchens". The Independent. London. Archived from the original on 12 May 2010.
[20] Smith, Lydia (2014-07-08). "Kim Il-sung Death Anniversary: How the North Korea Founder Created a Cult of Personality". International Business Times UK. Archived from the original on 6 October 2014. Retrieved 2014-10-01.
[21] Sang-Hun, Choe; Lafraniere, Sharon (27 August 2010). "Carter Wins Release of American in North Korea". The New York Times. Archived from the original on 30 June 2017.
[22] Suh Dae-Sook, Kim Il Sung: The North Korean Leader, Columbia University Press (1998) p. 7.
[23] Kim Il-Sung, "Let Us Repudiate the 'Left' Adventurist Line and Follow the Revolutionary Organizational Line" contained in On Juche in Our Revolution (Foreign Languages Publishers: Pyongyang, Korea, 1973)3.
[24] Yamamuro, Shin'ichi (2006). Manchuria Under Japanese Dominion. Archived from the original on 18 May 2016. Retrieved February 8, 2016.
[25] Kim Il-Sung, "Let Us Repudiate the 'Left' Adventurist Line and Follow the Revolutionary Organizational Line" contained in On Juche in Our Revolution, pp.1-15.
[26] Kim Il-Sung, "On Waging Armed Struggle Against Japanese Imperialism" on 16 December 1931 contained in On Juche in Our Revolution, pp. 17-20.
[27] Suh Dae-Sook, Kim Il Sung: The North Korean Leader, Columbia University Press (1998) pp. 8–10.
[28] Bradley K. Martin (2004). Under the Loving Care of the Fatherly Leader: North Korea and the Kim Dynasty. Thomas Dunne Books. p. 30. ISBN 978-0-312-32322-6.
[29] Robinson, Michael E (2007). Korea's Twentieth-Century Odyssey. Honolulu: University of Hawaii Press. pp. 87, 155. ISBN 978-0-8248-3174-5.
[30] Lone, Stewart; McCormack, Gavan (1993). Korea since 1850. Melbourne: Longman Cheshire. p. 100.
[31] Lone, Stewart; McCormack, Gavan (1993). Korea since 1850. Melbourne: Longman Cheshire. p. 100.
[32] Beria/Kim Il-sung Archived 28 May 2013 at the Wayback Machine.
[33] Mark O'Neill. "Kim Il-sung's secret history | South China Morning Post". Scmp.com. Archived from the original on 27 February 2014. Retrieved 2014-04-15.
[34] Bradley K. Martin (2004). Under the Loving Care of the Fatherly Leader: North Korea and the Kim Dynasty. Thomas Dunne Books. p. 51. ISBN 978-0-312-32322-6.
[35] Bradley K. Martin (2004). Under the Loving Care of the Fatherly Leader: North Korea and the Kim Dynasty. Thomas Dunne Books. p. 56. ISBN 978-0-312-32322-6.
[36] Armstrong, Charles (2013-04-15). The North Korean Revolution, 1945–1950. Cornell University Press.
[37] Lankov, Andrei (2012-01-25). "Terenti Shtykov: the other ruler of nascent N. Korea". The Korea Times. Archived from the original on 17 April 2015. Retrieved April 14, 2015.
[38] Formation of the KPA Archived 6 March 2016 at the Wayback Machine.
[39] Blair, Clay, The Forgotten War: America in Korea, Naval Institute Press (2003).
[40] DPRK Foreign Relations Archived 19 April 2014 at the Wayback Machine.
[41] Worker's Parties of Korea merge Archived 5 March 2008 at the Wayback Machine.
[42] Weathersby, Kathryn, "The Soviet Role in the Early Phase of the Korean War", The Journal of American-East Asian Relations 2, no. 4 (Winter 1993): 432
[43] Goncharov, Sergei N., Lewis, John W. and Xue Litai, Uncertain Partners: Stalin, Mao, and the Korean War (1993)
[44] Mansourov, Aleksandr Y., Stalin, Mao, Kim, and China's Decision to Enter the Korean War, 16 September – 15 October 1950: New Evidence from the Russian Archives, Cold War International History Project Bulletin, Issues 6–7 (Winter 1995/1996): 94–107
[45] Sudoplatov, Pavel Anatoli, Schecter, Jerrold L., and Schecter, Leona P., Special Tasks: The Memoirs of an Unwanted Witness—A Soviet Spymaster, Little, Brown, Boston (1994)
[46] Ho Jong-ho et al. (1977) The US Imperialists Started the Korean War Archived 29 April 2011 at the Wayback Machine.
[47] Mossman, Billy (June 29, 2005). United States Army in the Korean War: Ebb and Flow November 1950-July 1951. University Press of the Pacific. p. 51.
[48] Sandler, Stanley (1999). The Korean War: No Victors, No Vanquished. The University Press of Kentucky. p. 108.
[49] David Halberstam. Halberstam, David (25 September 2007). The Coldest Winter: America and the Korean War (p. 23). Hyperion. Kindle Edition.
[50] Halberstam, David (25 September 2007). The Coldest Winter: America and the Korean War (pp. 335–336). Hyperion. Kindle Edition.
[51] Bethany Lacina and Nils Petter Gleditsch, Monitoring Trends in Global Combat: A New Dataset of Battle Deaths Archived 12 October 2013 at the Wayback Machine., European Journal of Population (2005) 21: 145–166.
[52] Kim Il-sung and Chinese Troops
[53] Lankov, Andrei N., Crisis in North Korea: The Failure of De-Stalinization, 1956, Honolulu: Hawaii University Press (2004), ISBN 978-0-8248-2809-7
[54] Timothy Hildebrandt, "Uneasy Allies: Fifty Years of China-North Korea Relations" Archived 24 February 2015 at the Wayback Machine., Asia Program Special Report, September 2003, Woodrow Wilson International Centre for Scholars.
[55] Chung, Chin O. Pyongyang Between Peking and Moscow: North Korea's Involvement in the Sino-Soviet Dispute, 1958-1975. University of Alabama. 1978.
[56] French, Paul. North Korea: State of Paranoia. New York: St. Martin's Press. 2014.
[57] Chung, Chin O. Pyongyang Between Peking and Moscow: North Korea's Involvement in the Sino-Soviet Dispute, 1958-1975. University of Alabama, 1978, p. 45.
[58] Kim, Young Kun and Zagoria, Donald S. "North Korea and the Major Powers." Asian Survey Vol. 15, No. 12 (Dec., 1975), pp. 1017-1035 University of California Press. Stable URL: "Archived copy". Archived from the original on 7 November 2015. Retrieved 2015-05-04.
[59] Breznhev-Kim Il-Sung relations
[60] CEU.hu Archived 8 September 2009 at the Wayback Machine., Radio Free Europe/Radio Liberty Research 17 December 1979 quoting Hoxha's Reflections on China Volume II: "In Pyongyang, I believe that even Tito will be astonished at the proportions of the cult of his host, which has reached a level unheard of anywhere else, either in past or present times, let alone in a country which calls itself socialist." "Archived copy". Archived from the original on 8 September 2009. Retrieved 2008-10-30.
[61] Howard W. French, With Rebel Gains and Mobutu in France, Nation Is in Effect Without a Government Archived 30 June 2017 at the Wayback Machine., The New York Times (17 March 1997).
[62] "DPR Korea", Official site, Asia–Pacific Legal Metrology Forum, 2015, archived from the original on 9 February 2017.
[63] "Archived copy". Archived from the original on 19 March 2017. Retrieved 2017-03-19.
[64] North Korea and Eastern Europe Archived 10 March 2016 at the Wayback Machine.
[65] Cumings, Bruce, North Korea: Another Country, The New Press, New York, 2003, p. xii.
[66] Kim Il-sung halts DPRK nuclear program Archived 22 April 2012 at the Wayback Machine.
[67] Saxonberg, Steven (14 February 2013). Transitions and Non-Transitions from Communism: Regime Survival in China, Cuba, North Korea, and Vietnam. Cambridge University Press. p. 123. ISBN 978-1-107-02388-8. Archived from the original on 18 May 2016.
[68] Henry, Terrence (2005-05-01). "After Kim Jong II". The Atlantic. Retrieved 2014-10-01.
[69] Demick, Barbara: Nothing to Envy: Ordinary Lives in North Korea.
[70] Scenes of lamentation after Kim Il-sung's death on YouTube
[71] Portal, Jane; British Museum (2005). Art under control in North Korea. Reaktion Books. p. 82. ISBN 978-1-86189-236-2.
[72] "The Chosun Ilbo (English Edition): Daily News from Korea - N.Korean Dynasty's Authority Challenged". English.chosun.com. 2012-02-13. Archived from the original on 29 September 2012. Retrieved 2012-11-09.
[73] "Controversy Stirs Over Kim Monument at PUST" NK Daily. Archived 12 April 2010 at the Wayback Machine.. Retrieved 24 April 2010.

[74] Kim Il-sung Statue Traditions Archived 10 May 2012 at the Wayback Machine.
[75] Birthday of Kim Il-sung. Holidays, Festivals, and Celebrations of the World Dictionary (Fourth ed.). Omnigraphics. 2010. Retrieved 3 May 2015 – via TheFreeDictionary.com.
[76] Choi Song Min (16 April 2013). "Spring Art Festival Off the Schedule". DailyNK. Archived from the original on 13 March 2015. Retrieved 3 May 2015.
[77] "Immortal classical works written by President Kim Il Sung". Naenara. May 2008. Retrieved 2015-01-16.
[78] ""Complete Collection of Kim Il Sung's Works" Off Press". KCNA. January 18, 2012. Archived from the original on 12 October 2014. Retrieved January 16, 2015.
[79] 가극 작품 Archived 1 December 2005 at the Wayback Machine. – NK Chosun
[80] 2008年03月26日，金日成原创《卖花姑娘》5月上海唱响《卖花歌》 Archived 1 May 2011 at the Wayback Machine. – 搜狐娱乐

RHEE SYNGMAN - The First President of South Korea

[1] "KOREA: The Walnut". TIME. March 9, 1953. Retrieved 2010-03-20. In 1932, while attempting to put Korea's case before an indifferent League of Nations in Geneva, Rhee met Francesca Maria Barbara Donner, 34, the daughter of a family of Viennese iron merchants. Two years later they were married in a Methodist ceremony in New York.
[2] 이승만[李承晩] [Rhee Syngman]. Doopedia (in Korean). Doosan Corporation. Retrieved March 12, 2014.
[3] "Syngman Rhee". Encyclopædia Britannica. Retrieved March 13, 2014.
[4] "Syngman Rhee: First president of South Korea". CNN Student News. CNN. Retrieved March 13, 2014.
[5] "Syngman Rhee". The Cold War Files. Cold War International History Project. Retrieved March 13, 2014.
[6] Cha, Marn J. (September 19, 2012) [1996], "SYNGMAN RHEE'S FIRST LOVE" (PDF), The Information Exchange for Korean-American Scholars (IEKAS) (12-19): 2, ISSN 1092-6232, retrieved March 14, 2014
[7] 이승만 [Rhee Syngman]. Encyclopedia of Korean culture (in Korean). Academy of Korean Studies. Retrieved March 13, 2014.
[8] Breen, Michael (April 18, 2010). "Fall of Korea's First President Syngman Rhee in 1960". The Korea Times. KoreaTimes.co.kr. Retrieved March 14, 2014.
[9] Yu Yeong-ik (1996). [Rhee Syngman's Life and Dream] (in Korean). Seoul: Joong Ang Ilbo Press. pp. 40–44. ISBN 89-461-0345-0.
[10] Coppa, Frank J., ed. (2006). "Rhee, Syngman". Encyclopedia of modern dictators: from Napoleon to the present. Peter Lang. p. 256. ISBN 978-0-8204-5010-0.
[11] Jessup, John E. (1998). "Rhee, Syngman". An encyclopedic dictionary of conflict and conflict resolution, 1945–1996. Greenwood Publishing Group. p. 626. ISBN 978-0-313-28112-9.
[12] Breen, Michael (November 2, 2011). "(13) Syngman Rhee: president who could have done more". The Korea Times. KoreaTimes.co.kr. Retrieved April 7, 2014.
[13] "Japan surrenders". History. A+E Networks. Retrieved April 7, 2014.
[14] Cumings, Bruce (2010). "38 degrees of separation: a forgotten occupation". The Korean War: a History. Modern Library. p. 106. ISBN 978-0-8129-7896-4.
[15] Hastings, Max (1988). The Korean War. Simon and Schuster. pp. 32–34. ISBN 9780671668341.
[16] Wikisource link to United Nations General Assembly Resolution 112. Wikisource.
[17] "Details/Information for Canadian Forces (CF) Operation United Nations Commission on Korea". Department of National Defence and the Canadian Armed Forces. November 28, 2008. Retrieved April 8, 2014.
[18] "South Korea (1948-present)". Dynamic Analysis of Dispute Management Project. University of Central Arkansas. Retrieved April 8, 2014.
[19] Croissant, Aurel (2002), "Electoral Politics in South Korea" (PDF), Electoral politics in Southeast & East Asia, 370, VI, Singapore: Friedrich-Ebert-Stiftung, pp. 234–237, ISBN 978-981-04-6020-4, retrieved April 8, 2014
[20] Kyung Moon Hwang A History of Korea Palgrave Macmillan, 2010 page 204.
[21] Hastings (1988), p. 38
[22] Hastings (1988), p. 42
[23] Tirman, John (2011). The Deaths of Others: The Fate of Civilians in America's Wars. Oxford University Press. pp. 93–95. ISBN 978-0-19-538121-4.
[24] "The National Committee for Investigation of the Truth about the Jeju April 3 Incident". 2008. Retrieved 2008-12-15.
[25] Merrill, John, Korea: The Peninsular Origins of the War (University of Delaware Press, 1989), p181.
[26] http://www.koreatimes.co.kr/www/nation/2017/04/356_226873.html
[27] Hastings (1988), p. 235-240
[28] Hastings (1988), p. 235
[29] Cha (2010), p. 174
[30] Cha, Victor D (Winter 2010). "Powerplay: Origins of the U.S. Alliance System in Asia". International Security. MIT Press Journals. 34 (3): 158–196. doi:10.1162/isec.2010.34.3.158.
[31] James E. Dillard. "Biographies: Syngman Rhee". The Department of Defense 60th Anniversary of Korean War Commemoration Committee. Retrieved on September 28, 2016.
[32] "The Korean War armistice". BBC News. March 5, 2015. Retrieved on September 28, 2016.
[33] Buzo, Adrian (2007). The making of modern Korea. Taylor & Francis. p. 79. ISBN 978-0-415-41482-1.
[34] Cyrus Farivar (2011), The Internet of Elsewhere: The Emergent Effects of a Wired World, Rutgers University Press, p. 26.
[35] [Francesca]. Encyclopedia of Korean culture (in Korean). Academy of Korean studies. Retrieved April 7, 2014.
[36] "Syngman Rhee". South Korean President. Find a Grave. February 20, 2004. Retrieved Aug 19, 2011.

Printed in Great Britain
by Amazon

55883754R00127